Information Pr

Exces
Powel
Popula

An Ess

Copyright © 1995
Information Project For Africa, Inc.

EXCESSIVE FORCE: POWER, POLITICS, AND POPULATION
CONTROL

318 pages — includes index
1. International Relations — 2. Population — 3. Developing Countries
— 4. Economic Development — 5. United States Foreign Aid — 6.
Reproductive Rights — I. Title

ISBN: 1-886719-04-7

Information Project For Africa, Inc.
Post Office Box 43345
Washington, DC 20010
U.S.A.

TABLE OF CONTENTS

Preface

What could be more important than an overseas aid program that gets subsidized contraceptives to everyone of reproductive age? For most of us, there is at least *something* that would come first: food for famine victims, help to the sick and injured, sanctuary for refugees, or shelter for the homeless, perhaps.

So who would even argue that birth control takes precedence over these? The answer is: the United States government. More specifically, it is the Agency for International Development, The Department of State, the Pentagon, the Central Intelligence Agency, and, last but not least, that supreme executive body that coordinates the work of all these other bureaus, the National Security Council. These are joined by the far-reaching social agencies of United Nations, the powerful international lending institutions, innumerable private foundations and multinational corporations, and an increasing number of political leaders in other parts of the industrialized world.

To the average person, birth control is something intensely personal. In other words, most of us would feel terribly out of place lecturing others about their fertility. And to proclaim publicly that this group or that group is reproducing itself too fast puts a person in an awkward position: simply stated, it is insensitive, it is judgmental, and it smacks of prejudice.

But, private as it is, human reproduction is also intensely political. It has been said that because all of us will eventually pass away, *procreation determines the future of nations.* This is the key to understanding the exceptional interest that this issue generates among western policy planners.

And carefully-monitored birthrates around the world suggest some truly meaningful changes are about to take place in the "future of nations" and in the relative advantages enjoyed by different regions.

Since the start of the twentieth century, birthrates in the industrialized world have fallen to levels that are the lowest anywhere in all history. At the same time, fertility has stayed high in much of the developing world. This means that the constituency of the world is likely to change in ways that are difficult to imagine.

The following pages offer a brief history of the American foreign aid program with an emphasis on its objectives and consequences for the emerging nations of the south. It then reviews opinion about the importance of population change presented over the past half century by an assortment of scientists, academics, expert panels, military officials, and political leaders.

What happens when there are dramatic shifts in the world's ethnic and racial makeup? How will these trends alter the balance of power between north and south? What effect will population change have on the global distribution of wealth, resources, and technology? *Who will rule the world our children inherit?*

This text then looks beyond the theories and political analysis to the actual implementation of population programs. And its findings may come as a shock.

Indeed, the era is long past when international family planning meant establishing clinics, training providers, and shipping supplies. Today's population program, based in large part on intelligence assessments by the CIA, has assumed the characteristics and magnitude of the most aggressive political warfare campaigns of the 1950s — complete with the clandestine establishment of "indigenous" fronts, secret payments to affect political decisions, recruitment of "in-place" agents, the infiltration of academia, systematic intimidation of opponents, falsely-attributed communications, penetration of the news media, threats, targets, and ultimatums.

This work is the product of intensive research that spanned several years and required travel on four continents. The investigation also involved the filing of hundreds of federal Freedom of Information Act requests with several U.S. government agencies, along with the review of literally thousands of documents, reports, periodicals, and books. In 1990, this enormous task was taken over from several interested individuals and continued as an official activity of the Information Project For Africa. The IPFA is a reporters' collective made up of professional print and broadcast journalists and advisors representing several fields of learning, the majority of them from several African nations.

The purpose of this text is not to criticize individuals involved in family planning campaigns who neither fully understand nor share the motives of the international "population establishment" that plans and sponsors these activities. And it is certainly not intended as an attack on those who use birth control themselves. Rather, it examines the all-too-prevalent view held by many in the west that other people *ought* to limit their fertility because they are different in culture, class, religious affiliation, lifestyle, or political identity from the Anglo-Saxon "ideal." And, even more importantly, it explores the frightening consequences of extending this concept of "group superiority" into the arena of global politics where it becomes an instrument of power or even of conquest.

Human population growth may be the most critical issue facing the world today. There can be no doubt that the most important global events occurring during the twenty-first century will be, at least to a substantial degree, the result of changes in relative demographic strength between different groups. These emerging population patterns are virtually certain to create a "new world" in which major adjustments will have to be made in the allocation of resources among nations and peoples, the value of goods and labor in various regions, and the distribution of political power. Moreover, these adjustments will take place in a world in which people of color have a far greater voice.

Given the extraordinary political implications of current demographic trends, the worldwide campaign of reproductive intervention takes on astonishing importance. All people, regardless of place of residence, color, or class, have a stake in this process.

And there is a lot more to consider than just the abrupt decline of western potency foreseen by so many desperate policy makers in Washington, London, and New York. Indeed, the debate will by necessity include such matters colonization and the systematic impoverishment of what is now collectively called the "third world." And it must especially include the question of what might occur if population programs fail to stem the tide of geopolitical evolution now underway.

It is the belief of the writers and researchers who contributed to this report that the stakes are so high — involving nothing less than control over the world's political institutions and access to all its wealth — that a regime of mass genocide might at some point become a real possibility. And if this is a choice that western policy makers ultimately feel they must make, then it will be made — with or without the input of an informed public.

This book was prepared because its investigators believe that the peoples of the southern hemisphere have a right to information that has up until now been held mostly in secret by governments, and that they also have a right to know what is being contemplated for them. And, above all, it is intended to provide to all persons the background information they urgently need to play their rightful role in a debate over the future of humanity.

Chapter 1

Bosses With Visas:
Politics by Outsiders

*The most serious blow suffered by the colo-
nized is being removed from history and
from the community. Colonization usurps
any free role in either war or peace, every
decision contributing to his destiny and that
of the world, and all cultural and social
responsibility.*

Albert Memmi, quoted in
How Europe Underdeveloped Africa (1982)[1]

*Since absolute security for one power means
absolute insecurity for all others, it is obtain-
able only through conquest, never as part of
a legitimate settlement.*

Henry A. Kissinger in
World Politics, January 1956[2]

*It cannot be expected that the most powerful
military nations will sit still while other
nations reverse the balance of power by the
mere process of breeding.*

Bertrand Russell, in
Marriage and Morals (London, 1929)

---

[1] *How Europe Underdeveloped Africa* by Walter Rodney

[2] "The Congress of Vienna" by Henry A. Kissinger, *World Politics*,
January 1956, at page 164; quoted in *The Might of Nations: World
Politics in Our Time* by John G. Stoessinger, Random house, New
York, 1961, Rev. 1965, at page 219.

Since the earliest times in recorded history, governments have tried various means to influence the actions of other governments. However, during the past several decades, the opportunity for a small number of wealthy nations to exercise political control over others has increased enormously, and so have the implications of these activities.

Political influence can be sought through a variety of means. The economic approach — generally including measures that affect the allocation of resources through trade, credit or aid — is perhaps the most widely-utilized method by which industrialized states exert pressure for "reform" on developing countries. Diplomacy, too, plays an important role — usually supplementing economic actions — as does the use of a variety of channels of communications ranging from international broadcasting and the organized distribution of cultural and educational materials to the commercial exchange of information. At other times, a nation may try to produce an immediate or long-term impact on the behavior of another by resorting to various covert operations or military activities which create an incentive for a targeted country to respond in a certain fashion.

The standard definition of bilateral aid is the transfer of resources from one government to another. But the contemporary foreign aid system is much more than just a program by which the funds or commodities of one nation are applied to the use of another. For one thing, much of the economic "assistance" provided by the west to less-developed nations consists of "technical assistance" projects. These typically involve a minimum of actual goods put at the disposal of the recipient, and consist instead of activities carried out by the donor in the target country. More than a few of these activities are unwanted. Indeed, it is not rare for such "assistance" programs to be carried out without the consent or even the knowledge of the host country.

Moreover, the provision of technical and material aid has become a powerful force for political change — which was its essential purpose, anyway. Now more than ever, technical assistance includes activities that tend to have more than one set of objectives. The donor may describe a project's goals in terms of short-term benefits when approaching the host country government, while, at the same time, justifying the budgetary expenditure on the basis of a very different outcome.

Foreign aid, whether economic, military or "social" (as in the case of information and cultural programs), is explicitly intended to create an ideological atmosphere, to draw recipient nations toward a particular set of beliefs or alignments, and to open and maintain lines of access. These objectives, as a preponderance of the evidence suggests, far outweigh any good that recipients might ever get from the aid.

Even more importantly, one must consider the vast differences between the political and economic histories of the donor nations and those making up the so-called "third world" at whom these aid packages are directed. The latter have been left susceptible to external influences by from centuries of exploitation and destabilization, and often find it almost impossible to reject manipulative and highly unpopular programs.

It is generally accepted that the "under-development" of the southern hemisphere was a process that began centuries before the start of full-scale colonization. As Europe struggled to build a trade empire from the sixteenth century onward, it developed a "middleman" system of trade that could realize enormous profits from the products of others. Cloth made in India, for instance, would be transported to Africa for sale, while African cloth in turn would find its way to England, thus providing the British not only with a product that was superior to their own, but also availing them of that monetary gain which allowed them to increase their advantage in shipping. The system also had the effect of dismantling production systems in the producing countries. Europeans soon looked for ways to market their own textiles in countries that had been primary producers, creating trade incentives that favored their own economies. Over time, this practice left the non-European trading partners little option except to serve as sources of raw materials and to gradually abandon manufacturing.

As sociologist Agnes Riedmann has noted, "African labor created wealth in Europe and the New World. In return, African communities received products such as brandy, gin, and guns, which were not only potentially destructive but were soon consumed or worn out and offered no stimulus for production or technological advance."[3]

The lopsided trade situation eventually helped Europe to create new technologies that further tilted

---

[3] *Science that Colonizes: A Critique of Fertility Studies in Africa* by Agnes Riedmann, Temple University Press, Philadelphia, 1993, at page 21-22.

the balance in their favor. "Vital inventions and innovations appeared in England in the late eighteenth century, after profits from external trade had been reinvested," writes Walter Rodney in his classic study of the impact of colonization. "Indeed, the new machinery represented the investment of primary capital accumulated from trading and from slavery. African and Indian trade strengthened British industry, which in turn crushed whatever industry existed in what is now called the 'underdeveloped' countries."[4]

Most significantly, it was the access to raw materials in the southern hemisphere that made industrialization possible in the north, and ultimately led to the decline of trading.

With the advent of formal colonization, the Europeans established manufacturing outposts abroad in order to benefit from the abundance of cheap labor that resulted from the decline of indigenous industry during previous centuries. This, as Riedmann has noted, was the final step in creating the underdeveloped economy. "Precolonial blacksmiths had fashioned hoes, bolts, bells, and body jewelry, and later, modeled flintlock guns after European firearms. But by the 1950s, indigenous iron smelting and working had disappeared, primarily as a result of imported metal products."[5]

---

[4] *How Europe Underdeveloped Africa* by Walter Rodney. Howard University Press, Washington, D.C., 1982, at page 104.

[5] Riedmann, op. cit., at page 21.

Independence is the opposite of colonization, and the colonial powers did all within their power to subvert it. Formal political administration saw the systematic destruction of civic institutions that had been centuries in the making, and the forceful imposition of alien forms of government, education, and culture that would reflect European dominance. Where colonizers found mass settlement difficult, as in many parts of Africa, they carefully created networks of local collaborators to further their administrative control; conquered leaders were compelled to surrender positions of authority for pensions and meaningless titles. Through this process of reducing legitimate authorities to the level of bureaucratic subordinates, the colonial powers were able to render any form of nationalism or self-determination irrelevant.[6] Says Rodney, "The importance of this group cannot be underestimated. The presence of a group of African sell-outs is part of the definition of under-development."[7]

Ultimately, the colonized nations were reduced to a state of total dependency — a situation which, as one scholar has written, was fully intended to be permanent.

> Traditional society was distorted to the point of being unrecognizable; it lost its independence, and its main function was now to produce for the world

---

[6] See Riedmann, op. cit., at page 25.

[7] Rodney, op. cit., at page 27.

market under conditions which, because they impoverished it, deprived this society of any prospect of radical modernization. This traditional society was not, therefore, in transition to modernity; as a dependent, peripheral society it was complete, and hence a dead end, its progress blocked.[8]

In other words, the events that took place from the sixteenth through the twentieth centuries not only produced a "third world" that was under-developed, but one that was intended to be incapable of any form of development — and certainly one that remains to this day vulnerable to foreign interference of almost every conceivable kind.

Thus, the contemporary "technical assistance" activities sponsored by the west must be seen in the context of past exploitation and the enormous political advantage enjoyed by donors. But there is a great deal more to the picture than that. As the following pages will illustrate, the foreign assistance program evolved out an inter-related set of ideologies — notions about white superiority, the decades-long struggle between east and west for control of distant populations, and the desire of policy-makers in the industrial world to preserve their own dominance by curbing the rise to power of potential competitors.

Hence, the Washington power elite of the late 1950s openly debated the consequences of "the

---

[8]*Unequal Development: An Essay on the Social Formations of Peripheral Capitalism* by Samir Amin, Harvester Press, Sussex, Eng., 1976, at 328; quoted in Riedmann, op. cit., at page 23.

premature withdrawal of white men from positions of authority" in Africa.[9] An advisor to President Eisenhower who was instrumental in shaping the aid program justified the scheme on the grounds that western leaders have "more experience with the operations of war, peace, and parliamentary procedures than the swirling mass of emotionally supercharged Africans and Asiatics and Arabs that outnumber us."[10] And President Lyndon Johnson's Secretary of State worried: "If you don't pay attention to the periphery, the periphery changes. And the first thing you know the periphery is the center."[11]

But most importantly, development schemes were never intended to produce self-sufficiency in recipient economies at all, but rather to serve as instruments of bureaucratic surveillance and economic control. Indeed, the prevalent — if seldom spoken — view of U.S. government insiders was that a developing world no longer in need of American finance and American expertise would be "infinitely

---

[9] *Journal of Ethnic Studies*, Spring 1983. "Truman, Eisenhower, and South Africa: The 'Middle Road' and Apartheid" by Thomas J. Noer; cited in *Ideology and U.S. Foreign Policy* by Michael H. Hunt. Yale University Press, New Haven, 1987, at page 165.

[10] C. D. Jackson, quoted in Hunt, op. cit., at page 164.

[11] Dean Rusk at news conference of May 4, 1961, in *Department of State Bulletin*, May 22, 1961, quoted in Hunt, op. cit., at page 152.

capable of consuming resources desperately needed at home."[12]

In many ways, the foreign economic aid and lending program is the most influential — and the most coercive — tactic in the entire arsenal of political and economic weapons wielded against the developing world by the "big nations" of the north. Unlike direct military action, it is imminently suited to day-to-day intervention. It allows donors to take the moral "high ground," handing out discipline disguised as "advice" and defining the outcome of compulsion as "reform." And the more successful the program — that is, the greater the advantage it produces for the donor — the less will be the cost of execution.

The following pages contain examples of contemporary "technical assistance" programs that intentionally undermine democratic initiatives, increase poverty, feed corruption, and exacerbate conflict. The fact that these activities are intended to affect the future size of populations further suggests that their motivation is to preserve existing global power arrangements. And, above all, the extraordinary lengths to which U.S. leaders have gone to influence population trends over the past fifty years suggests the extraordinary importance they attribute to the issue.

---

[12] See Hunt, op. cit., at page 197.

Chapter 2

The Roots

*Each of our Presidents since foreign aid began
has repeatedly expressed his judgment that this
assistance is essential to the national interests
of the United States and to the curtailment of
Communist efforts in all parts of the world...A
foreign aid program is one instrument among
many which we and other developed countries
adequately can afford and vigorously must use
in the defense and advancement of free world
interests.*

Committee to Strengthen the Security of the Free World,
Report to the President, March 20, 1963[13]

*The process of great power emergence is under-
pinned by the fact that the economic (and technical and military) power of states grows at differential, not parallel rates. That is, in relative
terms, some states are gaining power while
others are losing it. ...over time, "the differential
growth in the power of various states in the
system causes a fundamental redistribution of
power in the system."*

Christopher Layne in *International Security*, Spring 1993[14]

---

[13] "The Scope and Distribution of United States Military and
Economic Assistance Programs." Report to the President of the
United States by the Committee to Strengthen the Security of the
Free World, March 20, 1963, at pages 1-2.

[14] "The Unipolar Illusion: Why New Great Powers Will Emerge." by
Christopher Layne, *International Security*, Vol. 17., No. 4, Spring
1993, at page 10.

American economic aid officially began with the Marshall Plan, named after former Secretary of State George Marshall, which was created for the purpose of rebuilding devastated cities and industries in western Europe in the aftermath of World War II.

The intent of the reconstruction campaign was not only to strengthen the major allies of the United States economically, but also to influence them politically. Indeed, the primarily justification for the massive European aid program was to ensure the loyalty of leaders to the west and thereby to prevent their being seduced by communism. As Peter Calvocoressi explains it in his history of contemporary international issues,

> In March 1947 the United States took over Britain's traditional and now too costly role of keeping the Russians out of the eastern Mediterranean. Truman took Greece and Turkey under the American wing and promised material aid to states threatened by communism. Three months later the United States inaugurated the Marshall Plan to avert an economic collapse of Europe which could, it was feared, leave the whole continent helplessly exposed to Russian power and communist lures.[15]

---

[15] *World Politics Since 1945* by Peter Calvocoressi. Sixth Edition. Longman Group UK Limited. London. Sixth edition. 1991. at page 14.

The Marshall Plan was at the time an innovative way to promote the political, economic and security goals of the United States. Its material objectives — the rebuilding of war-torn European cities — were achievable within a realistic period of time. But the political and ideological goals of the new foreign economic effort in Europe were far more subjective. Indeed, a former high-ranking Central Intelligence Agency official, in memoirs published in 1988, recalls:

> A ... systematic program was carried out by CIA within Western Europe itself, in effect as a covert annex to the Marshall Plan. The war had devastated the cultural and intellectual life of Europe as much as it had destroyed its industrial establishment. CIA's financial support was devoted to reviving the cultural groups that had survived the war. Subsidies were given to publications, meetings, congresses. Individual authors and artists were given help. Books were underwritten, travel grants supplied, lecture tours arranged. Organizations like the Congress for Cultural Freedom were founded.[16]

Although these activities declined progressively as the rebuilding effort neared completion, some of

---

[16] *The CIA's Secret Operations: Espionage, Counterespionage and Covert Action* by Harry Rositzke, Westview Press, 1988 edition, pp 158-159.

the ideological activities associated with the program were long-lasting. As the same account explains:

> A longer-range effort addressed itself in these early days to a more formidable task: to match and counter the 'Red fronts,' that vast Soviet apparatus of international front organizations devoted to bringing the democratic Left into the Soviet camp of anti-imperialism.... ¶ To provide an alternative forum for the non-Communist elements in these professional and social groups, the CIA's 'international organizations' program sought to establish counterfronts. Some of these democratic fronts survived to become viable organizations, others did not.[17]

In some respects, the foreign aid program for the developing world was an outgrowth of the Marshall Plan. But in many important respects it was radically different from the reconstruction effort in Europe.

Foreign aid to the southern hemisphere began in 1949 when President Harry S. Truman announced his "Four Point Plan." The idea was to build alliances by exporting "technical assistance" to poor nations. The provision of "technical assistance" requires an entirely different kind of approach than the aid program in Europe. Despite the ideological influence campaigns that accompanied the post-war reconstruction project, American aid in Europe was, in

---

[17] Rositzke, op. cit., at page 159.

theory at last, designed to allow the recipients "considerable responsibility for planning and implementation."[18] Another comprehensive history of U.S. foreign intervention describes the Marshall Plan as being...

> ... consistent with the principle of minimizing interference in the internal affairs of other countries. It also took into account American capabilities — given Washington's limited experience at that time with administering large foreign aid programs, it is questionable whether the United States could have done anything other than leave implementation largely up to the Europeans.[19]

The rebuilding of Europe, moreover, was a goal that could be easily defined. It had precise objectives which could be achieved, more or less, on a given time schedule and with a budget that could at least be forecast with some degree accuracy. "Technical assistance," on the other hand, has historically offered only the most vague of objectives — "development," for instance. Moreover, the program for the southern hemisphere has never been one that promised a clear outcome or one that would be completed after a particular goal was achieved.

---

[18] *Strategies of Containment: A Critical Appraisal of Postwar American National Security Policy* by John Lewis Gaddis, Oxford University Press, 1982, at page 37.

[19] Gaddis, op. cit., at page 37.

Rather, it has been from the start a campaign of continuing, sustained involvement on the part of donors — one in which the recipients have lacked the "valued ally" status of western Europe, and under which there was virtually no premium placed on local leadership and participation, except to the extent that host country officials could be co-opted to act in ways prescribed by the donors.

Against this backdrop, the American foreign assistance effort has taken on increasingly unpleasant dimensions, serving sometimes as a shield for covert operations, as was the case in Europe, and often running such activities under the guise of the "development aid" mission.

Chapter 3

Puppet Rulers and Client States

We must recognize, although we cannot say it publicly, that we need the strong men of Africa on our side. It is important to understand that most of Africa will soon be independent and that it would be naive of the U.S. to hope that Africa will be democratic. ...Since we must have the strong men of Africa on our side, perhaps we should in some cases develop military strong men as an offset to Communist development of the labor unions. The President agreed that it might be desirable for us to try to 'reach' the strong men in Africa... The President asked Stans whether he was now an expert on Africa since his trip to that continent. Mr. Stans, while disclaiming any expertness, said he formed the impression that many Africans still belonged in the trees.

Verbatim from the record of a
January 14, 1960 meeting of the
National Security Council[20]

---

[20] The text of the account of this meeting is published in the U.S. Government's *Foreign Relations, 1958-1960, Volume XIV,* at pages 73-78.

The foregoing exchange took place among some of the most powerful men in the world — men who helped to shape early American foreign policy toward the developing world in ways which are still evident and, by all appearances, permanent.

The suggestion that the U.S. establish ties to the "strong men" of Africa and even "develop military strong men" was put forward by Richard Milhouse Nixon, then Vice President of the United States and, from 1969 to 1974, its president. The President at the time, Dwight David Eisenhower, openly agreed about the political usefulness of dictators. "Mr. Stans" refers to Eisenhower's budget director, Maurice Stans, a powerful figure in political circles for at least three decades, who is best known as the "bagman of Watergate" for his involvement with Nixon as a fundraiser at the time of that historic scandal.

Also present at the meeting were Gordon Gray, the President's National Security Advisor and former head of the Psychological Strategy Board; Allen W. Dulles, Director of Central Intelligence; Deputy Executive Secretary of the National Security Council Marion W. Boggs; Livingston T. Merchant, Under Secretary of State for Political Affairs; Robert B. Anderson, Secretary of the Treasury; and Deputy Defense Secretary James H. Douglas, Jr.

At one point in the meeting, which was recorded by Boggs and classified at the time as "top secret," Central Intelligence Agency chief Dulles urged that a system be worked out for "rewarding the individuals who are assigned to give advice to native leaders." The Vice President added that a great deal could be accomplished in Africa if "the quality of our diplomatic representation were improved [and] if we sent politically sophisticated diplomats to that area."[21]

Gray advised the group that a total of $5 million in economic assistance to Africa and an additional $6 million for technical assistance had been budgeted for the years 1960 through 1963. Nixon then questioned whether this amount would be enough. And State Department official Merchant responded that "a Special Africa Fund for special technical assistance on a regular basis was under consideration as part of the Mutual Security legislation for 1961."[22] And all of this money was in the hands of people anxious to establish control of Africa through military dictatorships and capable of contemptuously stating that the African people "belonged in trees."

The use of the American economic presence — the provision of foreign aid and technical assistance, in particular — has always been seen as an effective means to provoke certain desired actions on the part of leaders or to dictate policy in less developed nations. And it serves another purpose, as well — one that is vital to the formulation of foreign policy: the gathering of intelligence.

The intelligence mission was already well underway during the early years of African independence. Indeed, an expert advised at an early 1958 meeting

---

[21] *Foreign Relations*, op. cit., at page 76.

[22] *Foreign Relations*, op. cit., at page 76. According to the text on pages 76-77, the administration intended to request an additional $25 million for the Africa Fund for the purpose of supplying "technical and limited related assistance."

of the National Security Council that, "in natural resources Africa South of the Sahara was potentially very rich."[23] A later assessment, contained in a secret National Security Council report dated August 26, 1958, elaborated on the matter of resources:

> The strategic value of Africa South of the Sahara stems principally from the area's geographic location athwart alternative air and sea routes to the Far East, and from its strategic materials.[24]

The matters of religion, nationalism and demographics were of particular interest at high levels of the U.S. government. A 1958 memorandum to Secretary of State Dulles went into excruciating detail about the relationship of these issues to western imperialist designs:

> Islam has a natural appeal to black Africans... the brotherhood of Islam is real ... it is adaptable to African customs and even superstitions, and it is *not* the religion of white Europeans. ¶ In West Africa there is a great band of

---

[23] Memorandum of Discussion at the 365th Meeting of the National Security Council,1 May 8, 1958, from *Foreign Relations, 1958-1960, Volume XIV*, at page 14.

[24] Statement of U.S. Policy Toward Africa South of the Sahara Prior to Calendar Year 1960, included in National Security Council Report NSC 5818, August 26, 1958, reprinted in *Foreign Relations, 1958-1960*, Volume XIV, at page 26.

Mohammedanism [sic.] in the savannas and desert areas... This population is largely composed of Hamitic, and Nilotic tribes, consciously differing in race, language, religion and mores from the Negroes of the coast. Mauritania, Senegal and the French Sudan are about 100% Moslem and the northern regions of the other territories are largely Mohammedan. In Nigeria, for example, there are approximately 16,000,000 Mohammedans in the Northern Provinces out of a country-wide population of 34,000,000. Increasing numbers of coast Negroes in the West African territories are being converted to Islam... ¶ On the East Coast there are large Islamic populations from Egypt south through Zanzibar and into Tanganyika... The Sudan, excepting the pagan South, the Somalias [sic] and somewhere near one-half of the Ethiopians are Moslem...[25]

These detailed demographic observations were not pointless, of course. Indeed, the confidential memorandum concluded with a warning:

I think that we should be alert to the emergence of another black Mahdi whom they might follow in an Islamic

---

[25] Memorandum from the Secretary of State's Special Assistant (Holmes) to Secretary of State Dulles, February 6, 1958, *Foreign Relations, 1958-1960, Volume XIV*, op. cit., at pages 7-8. Emphasis in original.

nationalist government. These are warlike folk, numbering 25 to 30 million, and if such a movement were to develop it might well upset the political structure all along the West Coast from Mauritania to the Congo.[26]

The United States, at this point in history, found itself facing a series of imperfect options for pursuing its interests. The African peoples obviously would not be anxious to open the door to an imperial power once they achieved independence, and most of the colonial regimes considered U.S. interference an unwelcome form of competition. The solution, of course, was to intervene in such a way as to keep the U.S. government one step removed from the process. This course of action essentially laid the groundwork for western intervention to the present day.

Among potential avenues for intervention mentioned in documents prepared during that era were various UN agencies, particularly the Economic Commission for Africa and the international lending institutions, which are described in a briefing prepared by the Operations Coordinating Board, a high-level unit charged with overseeing propaganda and

---

[26] Holmes to Dulles, *Foreign Relations*, at page 8. A footnote to the text explains that the writer was referring specifically to Muhammad Ahmad ibn Abd Allah, who "proclaimed himself the Mahdi in June 1881 and whose followers subsequently captured Khartoum, killing British General Charles George 'Chinese' Gordon in the process."

covert operations abroad.[27] In February of 1958, the government established a Foundation for Mutual Assistance in Africa South of the Sahara, under the State Department's Commission for Technical Cooperation in Africa. "Assistance to the colonies," added one "top secret" discussion paper, was often less offensive if offered in the framework of a multilateral organization so that it appeared as a mutual effort.[28]

But the promotion of "private" activities, including those related to investment, offered a unique opportunity for the U.S. government to accelerate its involvement on the continent without provoking objections on the part of the Africans or arousing the suspicions of European colonialists.

"The United States should encourage the removal of obstacles to private foreign investment, and explore new means of encouraging the flow of U.S. and other Free World investment to the area," said a 1958 policy guidance of the National Security Coun-

---

[27] Report of the Operations Coordinating Board, April 23, 1958, reprinted in *Foreign Relations, 1958-1960, Volume XIV*, at page 13. Another important study, included as a policy statement with an August 26, 1958 National Security Council Study (NSC 5818) went into greater detail about the use of the Multilateral economic organizations, explaining that they could be used to establish "a basis for a more rational integration of various bilateral aid programs." *See, Foreign Relations, 1958-1960, Volume XIV*, op. cit., at page 33.

[28] U.S. Policy Toward Africa South of the Sahara Prior to Calendar Year 1960, NSC 5719/1, memoranda to National Security Council from the Executive Secretary, July 29, August 5-6, 1958, reprinted in *Foreign Relations, 1958-1960, Volume XIV*, at page 19.

cil.[29] U.S. policymakers likewise urged efforts to encourage missionary activity and other private educational and cultural efforts in Africa. "Mr. Randall believed a great reservoir of good will for the United States was being created by the missionary movement in Africa," said the August 7, 1958 National Security Council study.[30] And a policy study, written less than three weeks later, included a set of concrete recommendations, including:

> Give special attention to education and training programs designed to develop Western-oriented leaders in the area... Encourage expanded support by private American institutions and foundations in the field of education and encourage the further development of missionary schools in the area. ... Encourage and assist in the development of training for Americans as experts in the African field.[31]

Ultimately, the foreign influence program in Africa, although later to start than similar operations in other regions, was no different than elsewhere. Projects were to be presented to the recipients as a

---

[29] Statement of U.S. Policy Toward Africa South of the Sahara Prior to Calendar Year 1960. NSC 5818. August 26, 1958. at page 35.

[30] U.S. Policy Toward Africa South of the Sahara Prior to Calendar Year 1960. NSC 5719/1. August 7, 1958. at page 20.

[31] National Security Council Report. NSC 58128. August 26, 1958. at page 36.

means to achieve rational, orderly development, but were in reality justified only by the concern that America's leverage in the region should be kept to a certain minimum level in order to prevent what the U.S. Mission at the United Nations described as "the catastrophe which we would confront if Soviet Communism established itself there [in Africa] ..."

Moreover, sensitive operations would be disguised as "multilateral" programs or even private activities. And eventually the most objectionable of these actions would come to be conducted in such a secretive way as to conceal the fact that they even existed at all. And in the early 1980s, the program reached a new phase in its evolution, beginning to rely more and more heavily on outright coercion to achieve its objectives.

Chapter 4

The Paramount Importance of People

The abrupt and massive changes in world population distribution resulting from the demographic trends of the next few decades will lead to a reshaping of world political geography whose general outline can already be foreseen. Young powers will emerge, basing their strength in large part on their population size and the stimulus it creates, and old powers will fade as their populations decline.

Jean-Claude Chesnais in
"The Africanization of Europe."
The American Enterprise. May/June 1990[32]

[W]orld population growth is likely to contribute, directly or indirectly, to domestic upheavals and international conflicts that could adversely affect U.S. interests. Population growth will also reinforce the politicization of international economic relations and intensify the drive of [less-developed countries] for a redistribution of wealth and of authority in international affairs.

The Central Intelligence Agency. 1977[33]

---

[32] *The American Enterprise.* May/June 1990. at page 24.

[33] Central Intelligence Agency. "Political Perspectives on Key Global Issues." March 1977 (Declassified in part. January 1995). at page 4.

America's strategic interests in the southern hemisphere have converged on a variety of concerns — access to critical minerals in Africa and oil in the Middle East, for example; the protection of U.S. investments and other financial interests, as in Latin America; usage of waterways and routes of transit throughout the world; and military base agreements, particularly in Asia.

At the heart of these issues, however, lies a single factor: population. Simply stated, large populations are capable of exerting more power than smaller ones do. Growing populations also produce more demands on their own natural resources, thus affecting the price of export goods such as metal ores, petroleum and so forth, that have traditionally been the backbone of western industrial superiority. Populous nations produce and consume a greater proportion of the earth's goods, thus establishing themselves as economic competitors in the realm of international trade. Moreover, they are capable of building large military forces and dominating regional (or even world) conflicts. In fact, the terms demography and democracy come from the same root. Even in a non-democratic society, it is the larger groups of people that possess the greatest potential to influence public activities.

The importance of power at the group and national level has been expressed this way:

> Politics is concerned with primacy in power. In international politics power is the ability of one actor, usually but

not always a government, to influence the behavior of others, who may or may not be governments. International primacy means that a government is able to exercise more influence on the behavior of more actors with respect to more issues than any other government can. ...[T]he amount of power an actor possesses is a function of weight (degree of participation in decision-making), scope (the values that are influenced), and domain (the people who are influenced).[34]

In other words, it is far more likely that a large group of people can exert control over a smaller group than vice versa. It was for this reason that the old National Security Council studies included repeated references to the relative size of particular population groups — the Islamic population of Africa, for example — both in absolute numbers and relative to other groups. As the same study notes:

To be powerful and to be viewed by others as such surely enhances the self-esteem of individuals and nations. Power enables an actor to shape his environment so as to reflect his interests. In particular it enables a state to protect its security and prevent, deflect, or defeat threats to that security. It also enables a state to promote its

---

[34] "Why International Primacy Matters," by Samuel P. Huntington, *International Security*, Vol. 17, No. 4, Spring 1990, at page 68.

values among other peoples and to
shape the international environment
so as to reflect its values.[35]

The subject of population and its relationship to
group power becomes of increasing concern to the
U.S. government and to other developed countries
when one considers that birthrates in northern
industrial countries are at record lows, while fertility
and rates of population growth in virtually all less-
developed regions are considerably higher. Such
trends would clearly suggest a dramatic change in
the balance of global power over a relatively short
time. Indeed, these concerns are expressed in the
north with ever-increasing frequency. Says Pierre
Lellouche, an aide to Jacques Chirac,

> The African population is projected to
> triple within the next 30 years, reach-
> ing an estimated level of 1.6 billion.
> Moreover, the Middle East, Central
> Asia and the Indian subcontinent all
> have volatile admixtures of acute pov-
> erty, demographic explosion and politi-
> cal instability. Together these regions
> will have some 4 billion people within
> 30 years, while due north sit 500 mil-
> lion aging Europeans already in a
> squall of demographic depression.[36]

---

[35] Huntington, op. cit., at pages 69-70.

[36] "France in Search of Security," by Pierre Lellouche, *Foreign
Affairs*, Spring 1993, at pages 123-124.

The impact of a stagnant or declining European census and continuing high birthrates to the immediate south is considerably more complex than Mr. Lellouche's vision of a future France teeming with Asian and African faces, alien religions, foreign languages, and radical ideas. Changes in the human constituency of the world have a direct bearing on the way in which social advantage and material goods are distributed throughout the world. Says one author,

> Regardless of what happens in the aggregate, within a nation or within the world, the component groups or nations will grow or maintain themselves at different rates. The consequence is almost certain to be changes in group relationships and international relations over time... ¶ If we conceive of each significantly differentiable group has having a stake in the larger society of which it is a constituent, then we can also conceive of its seeking to preserve that stake or to enlarge it over time... we can only be sure that over time change will take place in its relations with other groups that reflect the relative changes in populations.[37]

But even before such changes take place on a global scale, they are likely to produce changes

---

[37] *Beyond Malthus: Population and Power* by Neil W. Chamberlain, Basic Books, New York/London, 1970, at pages 11-12.

within countries that impact the international political environment. The examples of the Middle East and South Africa are given by one contemporary writer to illustrate the fears of ethnic groups who anticipate that, "as in a Darwinian struggle, the faster-growing species will encroach upon, and eventually overwhelm, a population with static or declining numbers."[38]

> Israeli anxieties that the Arab population within Israel's own (enlarged) boundaries is growing faster than the Jewish population, the alteration in the Christian-Muslim population balance in Lebanon (to the Muslims' advantage), and tensions and apprehensions in places as far apart as Quebec and Fiji all remind us of the political dimensions of population decline. ...[T]o what extent, one wonders, was the South African government's decision to abandon apartheid influenced by its recognition of the white's shrinking share of the total population, from one-fifth in 1951 to one-seventh in the early 1980s, and to a projected one-ninth or one-eleventh by 2020?[39]

Here, the fear of U.S. policy-makers is not just that national leaders in these countries may take

---

[38] *Preparing for the Twenty-First Century* by Paul Kennedy, Random House, 1993, at page 40.

[39] Kennedy, op. cit., at page 40.

- 32 -

different positions on domestic issues to reflect new demographic realities, but that the populations themselves may become "radicalized" — or, in the words of a 1984 Central Intelligence Agency report, "subject to manipulation by opposition elements."[40]

The CIA demographic assessment begins by advising that, "Population change and the buildup of demographic pressures are important underlying determinants of political instability in Third World countries vital to US interests." It lists four specific characteristics of high fertility societies — a high proportion of youth, migration across borders, urbanization, and changing ethnic structures — which might "lead to regime-threatening unrest."[41] The preponderance of youth in the developing world, the CIA adds, is especially important because younger people tend to be "receptive to recruiting by extremist politicians and religious zealots."[42] This "youth factor" is almost as important as the overall size of the population, according to many researchers:

> The youth of a growing population may
> very well play a major role in pressing

---

[40] CIA. Directorate of Intelligence. "CIA Views on Third World Population Issues." June 11, 1984 (declassified January 1995), at page 5.

[41] "CIA Views on Third World Population Issues." op. cit., at page 1.

[42] "CIA Views on Third World Population Issues." op. cit., at page 2.

for change. They are among those who are usually disproportionately disadvantaged; they have less at stake in the existing structure of authority, more idealism, more impatience, and in a society with a steady or rising rate of growth their proportion of the total population increases. The density of the number of youth relative to the total population may thus be one clue to the strength of pressures for change.[43]

And a 1986 book on *Population Growth in Latin America and U.S. National Security* was even more blunt:

In virtually all the countries of Latin America, half the population is under 18 years of age. In some of the countries, half of the population is under 15. The cause of these astounding figures is of course continued high birthrates accompanied by major improvements in infant and child care and in public health measures such as immunization. The implications for politics and foreign policy of these figures are enormous.[44]

---

[43] Chamberlain, op. cit., at pages 54-55.

[44] "Population, Internal Unrest, and U.S. Security in Latin America" by Howard J. Wiarda and Ieda Siqueira Wiarda, in *Population Growth in Latin America and U.S. National Security*, edited by John Saunders, Allen & Unwin, Inc., Westchester, MA.

The writer adds that the likely outcome of the situation will be "riots and revolutionary activities; the unraveling of political systems; and, finally, war, both civil and international."[45]

According to the same theory, once these "regime-threatening" elements in various nations gain sufficient strength and credibility to force a re-examination of national policies (their opposition to U.S. interests is taken for granted), new blocs and alignments will start to form. And it is at this juncture that "third world" population growth threatens the survival of the old order by stimulating competing ideologies and strengthening the relative power of the emerging nations. A demography text popular both before and after World War II explains the relationship of population to authority in these words:

> The thesis here is, then, that the changing rates of population growth in different nations help to create changes in the pressure of populations on the resources available to them and that as these changing pressures come to be felt more and more they are almost certain to lead to violent attempts to effect new adjustments more favorable to the growing peoples. Moreover, the tensions thus created are likely to become greater as the

---

1986, at page 161.

[45] Wiarda, op. cit., at page 159.

industrial power of these growing peoples increases and as their political organization enables them to act in a more unified manner to undertake to enforce what they come to feel are just demands for a larger share in the world's resources.[46]

In other words, national populations throughout the southern hemisphere are growing at rates far greater than those in the west, and this increase is occurring precisely at a time when these regions are on the verge of industrial and technological modernization. And development, along with enhanced numerical strength, virtually assures them the capacity to challenge the older powers. Another author explains:

It is common knowledge that those countries now going through the process of industrialization are also the ones that are growing most rapidly in population. This fact, known as the 'demographic transition,' significantly affects a nation's power. Industrialization leads to an increase in population, which in turn may make possible further industrialization.[47]

---

[46] *Population Problems* by Warren S. Thompson, McGraw-Hill Book Company, Inc., New York, Fourth Edition, 1953, at page 349.

[47] *The Might of Nations: World Politics in Our Time*, op. cit, at page 20.

Thus, it is hardly surprising that "development assistance" supplied by wealthy nations — and the grudging compliance with birth control "reform" it buys — has so utterly failed to produce the promised increase in wealth. Indeed, the donor nations are no more anxious to see the peoples of the south advance economically than they are to see their numbers increase. An this becomes all the more apparent when one considers the effect of population growth in Europe before and during the colonial period, and compares this history with future prospects in light of present low birthrates.

[I]t was the Industrial Revolution in Europe, simultaneously sustaining massive growth in population *and* producing enhanced forms of transportation and weaponry, that really stimulated the continent's outward thrust. Between 1846 and 1890, people emigrated from Europe at an average rate of 377,000 per year, but between 1891 and 1910 emigration soared to an average rate of 911,000 per year. Indeed, between 1846 and 1930, over 50 million Europeans sought a new life overseas. Since the European populations at home were also expanding rapidly in this period, their share of total world population steadily increased; according to one calculation, 'the Caucasian population was about 22 percent of the human species in 1800, and about 35 percent in 1930.' This was the demographic foundation of what would later be

termed 'the world revolution of Westernization.' Whether they liked it or
not, other societies across the planet
were compelled to respond to the expansion of Western man, his politics,
ideas, and economics. Many of them,
of course, fell under the direct political
control of the European immigrants.[48]

Numerous texts have been written over the past
few decades dealing with an epidemic of low fertility
in the industrial world. The situation has become a
subject of study for panels and commissions, an
object of pronatalist legislation in some countries,
and a topic of intensive research by various branches
of government. In essence, birthrates are at levels
that are historically unprecedented in most western
nations. In Germany, for example, the total fertility
rate has fallen to just 1.3 — meaning that German
couples will produce just slightly more than one child
each on the average. In raw demographic terms, this
means that every two persons in the current generation of young adults will be succeeded in the next
generation by only 1.3 — an actual one-generation
population decline of 35 percent. In Italy, the total
fertility rate has fallen to 1.5. Population growth
rates for virtually all parts of western Europe are well
below the "replacement" level of two children per

---

[48] Kennedy, op. cit., at page 42. The author's quotes are attributed
to *The Economic History of World Population* by C. M. Cipolla
(Harmondsworth, Middlesex, 1978) and *The World Revolution of
Westernization* by T. H. Von Lau (New York/Oxford, 1987).

couple and, in fact, the fertility rate of Europe as a whole is just 1.6.

The significance of this trend has not escaped the attention of the CIA and other government agencies involved in the formulation and implementation of U.S. foreign policy. "Chronic and potentially severe labor shortages" are likely to occur in western nations having "an insufficient pool" of young workers, advises the CIA in an unclassified report titled "Youth Deficits: An Emerging Population Problem," which was published in August of 1990. A "youth deficit," the study is explains, occurs when young people between the ages of 15 and 24 drop below 15 to 20 percent of a country's total population. This age group, it adds, is "particularly significant" because these are the people who make up the entry-level work force.[49] Say the experts at Central Intelligence...

> A population trend that portends new societal stress is beginning to emerge in a number of countries around the globe — the development of age structures with unprecedented low number of young adults. Since the early 1970s, the average number of children born to women in nearly every developed country has fallen below the number of children required for a population to 'replace' itself. The persistence of low

---

[49] "Youth Deficits: An Emerging Population Problem," Central Intelligence Agency, August 1990 (unclassified); reprinted in *Population and Development Review*, December 1990, at pages 801-807.

fertility means that successive infant
cohorts become smaller, eventually
resulting in a population with a small
proportion of young adults.[50]

According to the CIA analysis, there were no
countries with populations larger than 5 million that
faced youth deficits in 1980. But by 1985, seven
nations had already fallen into this category, and
nine more were added before the end of the decade.
"On the basis of the number of births over the last
two decades," the report continued, "we anticipate
youth deficits in at least 29 countries — including
almost all industrialized countries and a number of
key developing countries — by the year 2010."[51]

And a series of studies commissioned in 1988 by
the Office of the Director of Net Assessment at the
Department of Defense looked at fertility trends from
a similar angle, noting that a "significant demographic fact affecting the world today is the general aging
of the population," the consequence of "the decline of
previously high fertility rates and increases in life
expectancy."[52]

---

[50] *Population and Development Review*, op. cit., at pages 801-802.

[51] *Population and Development Review*, op. cit. at page 802.

[52] "Global Demographic Trends to the Year 2010: Implications for
U.S. Security" by Gregory D. Foster et. al., *The Washington
Quarterly*, Spring 1989, pages 5-24. A note appearing with the text
explains that the article is a summary, some parts inserted
verbatim, from a longer report prepared for the Commission on
Integrated Long-Term Strategy, under the Director of Net Assess-

The situation is especially pronounced in the developed world, where the median age by the year 2025 will be almost 39. In contrast, the median age in the developing world by that time will stand at about 30 (with some regions, such as Africa, appreciably lower). ¶ The significance of this pattern lies in the fact that aging implies a reduction in productivity and the possibility of economic stagnation. It produces a high ratio of retirees to workers and thus increased taxes and social security expenditures. Armed forces must compete for both money and people, but less overall money exists because the productive population base has shrunk.[53]

Here, again, the critical issue is not the unilateral decline of the rich nations but, more significantly, comparative rates of growth between the "old" powers of the north and the emerging states of the south. The same Pentagon study projects that fully 93 percent of population growth in the remainder of this century and the first decades of the next will occur in developing nations, boosting their share of the world's people to more then 80 percent by the first decade of the 21st. It adds:

---

ment, Department of Defense.

[53] *Washington Quarterly*, op. cit., at pages 6-7.

One of the most important issues in the years ahead will be the extent to which demographic developments are likely to affect the size and composition of military establishments around the world. On the whole, demographic factors will produce completely different concerns in the developed world than in the developing world. Declining fertility rates will make it increasingly difficult for the United States and its North Atlantic Treaty Organization (NATO) allies and the Soviet Union and its Warsaw Pact allies alike to maintain military forces at current levels. In contrast, exceptionally high fertility rates in most LDCs, if not matched by a commensurate growth of jobs, could lead to expanded military establishments in affected countries as a productive alternative to unemployment. In other words, where labor forces are significantly under-employed, military establishments may have a built-in momentum to capitalize on unused manpower for purposes of both internal and external security.[54]

The military researchers found that because "the types of conflicts likely to predominate in the years ahead are manpower-intensive regional conflicts," developing nations may indeed achieve "added power

---

[54] *Washington Quarterly*, op cit., at page 6.

Southside Pregnancy Help Center
4318 West Forest Home Avenue
Milwaukee, Wisconsin 53219

and influence" as a result of their growing populations.[55]

Population change is expected to diminish the relative advantage of the wealthy nations in just about every imaginable way. But contemporary literature suggests that four areas — culture, race, economics and military superiority — are of the greatest concern to the population establishment.

The future of Eurocentric culture as the global standard has become the topic even of commercial books like a 1987 contribution called *The Birth Dearth.* "Western culture was dominant forty-odd years ago after the end of World War II, when the West made up about 22 percent of the earth's population," argues author Ben Wattenberg, a scholar with the influential American Enterprise Institute in Washington. "Today, the West comprises 15 percent — and we are still dominant. [But] it is just about a sure thing that it will decline to under 9 percent by 2025 and probably down to about 5 percent by 2100 if present trends continue." Therefore, he continues, it becomes "unreal to suggest that our values will remain untouched as our numbers go down, and down, and down, if our economic and military power go down, and down, and down. It will be difficult for tiny minorities, growing weaker (we Westerners) to set the tone or values of the world."[56] Thus, Wattenberg concludes:

---

[55] *Washington Quarterly,* op cit., at page 6.

[56] *The Birth Dearth* by Ben Wattenberg. Pharos Books, 1987, at pages 97-98.

> Even if Western fertility should climb back to the replacement level in the decades to come, the population of the Third World will be a much greater proportion of the world's population than it is now. Those Third World nations will also likely be richer and more powerful than they are now... ¶ Do we know enough about the Chinese, the Indians, the Indonesians, the Nigerians, the Brazilians? Do we know their languages? Do we know their cultures? We ought to. These are the demographic superpowers of the next century.[57]

Equally crude and chauvinistic are some of the predictions made by "population professionals" — persons affiliated with institutions working under official contract to promote the use of birth control in the developing world.

The Population Council, founded by John D. Rockefeller III at the height of the cold war, receives major cash grants from the Agency for International Development to conduct psycho-social research into family planning attitudes, clinical tests of new contraceptives, and outreach to policy-makers in the developing world, as well as financing for a variety of population and family planning-related activities from the United Nations and several European countries. A working paper published by the Council's Center for Policy Studies in March of 1982

---

[57] Wattenberg, op. cit., at page 164.

examines the "sharp differences in observed and anticipated national and regional growth rates" between the rich and poor nations, and warns:

> From the point of view of the slower growing nations, this feature of global demographic growth is a source of obvious if ill-articulated long-term concern. In the domain of evolutionary theory, the consequence of any sustained difference between the rates of growth of two populations occupying the same ecological niche is straightforward: *the eventual complete displacement of the slower growing population by the faster growing one.* Since among human populations rates of growth are subject to social adjustment and relative magnitudes *may be reversed by conscious action,* the biological principle is not directly applicable. Nevertheless, the shifts in relative demographic weights can be remarkably rapid and, barring catastrophic developments (which, of course, may also reinforce the existing trend), non-reversible.[58]

In other words, those groups of people having sustained low fertility rates (persons of European descent) are counselled that their "eventual complete

---

[58] "International Aspects of Population Policies" by Paul Demeny, Center for Policy Studies, Working Paper No. 80, The Population Council, New York, March 1982, at page 8. Emphasis added.

displacement" at the hands of Asians, Africans, Arabs and Latin Americans is imminent — unless, of course, "conscious action" is taken to reverse the trend.

This race-survival theme has its parallel in the "privileged class" rhetoric of an official with another group having multiple engagements with the U.S. government's military and population control effort. According to Phyllis T. Piotrow, head of an elite psychological operations task force at the Johns Hopkins University in Baltimore,

> Wherever juxtaposed groups experience different fertility rates, the group with the highest per capita income and the greatest economic power is always the group with the lowest fertility. In these circumstances population growth represents a threat to the status quo: to political dominance and economic and social stability. This threat can easily erupt into a political crisis. When outbreaks do occur, of course, the immediate causes will always be perceived as political, but the underlying reasons may indeed be demographic.[59]

---

[59] Phyllis T. Piotrow in "Population Policies for the 80s: Meeting the Crest of the Demographic Wave." in *Six Billion People: Demographic Dilemmas and World Politics* by Georges Tapinos and Phyllis T. Piotrow. Council on Foreign Relations. McGraw-Hill Book Company. 1978. at page 143.

Piotrow envisions a "third world" at the boiling point: "Under conditions of growing unrest, aggravated by new masses of impoverished and dispossessed urban and rural populations, it will not be difficult to identify foreign scapegoats, to arouse great hostility toward the affluent countries, and to vent frustrations by sabotaging foreign interests and expropriating businesses, as well as kidnapping foreign business leaders, hijacking airplanes, and committing other terrorist acts."[60] Convinced that the fortress can only be secured by means of birth control, Piotrow laments the fact that the World Bank's policy of making population control compliance "one among many elements ... that indicate creditworthiness" has been "fraught with political difficulties."[61] And she insinuates that monetary "incentives" ought to be given to impoverished couples who accept family planning.[62]

Equally antagonistic is the UN-subsidized Population Institute in Washington, which sees "over-population" as a "cancer" eating away at white

---

[60] Piotrow, op. cit., at page 143.

[61] Piotrow, op. cit., at page 95. George Tapinos, Piotrow's co-author and a professor of economics and demography and the Institute of Political Studies in Paris, presents more of the same, cautioning (on page 16 of the same book) that "differential population growth among groups striving for greater control over economic and political resources heightens ethnic self-consciousness and serves to upset political bargains between groups worked out in earlier periods of time."

[62] Piotrow, op. cit., at pages 110-116.

military supremacy around the globe. "One of the overwhelming security issues of the 1990s and into the next century will concern resources and the struggle of the industrialized world to acquire all the necessary materials from the developing world," says a briefing paper prepared by the group in 1989. "More important to the United States' security is, and increasingly will be, the availability of ample strategic and critical materials for economic and military uses. The key competition in the next century will be a contest for resources between northern hemisphere and southern hemisphere, rather than the traditional confrontation — east vs. west."[63]

Here, the publication cites the fact that the U.S. must import most of its cobalt from two countries — Zaire and Zambia, both of which are likely to see a doubling of their populations within 23 years — to demonstrate that "the future of the majority of our cobalt imports is precarious, to say the least." The same is said about the "increasingly perilous" future of columbium imports, dependent mainly on Brazil, Nigeria, and Thailand.

Chromium, manganese, and platinum, too, must all be imported from such regions as southern Africa and Brazil, geographical hot-spots of the developing

---

[63] "Strategic and Critical Materials: The United States' Precarious Future." *Toward The 21st Century.* The Population Institute, Washington, November 4, 1989, at page 2.

world which the report characterizes as filled with "teeming masses of angry and disillusioned youth."[64]

Not only do growing populations in developing nations present competition for prized mineral resources, the briefing continues, but their aspirations are so contrary to the American vision that their mere existence intensifies our need for The Bomb:

> If major symptoms of unchecked population growth in the developing world include significant increases in political, social and economic instability, as experts in the U.S. and abroad have suggested, then supplies of strategic and critical materials will be increasingly important for American military and economic security in the future.[65]

In conclusion, says the same report, it is time for a family planning surgical strike: "The United States, as well as the rest of the nations of the world, have something available to them that no medical doctor fighting bodily cancer has yet to find: a cure for the cancer of overpopulation."[66]

Not surprisingly, the timing of population control efforts is discussed with "do-or-die" urgency by certain branches of government and private popula-

---

[64] *Toward The 21st Century*, November 4, 1989, op. cit., at pages 1-7.

[65] *Toward The 21st Century*, November 4, 1989, op. cit. at page 8.

[66] *Toward The 21st Century*, November 4, 1989, op. cit. at page 8.

tion lobby groups in the U.S. According to an official at Washington's largest population issues lobby:

> This decade presents the last chance to stabilize human populations by the middle of the next century, through humane and voluntary measures, at something less than double the current world population of 5.4 billion. Meeting that goal would require a massive and immediate international effort to implement family planning and development programs known to reduce birthrates rapidly.[67]

And columnist Cord Meyer, in a manifesto published in the *Washington Times* under the headline, "Warning to the West," writes:

> Whether the world population eventually stabilizes at a barely tolerable 10 billion people in 2050 depends in large measure on the extent to which the industrialized nations contribute adequately and promptly to funds needed for family planning in the developing countries.[68]

---

[67] "Population: The Critical Decade," by Sharon L. Camp, *Foreign Policy*, Spring 1993, at page 126. Camp is a director of Population Action International, formerly known as the Population Crisis Committee.

[68] "Warning to the West," by Cord Meyer, *The Washington Times*, June 18, 1993, at page F3.

Meyer, a senior official at the Central Intelligence Agency who for years headed the Agency's London bureau, knows, of course, that the real issue is not finding the needed first-world funds "adequately and promptly," but rather getting the leaders of target countries to adopt population policies and devising a strategy for getting contraceptives to the masses. Indeed, testimony submitted on behalf of the Director of Central Intelligence at a February 10, 1975 congressional briefing advised, "A future issue that the U.S. may have to grapple with is whether a viable population growth control program should be a condition for food aid and assistance for long-range agricultural development in LDCs [less-developed countries]."[69] And yet another CIA report, still partially classified, implies that the U.S. would even be willing to risk temporarily upsetting precious "stability" in pursuit of its population control agenda.

> Implementation of long-term goals for slowing world population growth will at times necessarily come into conflict with such immediate requirements as

---

[69] DCI Congressional Briefings, 10 February 1975, "Food and Population Problems" (released by the CIA January 1995), at page 5. A virtually identical statement was issued on May 7, 1977 by the CIA at another briefing: "Future issues facing the U.S. include (1) ways to soften the impact of large food exports on domestic price levels, (2) methods of allocating food exports between the affluent and poor nations in short supply years, and (3) decision on whether a viable population growth control program should be a condition for granting food aid and financial assistance."

maintaining stability in and effective
ties with certain poor countries.[70]

The pervasiveness of this eleventh-hour despera-
tion among Washington officials, however, is made
most emphatically clear by the Defense Department's
1988 threat assessment team, which recommended
that "population planning" be elevated to a status
comparable to the procurement of new weapons
systems.

> As difficult and uncertain as the task
> may be, policymakers and strategic
> planners in this country have little
> choice in the coming decades but to
> pay serious attention to population
> trends, their causes, and their effects.
> Already the United States has em-
> barked on an era of constrained re-
> sources. It thus becomes more impor-
> tant than ever to do those things that
> will provide more bang for every buck
> spent on national security. To claim
> that decreased defense spending must
> lead to strategic debilitation is fatuous.
> Rather, policymakers must anticipate
> events and conditions before they
> occur. They must employ all the in-
> struments of statecraft at their dispos-
> al (development assistance and popu-
> lation planning every bit as much as
> new weapon systems). Furthermore,

---

[70] CIA. "Political Perspectives on Key Global Issues." op. cit. at page
4.

instead of relying on the canard that
the threat dictates one's posture, they
must attempt to influence the form
that threat assumes.[71]

---

[71] *The Washington Quarterly.* op. cit. at page 24.

Chapter 5

Our Leaders Are Your Leaders: The Policy Development Initiative

The white man lives today at the peak of his power. Slow to start and late to flower, European civilization bestowed upon a pale minority of human beings the military, economic, and ideological power to dominate the globe. Although never a majority, Europeans and their descendants have increased their numbers greatly, multiplying more than sevenfold in the three centuries from 1650 to 1950, while the rest of the world's population grew less than fourfold.

Katherine Organski and A.F.K. Organski, in
Population and World Power (1961)[72]

Europe and more generally the industrialized countries seem to be in the midst of a complex process of evolution... and disastrous demographic consequences seem possible. The fate of the human species — or at least of certain national populations — is at stake in this process.

Jean Bourgeois-Pichat, "The Unprecedented
Shortage of Births in Europe" (1985)[73]

---

[72] *Population and World Power* by Katherine Organski and A.F.K. Organski, Alfred A. Knopf, New York, 1961, at page 85.

[73] "The Unprecedented Shortage of Births in Europe" by Jean Bourgeois-Pichat, from a conference on "Below-Replacement Fertility in Industrial Societies: Causes, Consequences, Policies," the Hoover Institution, Stanford University, November 1985; published by *Population and Development Review* as a supplement to Vol. 12, 1986, pages 24-25.

The U.S. government has long recognized that it cannot have a smoothly-functioning population control program without the cooperation of government officials in the host countries. And the likelihood is remote indeed of obtaining negotiated, voluntary agreements with foreign leaders to depopulate their own constituents. Thus, leaders in the industrialized world have sought a variety of alternate means to secure the collusion of heads of state and important ministries throughout the south.

Unquestionably, the single most important tool in the west's arsenal of coercive weapons has been its power to influence such international bodies as the United Nations, the International Monetary Fund, the World Bank and the various regional development banks and funds. By the mid-1940s — when the United Nations was founded and the Bretton Woods conference constructed the IMF and World Bank — population change had already emerged as a long-range security matter in the developed world. In fact, it was on the initiative of two countries — the U.S. and U.K. — that the population issue was incorporated as a subject of "policy" research at the UN. A brief overview of the way the population issues were seen by national leaders at that time is instructive.

On March 3, 1944, King George the Sixth of Britain assembled a Royal Commission on Population to "examine the facts relating to the present population trends in Great Britain; to investigate the causes of these trends and to consider the probable consequences; to consider what measures, if any, should be taken in the national interest to influence the future trend of population, and to make recommendations."[74]

A final report of the Royal Commission, circulated in June of 1949, confirmed what most Britons already knew — namely that there had been a monumental drop in the rate of national population increase over the preceding decades, and — more importantly — that falling fertility "is a phenomenon common to most of the peoples of Western civilization, and virtually confined to them."[75]

The panel took note of the fact that the rapid growth of the European population during the 18th and 19th centuries had been "largely responsible for the extension of European control over inhabited tropical and semi-tropical countries and their development as suppliers of food and raw material."[76] It added that consistent and substantial population increase ...

> was in fact an essential condition not only for the development of Britain itself as a great and rich nation, but

---

[74] Royal Commission on Population. Report, presented to Parliament by Command of His Majesty, June 1949. His Majesty's Stationery Office, London. The decree authorizing the work of the Commission appears on pages iii and iv of the final report.

[75] Royal Commission on Population. Report, page 134.

[76] Royal Commission on Population, op. cit., at page 7. The document further notes that the proportion of the world's people of European descent "has increased much faster than the part that lives in Europe, rising from 25 percent [of world population] in 1800 to 34 percent in 1900."

also of the growth of the new overseas countries inhabited mainly or largely by people of British descent and of the spread of British culture and influence all over the world through emigrants, commerce and capital investment.[77]

It is significant that the authors of the study attributed the trend toward small families among the English almost entirely to the practice of deliberate fertility limitation. "There is ... an overwhelming volume of evidence in this and other countries that the rates of childbearing are at present being greatly restricted by the practice of birth control and other methods of deliberate family limitation," the panel concluded, adding that "there can be no doubt that if the married couples of today wished to have much larger families than they now have, they would be able to do so."[78]

According to the Royal panelists, the impact of low fertility, particularly in the context of the relatively high birthrates of the world's non-white peoples, could be dramatic. The Commission declared:

> The establishment or continuance among Western peoples of sizes of family below replacement level would

---

[77] Royal Commission on Population. Report. page 8.

[78] Royal Commission on Population. Report. page 34. The Commission's findings also included a lengthy and sophisticated analysis of the social and economic factors responsible for the popularity of birth control in England.

accentuate a change in relative numbers which threatens in a few generations to be as radical as that between
France and Germany in the nineteenth
century, and might be as decisive in
its effects on the prestige and influence of the West. The question, it
should be observed, is not merely one
of military strength and security; that
question becomes merged in more
fundamental issues of the maintenance and extension of Western
values, ideas and culture.[79]

In other words, the momentum had gone out of
the European population "explosion," leaving them
without the catalyst which they credited with inspiring development at home and facilitating the conquest of territories and peoples around the world.
Even more frightening to the King's advisors was the
fact that population growth was now concentrated
precisely in those regions that had suffered at the
hands of the colonizers. Clearly, the Commission
considered the differential rates of fertility between
north and south to be a misplaced advantage, and
one more suited to action on the part of the UN than
the Crown.

On the other side of the Atlantic, public officials
and other experts were expressing the same ideas.
Frank Notestein, head of an elite Office of Population
Research housed at Princeton University, was soon
to become the first head of the United Nations

---

[79] Royal Commission on Population, Report, page 134.

Population Division — an honor bestowed on him for his keen insights into the relationship between "third world" birthrates and the future ability of the U.S. and its allies to affect the intellectual and economic domination of others.

Notestein had commented on the subject of fertility and national policy at an April 1944 conference of the Milbank Memorial Fund in New York, warning that the rise of the so-called third world "would adversely affect the immediate economic interests of this country and of other Western powers that are heavily dependent on the specialized products of these regions."[80]

Notestein acknowledged that one way to minimize the potential for conflict over resources might be "a highly complex and integrated program of modernization" in the developing countries.[81] But this, in the absence of counter-measures, could become a liability. Thus he wrote,

> By launching a program of modernization, the now dominant powers would in effect be creating a future world in which their own peoples would become progressively smaller minorities, and

[80] Frank W. Notestein, "Problems of Policy in Relation to Areas of Heavy Population Pressure," from *Demographic Studies of Selected Areas of Rapid Growth,* proceedings of the 22nd annual conference of the Milbank Memorial Fund, April 12-13, 1944, New York. Published by the Milbank Memorial Fund, New York, 1944. Page 155.

[81] Milbank Memorial Fund, op. cit. at page 155.

> possess a progressively smaller pro-
> portion of the world's wealth and pow-
> er. The determination of national poli-
> cy toward the under-developed regions
> must be made in the light of that
> fact.[82]

Equally relevant are Notestein's recommendations for ways to impose population control on
political leaders abroad, since they essentially became the blueprint for the UN population program.
"It is important that specific and widespread propaganda be directed to developing an interest in the
health and welfare of children rather than in large
families for their own sake," his research paper
stated. "Such education would also involve propaganda in favor of controlled fertility as an integral part of
a public health program."[83] And efforts to install
contraceptive-friendly political leaders would be even
more useful, according to Notestein.

> It is important to develop a native
> leadership that will acquire new values
> rapidly and serve as a medium for
> their diffusion. To this end, native
> political leaders, civil servants, and
> native middle classes are needed.[84]

---

[82] Milbank Memorial Fund. op. cit., at pages 155-156.

[83] Milbank Memorial Fund. op. cit., at page 154.

[84] Milbank Memorial Fund. op. cit. at page 154.

A number of specific roles are played by the UN — or more accurately, by its various social and scientific agencies — in pursuit of the global population program. It can exert pressure on leaders of developing countries to liberalize contraceptive distribution and access regulations, to adopt official family planning goals, and even to enact policies explicitly designed to reduce the size of future generations. It can provide data and information to political leaders in developing nations to support birth control as part of a larger public health scheme or arrange a mountain of "scientific" data to portray population growth rates as excessively high and burdensome.

Beginning with the creation of a special UN Population Fund in 1967, it can also supply funding and personnel for family planning programs, train project workers, and affect the dissemination of policy-relevant information to government officials. UN agencies also perform a vital function in the collection of population statistics and social science information that are used for both the initial development of population policies and for monitoring their implementation, once adopted. As one published study has noted, the UN compiles and publishes data on fertility and population change, supplies interpretation of statistics, and acts as "a source of guidelines and priorities, and an important influence on funding and project policies of governments throughout the world."[85] But all of these roles might just as

---

[85] Piotrow in *Six Billion People: Demographic Dilemmas and World Politics*, op. cit., at page 95.

well be — and nearly always are — performed by contractors accountable directly to the various aid-donor governments, as well.

What is special about the role of the UN is that it can act as a filter, so to speak, making the harsh pronouncements of officials at the State Department and Pentagon sound a little less biased and substantially less political. The use of "benevolent" United Nations agencies conceals the interest of the United States in the birth control issue, and thus makes the advice they convey look more like valid opinion and less like raw imperialism. Furthermore, because the United Nations theoretically speaks for all its member states, its active pursuit of population reduction schemes is markedly different from a campaign by the world's white rulers to prevent births among persons of color. And lastly, of course, the UN can effectively reach government leaders in nations with which the United States may not have diplomatic relations.

As for the duplication of efforts involved in running similar (or even identical) programs at both the bilateral and multilateral levels, this, too, is far from coincidental. Indeed, such duplication is the very essence of the "multiplier effect" strategy by which persuasion comes on many fronts. Developing countries are not only constrained through diplomatic and economic channels by the United States, the European Community, and other bilateral donors, but also by such lenders as the IMF and the World Bank, certain regional lending institutions and funds, and by virtually all the "social" institutes within the UN system. While the effort may be repetitious, it is also *universal.* In other words, virtually every source of advice, input, technical assistance, and financial aid appears unified in calling for plans and programs to reduce birthrates. This can make a critical difference, because one single voice of opposition — or even neutrality — could theoretically offer heads of state the latitude they need to opt out.

The international population control effort requires not just a uniformity of voices, but an enormous amount of patience, as well. Again, the United Nations helped by employing a "gradualist" approach, first relegating the matter of population to years of study and interpretation by "experts." Once the concept of conducting demographic research had become well entrenched at the UN, however, escalation followed in the form of admonitions that the various high-birthrate countries take steps to stem their growth. An important aspect of this phase was the international population conference, something which dates back even before the founding of the UN.

The first "world" population meeting took place in 1925, when an elite group of well-connected birth control advocates met in New York and passed a declaration calling upon the UN's predecessor, the League of Nations, to establish "a commission to study this question of birth control with a view to making recommendations to the constituent nations."[86] In 1929, under the guidance of the same U.S.-based birth control movement, a World Popula-

---

[86] *The United Nations and the Population Question 1945-1970* by Richard Symonds and Michael Carder. A Population Council Book. McGraw-Hill, New York, 1973, at page 11.

tion Conference was held in Geneva. Although the gathering lacked the explicit sponsorship of the League, many of its officials did attend in a personal capacity. In 1938, nine years after the Geneva conference, the League finally did pass a resolution creating "a special committee of experts to study demographic problems and especially their connection with the economic, financial and social situation and to submit a report on the subject which may be of value to governments in the determination of policy."[87] The committee was assembled the following year, but managed to meet only once before the outbreak of World War II.[88]

The UN's early focus on population research was not just a means of keeping a foot in the door, however. At the time the UN was born as the League's successor, western powers had little knowledge of fertility and population growth rates in the southern hemisphere, with the possible exception of India. The colonial nations were, however, in the words of one documented history, "preoccupied with falling birth rates [at home] and fears of population decline."[89] Therefore, their leaders had a keen interest in any data that might reveal rates of population growth abroad, and felt this would be most effectively

---

[87] *World Population and the United Nations: Challenge and Response* by Stanley P. Johnson, Cambridge University Press, New York 1987, at page 7.

[88] Johnson, op. cit., at page 7.

[89] Symonds and Carder, op. cit., introduction, at page xiv.

collected by an international organization professing the "neutrality" of the UN.

The first international population conference under the official banner of the UN was held in Rome from August 31 to September 10, 1954. A second took place at Belgrade from August 30 through September 10, 1965. Both were intended to accommodate the presentation of "scientific" data, and were attended by experts working in population-related fields rather than by representatives of developing countries or colonies. When the matter of birth control as a solution to population "problems" was raised at the 1954 conference, for example, speakers from communist nations attacked the concept as irresponsible.[90] The Belgrade meeting went only slightly farther, including one session devoted entirely to "studies relevant to family planning."[91] In neither instance was there an attempt to reach a consensus on the need for measures to restrict population growth. Indeed, the first to do so was the much-publicized Bucharest population conference in 1974.

It was at that meeting, to which the leaders of all nations were summoned, that a World Population Plan of Action (WPPA) was introduced which called for actions, including birth control and population policies, that would result in a "stabilized" world population. As one writer who attended the meeting has noted, "there was no way in which it could be

---

[90] Symonds and Carder, op. cit., at pages 84-85.

[91] Symonds and Carder, op. cit., at page 145.

said on the opening day that a global consensus existed already on the question of population and in particular on the draft WPPA. The high officials of the United Nations who spoke at the inaugural session may indeed have believed — or been led to believe — that such a consensus existed but the course of the debate was soon to show them to be wrong."[92]

Indeed, developing nations of Latin America, Africa, the Middle East, and parts of Asia, along with the communist bloc and the Holy See, were quick to attack the plan as the malicious outgrowth of "imperialism and hegemonism." Said one delegate, "Of all things in the world, people are the most precious."[93] The reaction, which may have genuinely surprised officials in Washington, led to further behind-the-scenes deliberations in Washington. And on December 10 of the same year, a lengthy plan was drawn up to outline a definitive strategy for the future of demographic intervention. The secret report was the product of input from several U.S. government agencies, including the Central Intelligence Agency, the Agency for International Development, the Department of Defense and the State Department. It was compiled at the National Security Council level as National Security Study Memorandum 200 (NSSM 200), with the title, "Implications of Worldwide Population Growth for U.S. Security and Overseas Interests." It stated,

---

[92] Johnson, op. cit. at page 91.

[93] Johnson, op. cit., at page 97.

The beliefs, ideologies and misconceptions displayed by many nations at Bucharest indicate more forcefully than ever the need for extensive education of the leaders of many governments, especially in Africa and some in Latin America.[94]

The confidential report, which remained classified for 16 years, further explained that, "Development of a worldwide political and popular commitment to population stabilization is fundamental to any effective strategy." This, it continued, makes imperative the "support and commitment" of leaders in target states — something which will happen only "if they clearly see the negative impact of unrestricted population growth and believe it is possible to deal with this question through governmental action." Furthermore, because the motives of the west were already suspect, the paper concluded that U.S. operatives would have to find a way to "encourage LDC leaders to take the lead in advancing family planning....."[95]

The National Security Council document warned, however, against taking any provocative action that might "give the appearance to the LDCs of an indus-

---

[94] "Implications of Worldwide Population Growth for U.S. Security and Overseas Interests." National Security Study Memorandum 200 (also known as "NSSM 200"). December 10, 1974, at page 96.

[95] NSSM 200, Introduction, at page 18.

trialized country policy directed *against* the LDCs,"[96] recommending instead that the U.S. use its leverage at the UN and other multilateral institutions to assist officials of developing countries "in integrating population factors in national plans, particularly as they relate to health services, education, agricultural resources and development," and that it attempt to "relate population policies and family planning programs to major sectors of development: health, nutrition, agriculture, education, social services, organized labor, women's activities, and community development."[97] It added that...

> ... providing integrated family planning and health services on a broad basis would help the U.S. contend with the ideological charge that the U.S. is more interested in curbing the numbers of LDC people than it is in their future and well-being. While it can be argued, and argued effectively, that limitation of numbers may well be one of the most critical factors in enhancing development potential and improving the chances for well-being, we should recognize that those who argue along ideological lines have made a great deal of the fact that the U.S. contribution to development programs and health programs has steadily shrunk, whereas funding for popula-

---

[96] NSSM 200, Introduction, at pages 21-22. Emphasis in original.

[97] NSSM 200, Introduction, at page 21.

> tion programs has steadily increased. While many explanations may be brought forward to explain these trends, the fact is that they have been an ideological liability to the U.S. in its crucial evolving relationships with the LDCs.[98]

But the text also frankly admits that rhetoric about "enhancing development potential" was a Washington device for disguising the real motivation behind population control:

> The US can help to minimize charges of an imperialist motivation behind its support of population activities by repeatedly asserting that such support derives from a concern with: (a) the right of the individual to determine freely and responsibly their number and spacing of children ... and (b) the fundamental social and economic development of poor countries....[99]

In this context, American leaders felt that the United Nations would be an ideal collaborator in the policy development process, but that western officials would also have a prominent role to play. The NSC report urged, for instance, that the U.S. arrange "familiarization programs at U.N. Headquarters in

---

[98] NSSM 200, at page 177.

[99] NSSM 200, at page 115.

New York for ministers of governments, senior policy level officials and comparably influential leaders from private life," and that American embassies abroad be on the alert for opportunities to promote policies that would be helpful to the U.S. population intervention scheme.[100] The text notes, for example, that...

> ...The USG [U.S. government] would, however, maintain an interest (e.g. through Embassies) in such countries' population problems and programs (if any) to reduce population growth rates. Moreover, particularly in the case of high priority countries to which U.S. population assistance is now limited for one reason or another, we should be alert to opportunities for expanding our assistance efforts and for demonstrating to their leaders the consequences of rapid population growth and the benefits of actions to reduce fertility.[101]

Moreover, other multilateral agencies not strictly under the UN charter were intended to participate in the policy development process. Said a section of the memorandum about the World Bank: "With greater commitment of Bank resources and improved consultation with AID and UNFPA [the United Nations Population Fund], a much greater dent could be

---

[100] NSSM 200. Introduction. at pages 21-22.

[101] NSSM 200. at page 128.

made in the overall problem."[102] The Bank, of course, had long before begun promoting population control policies as an integral part of borrower nation's development plans.

But "voluntary" cooperation on the part of host country governments — even in cases where policy statements had been made conditions for credit — was viewed as an unlikely occurrence. For this reason, the report suggested that "mandatory programs may be needed and that we should be considering these possibilities now."[103] Bilateral food aid, for example, might be used as a means of compelling national leaders to assist in the population control effort.

> Would food be considered an instrument of national power? Will we be forced to make choices as to whom we can reasonably assist, and if so, should population efforts be a criterion for such assistance? ¶ Is the US prepared to accept food rationing to help people who can't/won't control their population growth? ¶ ...Should the choice be made that the recommendations and the options given below are *not* adequate to meet this problem, consideration should be given to a

---

[102] NSSM 200, at page 149.

[103] NSSM 200, at page 118.

> further study and additional action in
> this field as outlined above.[104]

The idea of the imposing population policies on developing country leaders by force was not limited to the NSC policy statement.

The recommendations contained in NSSM 200 were made part of the U.S. government's official foreign policy on November 26, 1975, when signed by President Gerald Ford's national security advisor, Brent Scowcroft, in a binding document, National Security Decision Memorandum 314. Similar recommendations were issued again and again by top-level executive agencies in subsequent years.

Said one 1977 CIA report, for example, the United States "may be unable to avoid having to decide how to use food leverage to help manage global issues and cope with international challenges."[105] It asserted that the U.S. "has a fundamental interest in the health and welfare of its people and the preservation of their way of life,"[106] and advised,

> The ability of the U.S. to use food as
> an instrument of its foreign policy
> depends in part on the degree to which
> it controls the disposition of its agri-

---

[104] NSSM 200, at pages 119-120.

[105] CIA, "Political Perspectives on Key Global Issues," op. cit., at page 21.

[106] CIA, "Political Perspectives on Key Global Issues," op. cit., at page 20.

cultural production... Moral inclinations, economic considerations, and international political challenges posed by food and population trends, however, may lead to expanded and regularized government involvement.[107]

Still another CIA publication, issued just prior to the Bucharest population conference, suggested that a U.S. monopoly over global food distribution "could give the U.S. a measure of power it had never had before — possibly an economic and political dominance greater than that of the immediate post-World War II years."[108]

And a follow-up report to NSSM 200, prepared in May 1976 by a special population task force of the National Security Council's Under Secretaries Committee and transmitted to the White House January 3, 1977, clearly stated that the programs were intended to involve coercive measures of the most extreme sort. It listed three factors necessary in a useful population policy — "strong direction" from political leaders in target countries, the creation of a social environment which would stimulate "peer pressures" for small families, and a smoothly-running family planning operation in which birth control services actually "get to the people." On the subject

---

[107] CIA. "Political Perspectives on Key Global Issues." op. cit., at pages 20-21.

[108] Central Intelligence Agency. "Potential Implications of Trends in World Population, Food Production, and Climate." OPR-401, August 1974, unclassified, at page 39.

of national leadership and program commitment, the text stated:

> ... population programs have been particularly successful where leaders have made their positions clear, unequivocal, and public, while maintaining discipline down the line from national to village levels, marshalling government workers (including police and military), doctors, and motivators to see that population policies are well administered and executed. Such direction is the *sine-qua-non* of an effective program.[109]

---

[109] National Security Council Under Secretaries Committee, 1976, at Annex I, page 26.

Chapter 6

A First Step:
Political Intelligence

Unlike many traditional societies, those in Sub-Saharan Africa generally had no concept of having enough children... ¶ ...Consequently, the onset of premature sterility, whether from disease or planned operation, is regarded by most Africans with horror. ¶ African governments have given either no leadership or uncertain leadership to family planning programs...

...African politicians and public servants have also repeatedly been attacked on the grounds that population programs are a form of foreign intervention and that they are imperialist, neo-colonialist plots to keep Africa down... ¶ Such charges, however, are not the fundamental reason for opposition to the establishment or extension of family planning programs. The real problem is that politicians, civil servants, and political activists all feel that the programs may run counter to the basic spiritual beliefs and emotions of African society.

John C. Caldwell & Pat Caldwell in
"Cultural Forces Tending to Sustain High Fertility,"
the World Bank, 1990.[110]

---

[110] "Cultural Forces Tending to Sustain High Fertility," by John C. Caldwell & Pat Caldwell, in *Population Growth and Reproduction in Sub-Saharan Africa: Technical Analyses of Fertility and Its Consequences,* edited by George T. F. Acsadi, Gwendolyn Johnson-Acsadi & Rodolfo A. Bulatao, A World Bank Symposium; c. 1990.

The promotion of policies intended to reduce births has perhaps proceeded more cautiously in Africa than in any other developing region, in large part because of nearly-universal rejection of the concept of population control, both at the grass roots level and among leaders. In fact, it was not until the 1980s — just before the next major international population conference was held at Mexico City in 1984 — that the policy development offensive began to produce results.

The Agency for International Development's Office of Population, along with the various regional and country bureaus of USAID, has been the main branch of government charged with dispensing information and advice to foreign leaders about their role in population control. But not all policy changes are initiated by the Office of Population.

A report prepared for Congress in June of 1988 illustrates the process by which Economic Support Funds (ESF), the largest single item in the economic assistance budget, can be used to manipulate the political will of developing country leaders. It acknowledges, for example, "Sometimes AID conducts broad policy discussions with recipients without conditioning the aid on reform actions and other

---

the International Bank for Reconstruction and Development, 1818 H Street, N.W., Washington, DC 20433; chapter 13, at pages 199-214.

times conditions the aid on specific reforms.[111] It also discusses several factors that determine whether such initiatives have the desired impact. Among them are the questions of whether or not....

> Host government is able to weather dissent from unpopular reforms without jeopardizing its political stability; ¶ ESF is sufficient to leverage the anticipated policy reforms... ¶ the recipient government believes that AID will take the agreed-upon actions, such as withholding disbursements, if the recipient country fails to comply with ESF conditions.[112]

It is obvious that such tactics undermine fair and democratic government in recipient countries by forcing leaders to adopt repressive means to "weather dissent from unpopular forms" without hurting the "political stability" of the regime. Furthermore, the report strongly suggests that the impoverishment of aid-receiving nations is to the advantage of the U.S. because a smaller financial package would then be "sufficient to leverage the anticipated policy reforms." In other words, food — or at least economic develop-

---

[111] *Foreign Aid: Improving the Impact and Control of Economic Support Funds*, General Accounting Office, Publication No. NSIAD-88-182, Report to the Chairman, Subcommittee on Europe and the Middle East, Committee on Foreign Affairs, House of Representatives, June 1988, at page 3.

[112] *Improving the Impact and Control of Economic Support Funds*, op. cit., at page 28.

ment in the broad sense — is in reality being used as "an instrument of national power."

By 1990, the government was willing to state publicly that its "policy dialogue" approach had been largely successful. In a May 1990 report to Congress on the topic of "AID's Population Program," the General Accounting Office concluded that the "linkage" of population issues with economic matters, along with the "training" of political leaders, had caused many developing nations to reverse their earlier objections to birth control.

> Over the years, AID's population program has emphatically addressed this economic linkage in policy dialogue with LDC leaders in countries around the globe. Considerable technical assistance and training have been provided to LDC officials with regard to the impact of population growth on development and the positive effects of smaller family size. ¶ Partly as a consequence of AID's assistance, an international consensus has been formed on the importance of reducing population growth. ... 68 developing countries now support lower population growth compared to only nine when AID's population assistance was initiated.[113]

---

[113] *Foreign Assistance: AID's Population Program*, Report to the Chairman, Subcommittee on Foreign Relations, Committee on Appropriations, U.S. Senate, at pages 44-45.

But there is yet another mechanism in place by which the U.S. tries to compel political leaders to cave in on the issue of population control — the aid-funded "shadow lobbyist." These lobbying exercises can consist of a number of different activities — formal and informal conferences and briefings for ministry officials; the repeated presentation of biased data and projections, the establishment of quasi-governmental study centers which eventually take over the regulatory functions of government; the recruitment of key private sector leaders to act as advocates of U.S.-initiated change; the drafting of specific legislation conducive to expansion of family planning operations, and much, much more. Indeed, hundreds of millions of aid dollars have gone into this type of political influence just in the past several years.

A preparatory project designed to evaluate the attitudes and vulnerabilities of leaders in several African nations was completed in 1981. Under that program, a team of hand-picked "African advisors" was recruited to assist in the oversight mission, conducted under contract with the Battelle Human Affairs Research Centers of Washington, D.C. and funded by USAID. The policy "espionage" effort succeeded in enlisting the services of Dr. Fred Sai, a well-known advocate of population control policies who has headed both the World Bank's population section and the International Planned Parenthood Federation of London, and eight others from seven nations: Liberia, Cameroun, Kenya, Sudan, Ethiopia, Senegal, and Burkina Faso. The invitation extended to Sai read as follows:

International population assistance to Africa has been a subject of intense debate and oftentimes, controversy, for many years. My colleagues and I at Battelle Population and Development Policy (PDP), intrigued by and committed to population issues within the content [sic.] of Africa, therefore, developed a research project designed to carefully assess and analyze through personal interviews the current attitudes of African officials and policymakers regarding USAID population assistance. We also expect to measure levels of awareness and understanding regarding population phenomena. This effort is unique in that it emphasizes the participation of Africans in formulating strategies and policies in the complex and important field of population dynamics.[114]

A project report submitted by Battelle to USAID's Office of Population on December 8, 1980 focused mainly on four "pilot" study countries — Lesotho, Tanzania, Burkina Faso (then Upper Volta), and Senegal. But it set forth general guidelines for the aggressive policy development program that was unleashed on all of Africa over the next several years.

---

[114] Letter from Leonard H. Robinson, Jr., acting director of the Population and Development Policy Program, Battelle Human Affairs Research Centers, to Dr. Fred Sai, 8 December 1980.

When contemplating population assistance to Africa, the Agency for International Development must take into account the social, cultural, and economic realities of Africa and the challenges thrust upon those who seek to bring about social change, often through ill-advised shortcuts to complex socio-cultural conditions. Africans, especially politicians, government officials, and the educated elite, are politically and culturally sensitive to population issues, in particular family planning and population control. Cultural traditions, deeply rooted and constantly reinforced, dictate that large families constitute the norm, not the exception. ... Is there wonder, then, as to why Africa poses difficulties for those in the west who are frustrated at the lack of significant movement in the population arena? What is required is a commitment to assist in building an African constituency, in every country, for family planning and for the use of population variables in development planning.[115]

And, indeed, when the policy initiative achieved its major breakthrough of the decade — the launching of a massive, $100 million population reduction

---

[115] Report to Africa Bureau, Office of Regional Affairs, Agency for International Development, by Leonard H. Robinson, Jr., Battelle Human Affairs Research Centers, November 6, 1981, at pages 16-17.

scheme in Nigeria — it did so on the basis of an imaginative definition of "family planning" that made the program look like little more than an effort to help families to "achieve their wishes" with regard to "preventing unwanted pregnancies" and "securing desired pregnancies." The agreement with Nigeria also promised: "The methods prescribed shall be compatible with their [Nigerians'] culture and religious beliefs."[116] In reality, however, the U.S. government planning document described a far different set of objectives that was, by the U.S. government's own admission, incompatible with Nigerian culture and religious beliefs. Says an official project summary:

> By the end of this five-year project, it is expected that there will be a broad political and social constituency supportive of family planning policies and programs... This will be reflected in a nationwide contraceptive prevalence rate of 12 percent or approximately 2.5 million users... ¶ The project will ensure that a cadre of administrative, clinical, and educational personnel exists to plan, execute, supervise, and evaluate clinic-based family planning services in public facilities from teaching hospitals to basic [local government areas] and grass-root [sic] dispensaries... Trained community leaders will be actively promoting smaller

---

[116] U.S. Department of State and Agency for International Development, Sub-Project Paper, Family Health Initiatives II — Nigeria, Project 698-0462.20, Volume I, unclassified, at page 9.

family norms and the use of contraceptive methods. .. teachers will have been trained to include family life education in teacher colleges and urban secondary schools. More than 12,000 individuals in both the private and public sectors will be trained under this project... ¶ An innovative, broad-based information, education and communication (IEC) program will be in place to build social support, encourage smaller family norms, and explain the availability and use of modern family planning methods. Consequently, 80 percent of adults aged 15-44 will be aware of modern contraception and its benefits by 1992.[117]

While the entire focus of the document is on "persuading" Nigerians to abandon the traditional African large family, it does explicitly acknowledge that Nigerian women, if given the opportunity to "achieve their wishes" regarding family size, would have more children, not less. Indeed, the project document reports that the average Nigerian woman gives birth to 6.5 children in her lifetime, while average desired fertility is between eight and nine children per woman.[118] The project paper also reports

---

[117] Nigeria Family Health Initiatives II, Volume I, op. cit. at pages 1-2.

[118] Nigeria Family Health Initiatives II, Volume 1, op. cit. at pages 6 and 7.

that "[m]isconceptions as to religious bans on family planning are widespread."[119]

In fact, the Nigeria country plan sets out a detailed strategy for undermining pronatalist religious beliefs by holding "orientation" meetings and "motivational" sessions for influential people like "traditional and religious leaders," broadcasting "recorded testimonials from traditional and religious leaders" in the mass media, and preparing "special works addressed to specific groups" such as "Islam and family planning" — all of this making it clear that the U.S. government is not nearly so anxious to respect religious views as it is to change them.[120]

These and a host of other influence activities are, in the words of the sub-project paper, intended to satisfy a...

> ...need to broaden and deepen the extent of constituency support for the national program, with special attention to groups whose influence can have important impacts on program implementation and effectiveness. Activities in this area should aim not only at identifying potential obstacles and opposition groups to the expansion of family planning services, but at gaining group leaders' positive en-

---

[119] Nigeria Family Health Initiatives II, op. cit., Volume II, Appendix K, at pages K-3.

[120] Nigeria Family Health Initiatives II, Volume II, op. cit., Annex J, at pages J-8 through J-17.

dorsement of program goals, and where possible, to enlist various interest groups into actively contributing to policy, planning and program implementation activities.[121]

Similar attitudes toward fertility and family size can be found throughout the continent. Fertility preference surveys conducted during the 1970s and 1980s, for example, found that the average woman in Cameroun hoped to produce no fewer than eight children, while average completed family size measured just 6.5. In the Republic of Benin, where fertility again averaged 6.5 children per mother, desired family size was 7.6. In similar fashion, Senegalese women, who have an average of 6.6 children in a lifetime, prefer families of between 6.8 and 7.3 offspring. In Cote d'Ivoire, desired fertility was nearly two children per family higher than actual fertility, and in Mauritania, the average woman wanted nine children, three more than were typically born.[122]

A multitude of comparable attitude studies has shown beyond question that the concept of "too many" children is alien to African society, whereas sterility is regarded with horror. Yet sterility rates are surprisingly high in several parts of Africa. One study

---

[121] Nigeria Family Health Initiatives II, op. cit., Volume II, Appendix K, at page K-3.

[122] *The State of African Demography*, International Union for the Scientific Study of Population, Liege, Belgium, 1988, at pages 31, 38.

of African infertility, conducted in 1983 and published by the United Nations in 1989, found that more than 11 percent of all women in Angola remained childless at the end of their reproductive lives. Nearly 14 percent had the same experience in Mozambique. In the Central African Republic and in Cameroun, the figures were slightly above 17 percent, and in Gabon nearly one-third of all women were found to be infertile.[123]

And where African leaders gave in to early population policy overtures, public outrage soon forced them to withdraw their endorsements. In Kenya, for instance, a National Family Planning Program was adopted in 1967. Based on a program design drawn up by the Population Council in New York, it cautiously avoided such controversial features as the payment of incentives to birth control users, permanent sterilization, and abortion. Nonetheless, it provoked a rebellion. One writer describes the aftermath as follows:

> Critics soon charged that Kenya's efforts at population control were colonialism in economic clothing and might even have genocidal intent. The Catholic archbishop of Nairobi claimed that there was no population problem in Kenya, for there were vast lands yet to be inhabited. Oginga Odinga, once Kenyatta's vice-president, stated during parliamentary debate on the health

---

[123] *World Population at the Turn of the Century*, the United Nations, New York, 1989, at page 112.

budget: 'We oppose family planning and don't even want to hear of family planning in Africa.' .. Others criticized the speed with which the Population Council report had become national policy, especially without public hearings or debate... ¶... Before long, key figures pulled back from their espousal of family planning.[124]

The same writer concludes, "The early emphasis on population control proved disastrous, as it conjured up images of a white plot to limit African numbers or a Kikuyu design to consolidate power."[125]

The 1981 USAID-Battelle political surveillance project grew out of experiences like the one in Kenya. Thus it was particularly concerned with devising tactics that would prove useful in breaching cultural and political barriers. It suggested, for example, that population projects "should be integrated with maternal and child health care delivery" because those that "focus too narrowly on family planning as a solution" only increase suspicions on the part of host country officials.[126] It remarked that "ample cadres of statisticians, demographers, and other technicians" have not been present in Africa "to assist the persua-

---

[124] *Bitter Pills: Population Policies and Their Implementation in Eight Developing Countries* by Donald P. Warwick, Cambridge University Press, New York, 1982, at page 14.

[125] *Bitter Pills*, op. cit. at pages 14-15.

[126] Battelle report, op. cit. at page 15.

sion effort," and therefore "training assistance from AID and other donors is urgently required."[127] It also stated that, "There is a lack of adequate and relevant social science research and analysis, the data of which could be used for more effective development planning."[128] And it concluded that exhaustive efforts should be made to convince African politicians of the "linkages between population dynamics and development," saying that, "Workshops and seminars need to be designed to fill this void."[129]

In addition, the paper made specific recommendations to USAID as to the sort of interventions that would be feasible for Africa. It said, for instance, that

> Indigenous systems of maternal and child health care and family planning service delivery should be fully investigated and tried on an experimental basis, to enhance the acceptance and credibility of services.[130]
>
> Contraceptives should be packaged according to local customs and requirements, using local motifs and advertising slogans...[131]

---

[127] Battelle report, op. cit. at page 16.

[128] Battelle report, op. cit., at page 16.

[129] Battelle report, op cit., at page 16.

[130] Battelle report, op. cit. at page 17.

[131] Battelle report, op. cit., at page 17.

USAID Missions should actively recruit and hire Africans as population and health officers...[132]

Social science research, analysis, and dissemination is urgently required, using local research institutions and research scientists...[133]

Parliamentarians, politicians, and government decision makers should be exposed to population and development theory, actual country-specific case studies, and research findings. This process will facilitate the requirement to build a constituency for population and family planning. Seminars and one-day workshops are excellent mediums for this input.[134]

Educational tours should be provided for high level officials to countries where governments have adopted active and effective policies and programs. The multiplier effect may foster definitive action on the part of participants.[135]

---

[132] Battelle report, op. cit., at page 18.

[133] Battelle report, op. cit., at page 18.

[134] Battelle report, op. cit., at page 18.

[135] Battelle report, op. cit., at page 18.

In addition, the study urged what could fairly be called a cover-up of the medical hazards associated with western-financed birth control methods.

> We also need to counter the impact of frequent western-based news reports concerning documented side effects of orals and IUDs, and the continuing saga of Depo Povera, issues which make front page headlines in every African country, often precipitating political hassles with local IPPF [International Planned Parenthood Federation] Associations because of the active dissemination of various contraceptive methods.[136]

Because Battelle was relatively open about its association with the U.S. government during its research, the perception existed in several nations that staff members were acting as "brokers" for the Agency for International Development.[137] Although the group generally tried to deny such charges, it also found the situation advantageous to its mission of identifying population control "obstacles."

> In one country, Tanzania, the assessment team member was viewed as an AID official, despite the indirect affiliation. This prompted some respondents

---

[136] Battelle report, op. cit., at page 17.

[137] Battelle report, op. cit., at page 23.

to strongly allude to their suspicions concerning United States motivations in population assistance and to otherwise vent their displeasure at AID in general on many population related issues. Serving as a "lightening rod" was not an inappropriate role for the American team member to assume, for it did tend to foster candor.[138]

The report closed with the suggestion that several additional African nations be chosen for an augmented policy study and future action. Listed in order of importance were: Nigeria, Cameroun, Cote d'Ivoire, Zambia, Sierra Leone, Burkina Faso, and Niger.

---

[138] Battelle report. op. cit., at page 20.

Chapter 7

The "OPTIONS" Project:
"Heads We Win, Tails You Lose"

*Personally, I am of the view that unless
there is some compulsion and disincentives
are enforced, there is no way that the population control program will succeed in India,
as past experience has shown. ...The program should be strictly enforced in all sections of the society, transcending religious
and moral grounds and reservations.*

N. Kanna, Secretary, the Madras Chamber of
Commerce & Industry, Madras India[139]

The effort by the U.S. government to persuade
heads of state and government ministries in developing nations to adopt population reduction plans
involves much more than coercive policy negotiations
by aid donors and by lenders like the World Bank.
Also active in the same effort are several teams of
"influence peddlers" who seek ties to high-level
officials in targeted countries and who use their

---

[139] N. Kanna, Secretary, the Madras Chamber of Commerce &
Industry in Madras India, from World Population Day Replies, a
solicitation of opinions from community & business leaders
initiated and published in preparation for the planned UN's 1994
population conference in Cairo, Egypt, by Population Communication, Pasadena, California. The responses are undated.

extravagant budgets to present a false picture both of the relationship between population and development and of the U.S. government's motives in pursuing population control in the southern hemisphere.

One such USAID-funded initiative is called the "OPTIONS" project, conducted under contract by the private Futures Group, which also receives substantial funding from the Pentagon. The OPTIONS project has received awards totalling approximately $23 million from USAID headquarters in Washington since initial activities began on September 29, 1986. This figure does not include additional revenues poured into the project at the local level through USAID missions in target countries or USAID regional bureaus.[140]

The purpose of the program, according to the 1986 contract document, is to "strengthen the capacity to develop and evaluate operational policies and improve links between policy institutions and

---

[140] Extra funds contributed by USAID contract offices overseas are called "buy-ins." According to a preliminary evaluation of the OPTIONS project, substantial additional financing was made available to OPTIONS under USAID's country and regional budgets. An additional $350,000 was allocated to OPTIONS for work solely in Niger, for example, and in Morocco, more than $400,000 in added funds were supplied for in-country work. In Zaire, buy-ins totalled $680,000. Lesser amounts were provided by USAID missions in Botswana, Burkina Faso, Cameroun, Chad, Cote d'Ivoire, Haiti, Madagascar, Nigeria, Papua New Guinea, Rwanda, Sudan, Togo, and Zambia. See "OPTIONS for Population Policy Midterm Evaluation," the Population Technical Assistance Project Report No. 89-048-099, August 10, 1990, at page 11.

program and financial decision-makers."[141] The written agreement explains further that:

> These objectives will be achieved by shifting the focus of current data and policy analyses to resource allocations and operational policies... ..the contractor will continue to provide technical support for the development of national policies where national policies do not yet exist.[142]

The program is also to consist of "training, special studies and seminars, observational travel, and [provision of] long-term advisors," says the USAID contract. "A modest fellows program for developing country graduate students in the U.S. will be supported as well. Support will be provided to institutions to promote any component of the policy process."[143]

The USAID project description advises that the program is to begin with political surveillance similar to that conducted by Battelle. It notes that the "first step" in launching the policy campaign is to ...

> ...carry out an analysis of the institutional strengths and weaknesses in the

---

[141] USAID-Futures Group, OPTIONS Contract, #DPE-3035-C-00-6062-00, at page 6.

[142] USAID Contract #DPE-3035-C-00-6062-00, at page 6.

[143] USAID Contract #DPE-3035-C-00-6062-00, at page 6.

policy system including an identification of bottlenecks in the policy process. This analysis will also result in the identification of for-profit private sector organizations and firms such as personnel managers associations that can influence operations policies.[144]

The contractor is also obligated under the USAID agreement to prepare "guides to helping population policies," "guides to sectoral policy development," "model legislation," "compilations of doctrines issued by international organizations (e.g. World Population Conferences, Regional Conferences, etc.) which can form the bases of policies," and "broad analyses of the literature" on population and policy.[145]

Project targets, according to a report prepared by the Futures Group and submitted to USAID in connection with the program, include "heads of state, ministers, parliamentarians, private sector leaders and others who exercise decision-making power or who control the allocation of significant amounts of resources."[146]

The OPTIONS project was active in 24 countries during its first phase, 1986 to 1991. As a listing of target countries illustrates, these included two Arab

---

[144] USAID Contract #DPE-3035-C-00-6062-00, at page 7.

[145] USAID Contract #DPE-3035-C-00-6062-00, at pages 8-9.

[146] "Tools for Population Policy Development" by James C. Knowles, the OPTIONS for Population Policy Project, undated, at page 15.

nations; one in southeastern Asia; three in Latin America; one, Papua New Guinea, inhabited mainly by indigenous peoples; and seventeen whose populations are African or of African descent.

Bolivia	Morocco
Botswana	Niger
Burkina Faso	Nigeria
Cameroon	Papua New Guinea
Chad	Peru
Cote d'Ivoire	Rwanda
Ecuador	Senegal
Egypt	Sudan
Haiti	Togo
Indonesia	Zaire
Liberia	Zambia
Madagascar	Zimbabwe

Indeed, it is not surprising that population programs often struggle to fend off charges of racism. Under the OPTIONS project, the real targets — not the ministries and presidents, but the people who would be expected to expected to comply with the intrusive and demeaning policies — are 83 million Arabs, 40 million Latin Americans, 195 million Indonesians, 4 million citizens of Papua New Guinea, and 866 million Africans, including the Haitian people.[147] And it cannot be over-emphasized that it is precisely because birth control enjoys such little support among these people that population policy

---

[147] Population statistics from *The World Almanac and Book of Facts*, 1994 edition.

has become the political imperative it is for western leaders.

The extent to which the foreign policy establishment will go to reduce the numbers of children born to people of color is illustrated by still other activities described in the Future Group/OPTIONS contract. There are, for instance, "operational policy tools" that serve the purpose of "raising awareness about the role of the private sector in social service and family planning delivery [and stimulating] private sector participation." These actions, in the words of the project document, might "involve high-level sector seminars for governments, labor and industrial leaders..."[148] Other activities, the contract continues, will be directed toward those who balk at American discipline, being ...

> ....targeted specifically at policy bottle-necks which could be alleviated by additional information and discussion. These activities are aimed at promoting "policy dialogue" with developing country organizations and governments. Policy dialogue can be defined as any activities involving the interaction of LDC public and private sector leaders, and international experts which lead to policy improvements or reforms.[149]

---

[148] USAID Contract #DPE-3035-C-00-6062-00, at page 10.

[149] USAID Contract #DPE-3035-C-00-6062-00, at page 11.

The funding agreement between the Futures Group's "international experts" and the U.S. government also advises that there are to be a "minimum of 30 subprojects" conducted during the first five years of operations alone. These will produce "research review papers, short-term studies, policy development and evaluation papers, cost/benefit studies," and other materials, all designed to build...

> ...heightened public support for population policy, increased commitment by national leadership, specific policy recommendations for national and operational policies, specific operational plans for private sector organizations, and blueprints for further policy and program development.[150]

Other Futures Group responsibilities include "observational travel" aimed at "motivating decision-makers" to opt for population control and "providing them with contexts within which to plan and implement policies."[151] With regard to the latter, the contract adds: "This type of travel is especially important in Africa where nations have tended to move quickly through the national and operational policy stages...."[152]

---

[150] USAID Contract #DPE-3035-C-00-6062-00, at pages 11-12.

[151] USAID Contract #DPE-3035-C-00-6062-00, at pages 12-13.

[152] USAID Contract #DPE-3035-C-00-6062-00, at page 12.

A simultaneous scholarship project is also intended to produce a "leadership" constituency for population control abroad. "Past experience has shown that many of these students return to their countries and become key actors in policy systems," says the funding agreement.[153]

But the project. as the contract openly concedes, is not without political risk. So the involvement of the contractor must at all times be discreet :

> Because the Policy Formulation stage is more political than technical, extensive external assistance and involvement is perhaps less appropriate here than at other stages of the policy development process. Policy interventions at this point should be designed to support an essentially national process.[154]

Therefore, approaches are carefully tailored to specific targets, and the objectives of the population program are often presented — *deliberately* — as having little or no impact on population growth. For instance, a 45-page OPTIONS project report on "Tools for Population Policy Development" advises:

> In some countries (particularly in Africa). family planning as a fertility

---

[153] USAID Contract #DPE-3035-C-00-6062-00. at page 13.

[154] "Tools for Population Policy Development." op. cit.. at pages 24-25.

reduction measure may not be acceptable for cultural or political reasons. At the same time, the use of family planning to space births for maternal/child health reasons may be quite acceptable. In such cases, Child Survival Presentations can be an effective policy tool. These computer-assisted presentations use international demographic data to show the close relationship between fertility patterns, on the one hand, and infant, child and maternal mortality, on the other hand....[155]

Even more importantly, the policy change process does not begin or end with a state-approved family planning campaign. What may initially seem a rather modest effort to "space" births will almost certainly escalate into a more ambitious program of propaganda intended to alter opinions about family size. And once this is in place, still more aggressive steps will be taken to establish and meet contraceptive distribution targets.

In some Asian nations where western population programs already have slashed birthrates by more than half, the policy development process is nowhere near its conclusion. Even as reports of widespread coercion surface in nations with mature population policies, foreign aid contractors are now trying to build on previous policy "reforms" by promoting

---

[155] "Tools for Population Policy Development" op. cit., at page 23.

legislated birth limits.[156] And there is no evidence of any kind to suggest donors ntions have ever disclosed to host country leaders their intent to incrementally increase their levels of interference in the reproductive autonomy of developing country subjects.

In reality, there is little difference between the Agency for International Development's policy development operation and the hostile infiltration tactics of the CIA in the early years of the cold war. In fact, the latter is described in words bearing an eerie similarity to the Futures Group contract by former CIA Chief of Station Harry Rositzke in *The CIA's*

---

[156] As will be noted in the following chapter, Indonesian woman are routinely picked up by police and taken to family planning centers where contraceptives are administered, if necessary, at gunpoint. Yet money is still poured into the Indonesian population policy development operation in an attempt to get a permanent "population law" enacted. See, i.e., *Inventory of Population Projects in Development Countries Around the World 1990-1991*, UN Population Fund, United Nations, New York, at page 277. The *Inventory of Population Projects in Development Countries* contains brief descriptions of population-related sub-projects, arranged by country and sub-headed according to sponsoring nation or agency and contractor, sometimes including activity costs and scheduled start/finish dates. The entry for the Indonesian population law appears under the name of "Pathfinder," a major USAID-financed family planning agent. The full text of the entry is as follows: "Development of Population Law in Indonesia. Support to construct an agenda for drafting a general population law in Indonesia through the establishment of a Population Law Council and a framework for convening of working groups and preparation of an integrated draft. Amount: $40,090. Dates: January-September 1990."

Secret Operations: Espionage, Counterespionage and Covert Action:

> Covert political action in its broadest sense involves the use of secret contracts and secret funds to affect the power and policies of another nation...
> ¶ Political action contacts can range from the chief of state to the leader of a political party, from a cabinet minister to the secretary of a labor union, from the chief of a security service to an influential cleric.[157]

Another author explains, "Traditionally, covert action, which has often been the most visible aspect of U.S. intelligence activity, involves activities designed to influence foreign governments, events, organizations, or persons in support of U.S. foreign policy in such a way that the involvement of the U.S. government is not apparent."[158] The same text adds,

> U.S. covert actions have taken place in all major (and many minor) areas of the world: Europe and the Soviet Union, Africa, the Middle East, Asia and Latin America. The operations have included: (1) political advice and coun-

---

[157] *The CIA's Secret Operations: Espionage, Counterespionage and Covert Action,* by Harry Rositzke, Westview Press, 1988 edition, at pages 185-186.

[158] *The U.S. Intelligence Community* by Jeffrey T. Richelson, Harper Business, 1989, at page 333.

sel; (2) subsidies to an individual; (3) financial support and technical assistance to political parties; (4) support to private organizations, including labor unions and business firms; (5) covert propaganda; (6) training of individuals; (7) economic operations; (8) paramilitary or political action operations designed to overthrow or support a regime; and (9) attempted assassination.[159]

Rositzke concedes that a moral dilemma is posed by such interventions, but justifies the use of covert political intervention (by the CIA and presumably by other branches of government, as well) on the following grounds:

The world we live in is not a moral world. It is a world of more power and less power, of more goods and less goods, of greater security and lesser security, a world in which war is the final immorality. Nations are inevitably committed to the motto: Better bad than dead. In this world American foreign policy has been and will continue to be pragmatic...[160]

Without question, the OPTIONS project is "pragmatic." And, to a large degree, it is also covert

---

[159] *The U.S. Intelligence Community*, op. cit. at page 333.

[160] Rositzke, op cit., at page 206.

— at least in the sense that neither the source nor the purpose of the intervention is fully disclosed to the "recipients." The policy development report, for instance, states that the implementation phase of the "national" population program will ultimately require that responsibility be assigned to institutions within the host country government, "*some of which may need to be created.*"[161]

And it adds that "information campaigns" can be directed to special interest groups through the mass media, and that such outreach endeavors are expected to "facilitate attempts to change leaders' minds and to develop effective coalitions of interest groups in support of new policies."[162]

Above all, the purpose for allocating such exorbitant financial aid to population control is carefully concealed from target governments and ministries. Extraordinary precautions are taken wherever necessary to avoid disclosure that the program consists of American specialists and U.S.-trained and paid recruits actively pursuing a planned depopulation offensive. And the same prefabricated messages and themes are stressed over and over again, year after year, to one official after another, on the grounds that if they hear the idea enough times from enough sources, they may eventually drop their opposition.

---

[161] "Tools for Population Policy Development," op. cit., at page 24. Emphasis added.

[162] "Tools for Population Policy Development," op. cit., at page 13.

The Futures Group OPTIONS project is just one of many similar population policy development campaigns. There are scores of others which have population policies as their primary or secondary objective.[163] But even this massive volume of foreign influence activities must be backed up by other, more concrete measures to ensure the compliance of developing country leaders. Indeed, the World Bank, which controls the purse strings of many less-developed nations, often plays a definitive role.

---

[163] See Appendix B of this book.

Chapter 8

The Bank Mandate: Ending
The Mirage of Independence

On August 11, 1987, in Bangladesh, an eighty-year-old peasant named Osman Ali traveled to the town of Mymensingh to see his brother. On Ali's way back home, a sterilization agent accosted him, promising a free sarong and cash payment of 175 taka — the equivalent of several weeks' wages — if Ali agreed to a vasectomy. These are the standard incentives offered by the government's population-control program, which is funded by the World Bank and a consortium of other foreign donors. ¶ *... After the operation, the agent collected his referral fee from the clinic staff and then proceeded to steal the sarong and cash from Osman Ali. The old man suffered an immediate stroke and died the next day.*

Betsy Hartmann in
The Progressive, September 1990

Evolutionary principles, based on competitive reproduction and competitive survival, are still in force among the majority of the peoples of today's world. Thus, any birth control program is a 'bone in the throat' to such people, who will cry 'genocide' when they are actually quite happy to outbreed those whom they consider their rivals, and take over by sheer weight of population their rival's territorial property.

Mankind Quarterly, Summer 1992[164]

---

[164] "Malthus Revisited" by J.W. Jamieson, *Mankind Quarterly*, the Institute for the Study of Man, McLean, Virginia, Summer 1992, at page 432.

The United States has been concerned for more than 50 years with its eventual decline as a world leader, coming as a consequence of shifts in population size and distribution. Nothing less than the leadership of the world is at stake. It is therefore not surprising that all avenues of influence and all available resources would be directed toward activities that have a bearing upon population growth trends in high-fertility societies.

Indeed, the U.S. has most effectively used its influence over the World Bank to force unwanted population policies on less-developed nations, and intends to do much more. In fact, the Bank, which provided slightly under $100 million (U.S.) per year for population control activities during the early 1980s, plans to increase lending in the "population sector" to at least $2.5 billion dollars per year by 1995.[165]

Coercive lending policies are no secret at the Bank. In numerous publications distributed by the Bank, it is made clear that population loans are imposed on unwilling nations as a condition for receiving more desirable development credits — funds for public education, electricity, irrigation systems, and agriculture, for example.

No less than the foreign military and economic aid program, the World Bank's interference with the private lives of citizens in developing countries was

[165] Statement of World Bank President Lewis Preston, March 9, 1992, at the opening of a World Bank conference on the Safe Motherhood project, World Bank auditorium, Washington, D.C.

engineered by the "secret" agencies of the United States government. For example, a classified National Security Council memorandum, signed by then-President Richard Nixon's security advisor Henry Kissinger in the summer of 1970, elevated population control to "a top priority item" on the multilateral agenda.[166] That year, the World Bank made its first population control loan — a $2 million dollar credit to Jamaica.[167]

Four years later, the National Security Council, in its 1974 study of the political and security implications of population growth in the south, recommended that the U.S. use its leverage with international financial institutions to promote political change on the part of recipient country leadership. The involvement of "multilateral" agencies, the study reasoned, would help to conceal the U.S. role in implementing such programs.[168] "It is vital that the effort to develop and strengthen a commitment on the part of the LDC leaders not be seen by them as an industrialized country policy to keep their

---

[166] National Security Decision Memorandum 76, August 10, 1970, at page 5. The directive stated: "The U.S. should recommend that the UN Fund for Population Activities undertake a study of world population problems and measures required to deal with them, as a top priority item in the Second Development Decade." It was declassified on December 18, 1989.

[167] See, e.g., *Strengthening the Bank's Population Work in the Nineties* by Steven W. Sinding, World Bank Population and Human Resources Department, Working Paper WPS 802, November 1991, at page 31.

[168] NSSM 200, op. cit. See, e.g., pages 106, 113-114, 149.

strength down or to reserve resources for use by the 'rich' countries," the report stated.[169] The same study also advises:

> The World Bank Group is the principle international financial institution providing population programs. However, the Bank's policy prevents it from financing consumables such as contraceptives and other family planning commodities. This restricts its ability to finance population projects with its available funds. At present a high level outside consultant group is evaluating the Bank's population programs. This evaluation and our review of it should help provide a clearer picture of what improvement there might be in the Bank's role and activities in the population field.[170]

The "external review" discussed in the memorandum was begun in late 1975, at about the same time the CIA-National Security Council policy study was endorsed by the White House and made an official instrument of American foreign policy.[171] It was

---

[169] NSSM 200. op. cit. at page 114.

[170] NSSM 200. op. cit., at pages 10-11.

[171] The recommendations contained in NSSM 200 were officially adopted as guidelines for U.S. foreign policy under another National Security Council directive, (NSDM 314), which was signed on behalf of the president (then Gerald Ford) on November 26.

completed in August of 1976. Among the panelists assembled to conduct the review was Dr. Fred Sai, the same "advisor" who participated in the Battelle population policy research project, and who later was rewarded with a senior population advisor post at the World Bank.[172]

Among other things, the review committee recommended that the Bank work to develop "more satisfactory relationships" with donors (not borrowers), and urged that it "include population considerations on a substantial and consistent basis in its economic reports, particularly with regard to key countries, and ... reach for collaboration with population policy units in key countries."[173]

The panel argued that the Bank's population activities at that time offered only a relatively minor opportunity for the imposition of western-dictated policies on less-developed countries, and suggested a general overhaul of Bank policy to permit greater

---

1975 by National Security Advisor Brent Scowcroft.

[172] The panel consisted of five persons. Bernard Berelson, president emeritus and senior fellow at the Population Council in New York was its chairman. Other participants included Dr. Frederick T. Sai, then assistant secretary general at the International Planned Parenthood Federation in London; A. Chandra Sekhar of the Ministry of Health and Family Planning in India; Goran Ohlin, a professor of economics at the University of Uppsala; and Ronald Freedman, a professor sociology at the University of Michigan's Population Studies Center.

[173] "Final Report of the External Advisory Panel on Population," August 1976, at page 51.

financial and political involvement in population control schemes.[174]

The ease with which the United States gets its way at the Bank is no coincidence. Since the World Bank was created in 1944, the U.S. government has maintained a special office to monitor and influence its activities. This body, the National Advisory Council on International Monetary and Financial Policies (or "the NAC" to insiders), is part of the U.S. Department of the Treasury, and is assigned the task of ensuring that U.S. investments in the World Bank, IMF and regional development banks "provide for support which does not fall below levels at which U.S. influence would not be adequate to defend or promote our interests," in the words of a 1978 study by the General Accounting Office.[175]

While the Treasury Department connection is technically not privileged information, it is something about which officials almost never speak publicly. However, a recent NAC annual report does explain that...

> ...the NAC is an advisory body, authorized, inter alia, to review proposed transactions and programs to the extent necessary or desirable to coordinate U.S. policies. With regard to the

---

[174] "Final Report of the External Advisory Panel on Population." See, e.g., pages 51-56.

[175] *Multilateral and Bilateral Assistance for Developing Foreign Mineral Projects.* The General Accounting Office. August 15, 1978. Document No. ID-78-50, at page 1.

international financial institutions, such as the World Bank, the Inter-American Development Bank, the Asian Development Bank, and the African Development Bank and Fund, the Council seeks to ensure that, to the maximum extent possible, their operations are conducted in a manner consistent with U.S. policies and objectives and with the lending and other foreign financial activities of U.S. government agencies.[176]

Earlier reports explain more specifically that the Council "operates mainly through a Staff Committee," which consists of "representatives of other agencies of the U.S. Government such as the Departments of Defense and Agriculture, and representatives of the National Security Council..."[177] In other words, it is in the hands of the same government bodies that engineered the population program.

Thus Bank policy reflects U.S. overseas policy. This is vital because, among other things, it allows U.S. officials to exert influence even in nations with which diplomatic relations are limited. Furthermore, it permits the use of coercive tactics which can, when

---

[176] Annual Report for Fiscal Year 1988, the National Advisory Council on International Monetary and Financial Policies, at page 31.

[177] This description appears in NAC annual reports for 1985 and earlier. See also Executive Orders No. 11238 and 11269, which established the process for review of multilateral financial transactions.

they become a political liability, be disclaimed by U.S. officials on the grounds that the Bank is "multi-lateral" and the projects are those of the borrowing countries. Moreover, the use of Bank funds to control policies in borrower countries cannot be thwarted by Congress, as the relationship between the Bank and the U.S. government is orchestrated at the executive level.

Thus, using credit as a "carrot," and withdrawal of development funds as a "stick," the Bank is in a position to enlist the reluctant cooperation of heads of state and key ministries in a planned program of population reduction, making it possible that the developing countries will suffer sufficient losses in births to forestall the demographic marginalization of the west.

Furthermore, such policies are imposed "over the heads" of the affected communities, with no public debate whatever, and often — at least in the beginning — without a clear acknowledgement that such plans have even been adopted. Thus the governments of borrowing countries are pitted against the very people they are supposed to protect, and the inevitable public criticism almost always results in increased repression and state control over citizens.

The Bank's population policy dialogue and its destructive impact on national self rule in developing nations is perhaps best illustrated by the case of Senegal. A 1992 Bank publication called *Population and the World Bank: Implications from Eight Case Studies* gives a history of the Bank's activities in the predominantly Muslim West African nation.

The Bank's first family planning-related loan to Senegal was granted in 1982 as part of a health project, the report notes, and it included a stipulation that contraceptives were to be distributed as part of the maternal care package. The Senegalese government simply ignored the birth control requirement.[178]

The Bank report reasons that the forceful way in which the population program was introduced may also have prompted the government to dodge the family planning provision. It notes, for example, that the obligation...

> ...was not a part of the original Government submission, but was introduced at the behest of the Bank staff on the basis of correspondence and discussions during brief visits. It was not developed in a collegial, problem-solving atmosphere which might have led the Government to assume ownership of the idea. The Bank also did less than it could have during implementation to follow up and encourage the Government to proceed with this and other software elements.[179]

In 1985-86, the Bank conducted a population sector review for Senegal, and concluded that its population officials should concentrate on policy

---

[178] *Population and the World Bank: Implications from Eight Case Studies.* A World Bank Operations Evaluation Study. Operations Evaluation Department. The World Bank. 1992. at page 58.

[179] *Population and the World Bank: Implications from Eight Case Studies.* op. cit., at page 58.

development rather than make further attempts to directly fund birth control activities. To this end, it was determined that pressure would be placed on the government to issue a "statement" approving of population control.[180]

This tactic is fairly common in countries that balk at accepting funding for the actual promotion of birth control According to the 1992 World Bank publication, the suggestion was accepted by Bank leaders and was "implemented by making the development of such a policy statement a condition for release of the second tranche of the third structural adjustment loan." The pronouncement in favor of fewer births, which had literally been extracted by force from Senegalese officials, was eventually published in 1988.[181]

In April of 1991, the Bank decided it was time to make another move, and followed up on the statement by approving a broad Human Resources Project for Senegal. But again, there were strings attached — in fact conditions were imposed first at negotiation and then again as a requirement for approval.

> A *condition of negotiation* was liberalization of restrictions on provision of [family planning] services. As a result, nurses can now provide all services except sterilization and traditional

---

[180] *Population and the World Bank: Implications from Eight Case Studies*, op. cit., at page 58.

[181] *Population and the World Bank: Implications from Eight Case Studies*, op. cit., at page 58.

birth attendants can distribute pills. These are radical changes from earlier, when only doctors could provide such services. A *condition of approval* was official adoption of the NPFP [the national program in family planning].[182]

The same publication confirms that the Bank is on the verge of launching a major campaign of population control in Senegal, against the wishes of the nation's leaders. "Much will depend on whether the momentum on policy of recent months is sustained," it says, "and more important, how well these policy decisions are implemented. So far, there has been little public support by high-level government officials."[183]

Therefore, it continues, it is imperative that the Bank "consider ways to more intensively and intimately assist the Government to implement this project that its typical supervision procedures allow. If the urgency of the problem warrants taking additional risks in this case, it also warrants a more intensive effort to ensure a successful outcome."[184]

Similar histories are available regarding the Bank's role in promoting population policies and

---

[182] *Population and the World Bank: Implications from Eight Case Studies,* op. cit., at page 58. Emphasis added.

[183] *Population and the World Bank: Implications from Eight Case Studies,* op. cit., at page 59.

[184] *Population and the World Bank: Implications from Eight Case Studies,* op. cit., at page 59.

activities in numerous other nations. A brief evaluation of the Bank's history in Kenya describes ...

> ... successful efforts to persuade the Government to establish an inter-ministerial coordinating agency for population outside the MOH (included as a condition in the second structural adjustment loan), and then provide it with more responsibilities; and efforts to persuade the MOH to liberalize guidelines for providing contraceptives, to integrate FP into the mainstream of MOH activities, and to offer sterilization services.[185]

Another inside report on Bank activities mentions that "Malawi and Zambia were both pro-natalist in the late 1970s," and that Bank officials had been "instrumental in raising population issues and having them discussed openly. Both of these countries," it concludes, "organized seminars to discuss the Bank's sector work and subsequently revised their stance regarding family planning."[186]

In Nigeria, the Bank used a different tactic. There, the discussion paper says, "Bank support helped lay groundwork for policy formation," the

---

[185] *Population and the World Bank*, op. cit. at page 5.

[186] *The World Bank's Role in Shaping Third World Population Policy* by Fred T. Sai and Lauren A. Chester, The World Bank, Population and Human Resources Department, November 1990, WPS 53, at page 9.

publication reveals, but the follow-up was done in a "somewhat different" way. Says the report, "Nigerian consultants, funded by the Bank, conducted the research necessary to suggest a reasonable population policy to the government." This opened the way for the USAID-financed Futures Group to recruit and train local demographers and to "demonstrate why the government was developing a population policy to government officials, religious leaders, etc." The same USAID contractor, this time working as an agent for the Bank, "helped pave the way for eventual approval the policy," the document concludes.[187]

And in Malawi, says yet another World Bank publication, "government policy has shifted from a pre-1981 pro-natalist stance to the acceptance of child spacing as a formal policy, and a low key discussion of population issues among the top civil servants and policy makers has even begun." The Bank, it concludes, "played a significant role in this process."[188]

If this massive and carefully-orchestrated interference raises serious questions about the sovereignty of independent states, it also raises equally serious debate about human rights. Indeed, if loan conditioning is a coercive way of dealing with govern-

---

[187] *The World Bank's Role in Shaping Third World Population Policy,* op. cit., at pages 10-11.

[188] *The World Bank's Population Lending and Sector Review* by George Simmons and Rushikesh Maru, The World Bank, Population and Human Resources Department, Washington, DC, September 1988, at page 11.

ments, the means by which the programs reach the people are often even more so.

In Indonesia, another country in which the Bank freely admits to having played a substantive policy development role, observers have documented abuses comparable to those widely reported in China. An "information, education and communication" component of the Indonesian population program, for instance, agents "have been known to try intimidation with statements such as 'those who refuse will have to joint the transmigration program to the outer islands.'"[189] The report adds:

> *Safari* is a far more potent recruitment measure. Village and sub-village heads are assembled and expected to submit the names and numbers of targets in their areas. These people are summarily 'enrolled,' then taken to a place where the contraceptive is inserted, usually the village head office. Where villagers are reluctant to comply with the summons military or police personnel will come and pick them up... ¶
> In 1988 during a safari a group of women were taken into a locked room where they were held at gunpoint. The women panicked and tried to escape through the locked glass windows, which resulted in a number of injuries from shattered glass. In one safari

---

[189] "Family Planning in Indonesia: The Case for Policy Reorientation" by Wardah Hafidz, Adrina Taslim and Sita Aripurnami, in *Inside Indonesia*, March 1992, at page 20.

> during our study in 1990, IUDS were
> inserted at gunpoint to those who
> continued to resist.[190]

In fact, the notorious Chinese one-child policy —
complete with sterilizations and late-term abortions
on a compulsory basis — has been implemented with
massive World Bank support, more than $200
million from the Bank's Population, Health & Nutrition sector in the 1980s alone. And the "population
emergency" in India which resulted in millions of
involuntary sterilizations and thousands of deaths
followed a 1972 population sector project worth $21
million negotiated by the Bank.[191]

Official Bank literature is ambivalent, at best,
about human rights. An official working paper on
Ethical Approaches to Family Planning in Africa
debates the "human rights" problem in a way that
suggests the only "unethical" practices are those that
somehow inhibit the distribution of birth control
drugs and devices. In one example, it relates events
that took place during a family planning campaign in
Zaire: "After encouragement by members of the
health team, several of whom accepted IUDS themselves, a number of women accepted them. Subsequently two local women suffered excessive bleeding,
after which there were almost no new acceptors." The
outcome of the case is this: "In may parts of Africa

---

[190] "Family Planning in Indonesia," op. cit., at page 20.

[191] *Strengthening the Bank's Population Work in the Nineties,* op.
cit., at pages 31-33.

there are service staff who are not well informed about contraceptives and who pass on their prejudices and ignorance to clients. It should be part of staff training to show that this is unethical."[192]

Sterilization programs, too, can infringe on human rights, the authors admit. But the acknowledgement is made in the context of attacks by opponents of family planning programs. "For sterilization to be tainted, possibly deterring couples from using it, is to deny them their right to choose it," the text lectures. And it concludes: "Doctors who refuse to discuss this option for highly fertile African couples, even with parities of five and above, ought to examine their ethics."[193]

Still another World Bank study, *Costs, Payments, and Incentives in Family Planning Programs*, takes a "what-the-hell" approach to the human rights controversy. "A crucial aspect of the ethical dilemma is found in the tension between a government's proper function of protecting the welfare of current and future generations, versus the right of individuals now alive to freely determine the size of their families," the writers explain. Here they quote the World Population Plan of Action introduced at the UN's 1974 population conference in Bucharest: "All couples and individuals have the basic right to

---

[192] *Ethical Approaches to Family Planning in Africa* by F. T. Sai and K. Newman. The World Bank, Population and Human Resources Department, WPS 324, December 1989, at pages 16-17.

[193] *Ethical Approaches to Family Planning in Africa*, op. cit., at page 18.

decide freely and responsibly the number and spacing of their children..." The publication comes to a puzzling — but frighteningly understandable — conclusion:

> The contradictions are apparent: couples and individuals can decide 'freely,' but also 'responsibly,' and in light of other 'needs.' As with most other human rights, the fact that people have the right to determine the number and spacing of their children, *does not mean that the government can never infringe it.*[194]

If all this isn't bad enough, the World Bank carries out these programs with the explicit — and sometimes even *explicitly-stated* — understanding that population control is unnecessary and potentially harmful to the developing economies of the southern hemisphere. "With sound practices and technological innovations Africa might eventually accommodate several times its present population," says one lengthy publication, *Sub-Saharan Africa, From Crisis*

---

[194] *Costs, Payments, and Incentives in Family Planning Programs* by John A. Ross and Stephen L. Isaacs, The World Bank, Population and Human Resources Department, WPS 88, September 1988, at page 15. Emphasis added.

to Sustainable Growth.[195] And the Bank's 1990 *Development Report* remarks:

> In the short run an increase in population will result, almost by definition, in lower per capita income growth, but in the longer run the larger number of productive workers may accelerate growth. It can even be argued that some countries — particularly in the West — need faster population growth even to sustain their current economic performance.[196]

The same report states that, "Rapid growth of the labor force does not necessarily lead to unemployment and poverty: if investment in capital is adequate, an expanding economic could absorb the additional labor and may indeed depend on it."[197]

---

[195] *Sub-Saharan Africa, From Crisis to Sustainable Growth: A Long-Term Perspective Study.* The World Bank, Washington, DC, 1989, at page 41.

[196] *World Development Report 1990.* The World Bank/Oxford University Press, 1990, at page 82.

[197] *World Development Report 1990,* op. cit., at page 82.

Chapter 9
Seamless Web of Influence

Given the strictly formal nature of instrumental rationality, given further its indifference to moral values, it is unfortunately possible to imagine plausible scenarios in which, in a time of acute social stress, decision-makers in a desacralized society conclude that genocide is the most rational means of 'solving' the problem of surplus people. Put differently, as long as impersonal, value-free, cost-benefit calculations form the basis of large-scale decision-making by anonymous state functionaries, there may come a time when the functionaries may conclude that the 'benefits' of a program of mass population elimination outweigh the 'costs.'

Richard L. Rubenstein in *The Age of Triage* [198]

[E]ven though it is quite true that any radical eugenic policy will be for many years politically and psychologically impossible, it will be important for UNESCO to see that the eugenic problem is examined with the greatest care, and that the public mind is informed of the issues at stake so that much that now is unthinkable may at least become thinkable.

Julian Huxley, in *UNESCO: Its Purpose and its Philosophy* [199]

---

[198] *The Age of Triage* by Richard L. Rubenstein. Beacon Press. Boston. 1983. at page 32.

[199] *UNESCO: Its Purpose and its Philosophy* by Julian Huxley. Director General. United Nations Educational. Scientific and Cultural Organization. The Public Affairs Press/American Council on Public Affairs. Washington. DC. 1947. at page 21.

The reality of total control in the post-colonial world dictates that all gaps be closed. Economic assistance agencies, credit sources, and multilateral donors must all align themselves behind the same policy objectives and adopt the same conditionality. There can be no escape hatch for borrowers, no one source of funds that exempts the borrower from the rules imposed by the rest.

The African Development Bank (ADB) is head-quartered in Abidjan, Cote d'Ivoire, and was founded by some 30-plus independent African states in 1963 to finance the economic development of the conti-nent. Membership in the ADB was (wisely) restricted to African nations in the early years of the Bank's existence. In 1973, non-African nations joined African countries in establishing the African Develop-ment Fund, essentially a competitor to the Bank. In 1982, by which time 50 African nations were mem-bers of the Bank, non-African members of the Fund were formally permitted to become members of the Bank. The U.S. joined the Fund in 1976 and became a member of the Bank on February 8, 1983.[200]

The frequently-stated views of African leaders make clear the fact that the Bank was never intend-ed to be an instrument of population control. "The relation between the degree of destitution of peoples of Africa and the length and nature of the exploita-tion they had to endure is evident," said Guinea's

---

[200] *The United States Government Manual 1990/1991.* U.S. Government Printing Office, at page 783. See also Executive Order 12403, "African Development Bank, February 8, 1983.

President, Ahmed Sekou Toure, in 1962. "African remains marked by the crimes of the slave-traders: up to now her potentialities are restricted by under-population."[201]

A prominent Kenyan writer dismissed the introduction of "family planning" to Africa Kenya as a plot against the African people: "colonialism is still fresh in the minds of East Africans and it would, therefore, not be difficult to interpret the foreign experts' enthusiasm as a kind of neocolonialist trick to keep the African population down."[202] And the country's opposition leader bitterly charged, in the words of one written history, that the African people were already being systematically "eliminated from a sparsely population continent and... birth control would only speed up this trend."[203]

The view was echoed by others across the continent, political leaders as well as intellectuals. But it was, by no means, confined to Africa. "Just when science and technology are making incredible advances in all fields, they resort to technology to suppress revolutions and ask the help of science to prevent population growth," said Cuban leader Fidel Castro in 1968, mocking comments from then-U.S. Secretary of State Dean Rusk about supplying birth control in the name of stability. "In short, the peoples

---

[201] Ahmed Sekou Toure, 1962, quoted in *How Europe Underdeveloped Africa*, op. cit., at page 95.

[202] Grace Ogot, 1967, quoted in *Bitter Pills*, op. cit., at page 98.

[203] Oginga Odinga, quoted in *Bitter Pills*, op. cit., at page 98.

are not to make revolutions, and women are not to give birth. This sums up the philosophy of imperialism."[204]

Indeed, these consistent objections to population policy have been duly noted by donors over the years. "Few African are yet persuaded of the advantages of smaller families; they see land as abundant and labor as scarce," says a 1989 World Bank publication.[205] And a 1972 cable from Lagos instructed officials at the Department of State that opposition to population control in Nigeria was virtually universal. "They discount the danger of continued population growth ... question the motives of externally supported family planning programs, and dismiss birth control as alien to Nigerian values." It added that Nigerian officials had cited "a considerable amount of unused land" to justify their view that "population growth should be encouraged."[206] Indeed, even one former USAID official was forced to agree that their position made sense, in light of the "insensitive" and

---

[204] Fidel Castro, January 12, 1968, to Havana Cultural Congress, quoted in *Ideology, Faith, and Family Planning in Latin America: Studies in Public and Private Opinion on Fertility Control* by J. Mayone Stycos, A Population Council Book, McGraw-Hill Book Company, New York, 1970, at page 126.

[205] *Sub-Saharan Africa, From Crisis to Sustainable Growth*, op. cit., at page 41.

[206] Cable to State Department, March 30, 1972, quoted in *Nature Against Us: The United States and the World Population Crisis 1968-1980* by Peter J. Donaldson, University of North Carolina Press, 1990, at pages 118-119.

"genocidal" style of the government's population program. "If AID has not been so prominent and so noisy it could have assisted a lot of programs it was not able to assist because AID was seen has having such an insensitive genocidal policy," says David Bell, USAID administrator in the early years of the program.[207]

The initial response of donors to such insubordination was to try to mask their demographic goals by wrapping birth control — rhetorically at least — in a larger package that consisted of maternal and child health, human services, and fertility planning. "The progressive integration of programs in health, nutrition and family planning has partly been a response to the failure (and political costliness) of past attempts to run population programs separately," write two World Bank consultants. But, for the most part, the concept did not work. Say the same authors, "although population policy was often supposed to involve other elements, especially after the post-Bucharest consensus that 'development is the best contraceptive,' it was in fact often identical to family planning policy."[208] Thus,

> ... over the decade of the 1970s a
> number of factors forced a change in

---

[207] Donaldson, op. cit., at page 102.

[208] *Maternal Education and the Vicious Cycle of High Fertility and Malnutrition: An Analytic Survey* by Matthew Lockwood and Paul Collier. The World Bank, Population and Human Resources Department, Washington, DC, WPS 130, December 1988, at pages 47-48.

the packaging of population policy and
showed the true nature of the implementation of family planning programs
under conditions which threatened
their success. Popular resistance,
fuelled by political, often nationalist,
rhetoric, brought quick retraction of
the notion that population policy
aimed to control and restrain population growth...[209]

In other words, the strategy of coupling population planning operations with more desirable social
programs had little or no lasting impact on their
acceptance — and sponsors often found it necessary
to issue denials that a reduction in birthrates was an
objective.

The U.S. and other donors faced a dilemma. It
had become apparent that persuasion was not going
to work, but that overt compulsion could be an even
greater political liability. The solution, then, was to
force developing country leaders to issue procla-
mations calling for slower rates of growth, and then
to build on these pronouncements in a way that
would make it appear that population control "assistance" had been *requested* by these same governments. This, in essence, is the blueprint for the
credit-control strategy.

But, in order for this to work, there must be "full
coverage." Regional development banks, many of
them under the direction of governments within their
respective parts of the world, might be an alternative

---

[209] Matthews and Collier, op. cit., at page 48.

to borrowing from those western-controlled institutions that increasingly made an active family planning program a prerequisite for operational funds. Equally troublesome was the possibility that lack of interest on the part of regional banks might signal to the rest of the world the continuing distaste for population control in the southern hemisphere. And furthermore, such gratuitous duplication is necessary because the collaboration of many bilateral, multilateral and private agencies makes it difficult to pin the blame for a disastrous policy on any one donor.

Thus, the opening of the African Development Bank to outside investors was a long-awaited opportunity for the United States. As part of its policy development campaign, USAID, again using its OPTIONS project, worked from within the African Development Bank (ADB) to bring that institution more closely in line with other donors in the field of population lending. According to a "final report" prepared in 1992, the end of the first five-year OPTIONS phase, the OPTIONS project was able to "integrate population variables into [the] planning process" of the ADB and even to secure funding from ADB itself for still more Futures Group influence operations at the Bank.[210]

---

[210] "OPTIONS for Population Policy I Final Report." The Futures Group, May 15, 1992, at pages A3-A4. The "OPTIONS I" signified the first phase of the operation, conducted between September 1986 and September 1991, at which time the second phase, or "OPTIONS II" (essentially a continuation of the program), was inaugurated.

Under this situation, a borrower interested primarily in education, for example, or electricity and highways, might be told that the activity will only be approved as part of a package deal which will include a new health and family planning budget. The latter will allocate a fixed amount for population activities, and the borrower will agree, as part of the deal, to obtain additional grant financing from USAID or a supplemental loan from ADB.

Thus a condition *imposed* on the borrower, the birth control program, is converted to a "request for assistance" from other lenders and donors. Indeed, the purpose of the OPTIONS work with the ADB was, in the words of the Futures Group report, "to encourage the ADB to actively solicit requests for loans for population projects from the member countries and, ultimately, for the ADB to become a significant financier of population projects in Africa."[211]

The OPTIONS report on its USAID-funded activities at the African Development Bank further explains:

> The desired outcome for OPTIONS work with the African Development Bank was a substantial, measurable increase in ADB financing of population activities. Towards this end, the Futures Group was retained under separate contract by the ADB to provide technical assistance that will allow the Bank to expand its population portfolio. A number of ADB per-

---

[211] OPTIONS Final Report, at page A3.

sonnel were trained in incorporating demographic factors into rural and agricultural project design.[212]

A summary of activities in the same report reveals that the project consisted of various "informational" sessions for ADB professional staff, a seminar on Population and Development in Africa, the design of a training program on the integration of population into other sector projects, the recruitment of a population specialists to work at the Bank, and staff presentations.[213] A commentary on one population-development meeting, held in 1987, attempts to portray compliance as a shift in attitudes:

> Approximately 65 people attended; they included ADB senior professional staff and resource persons from selected foreign national and international organizations. The summary report of that seminar took note of the pronounced shift from negative to positive attitudes by African governments about the importance of the population factor in development. The report also affirmed the African Development Bank's commitment to support population-related activities and detailed

---

[212] OPTIONS Final Report, at page A4.

[213] OPTIONS Final Report, at page A3.

the measures the Bank intended to take.[214]

A similar event held the following year was attended by 41 members of the Bank staff, but only one of the Bank's directors — the one from the U.S. Nonetheless, says the OPTIONS report, the 1988 seminar resulted in "requests" for additional training of "up to 150 people" and for "consultants" to assist with the preparation of "the first ADB population project," as well as future population loans.[215]

It is virtually impossible to overestimate the power exercised by external forces under such arrangements. Decisions about issues of concern to donors simply cannot be made without the prior knowledge and approval of outsiders.

Indeed, USAID alone has funded more than 15 major population policy programs in Africa (or large population projects with a significant policy component) since the early 1980s, and most of them are intended to remain active in one form or another well into the 1990s.

There is the Johns Hopkins Population Information Program ("PIP"), for instance, a $23 million intervention designed to "inform" policymakers worldwide of major developments in contraceptive technology and to conduct demographic evaluations and assist in the development of new program initiatives. Like many others, the PIP activity uses

---

[214] OPTIONS Final Report, at page A3.

[215] OPTIONS Final Report, at page A3.

the "contagion" theory of political change, making a special effort to inform the policy elite in developing nations of legal and public policy changes elsewhere in the hopes of generating a "bandwagon" effect. In December of 1992, PIP activities were merged with a larger effort by the same contractor, the Population Communication Services program, which is essentially a large-scale propaganda operation.[216]

The IMPACT project is similar to OPTIONS, but conducted by a different contractor, the Population Reference Bureau in Washington. Like OPTIONS, it is essentially an outreach campaign to persuade ministers and government officials of the "need" to adopt efficient birth control schemes. IMPACT received about $6 million from the USAID Office of Population in Washington between 1985 and 1990 for the preparation and distribution of publications and for technical assistance to population bureaucrats in developing countries.[217]

The RAPID policy program is another Futures Group activity, scheduled to receive about $11 million in "central funds" (from USAID-Washington) between 1991 and 1996; it holds seminars and gives presentations to policymakers for the purpose of

---

[216] U.S. Agency for International Development Project No. 936-3032.

[217] U.S. Agency for International Development Project No. 936-3035.02.

"assisting" them to develop and implement population control programs.[218]

A second policy contract to the Washington-based Population Reference Bureau is intended to "bridge the gap between the population research community and policy audiences who need the research findings to make informed policy choices," according to a directory of Washington-funded population programs published by USAID. The group also is responsible for "arranging briefings and meetings for developing country officials visiting Washington, D.C.," and for providing "wire service stories, press releases, news packs, and seminars" for journalists. The project is currently active worldwide.[219]

Another campaign to change policy and law in aid-recipient countries was the Columbia University project, active in the mid 1980s, and directed mainly toward legislation. Its "cost-reimbursement" agreement with USAID covered the preparation of "model legislation," "study tours" for policymakers and lawyers, assistance to "indigenous" organizations favoring population control, and other activities involving "parliamentarian groups."[220]

---

[218] See U.S. Agency for International Development Contracts No. DPE-3046-C-1047-00 and DPE-3-46-Q-00-1048-00.

[219] *User's Guide to the Office of Population*, USAID, 1993, at page 35. See also U.S. Agency for International Development Contract No. DPE-0502-A-00-7066-00.

[220] U.S. Agency for International Development Contract No. DPE-0643-C-00-3063.

The Population Council, which does extensive work with experimental contraceptive technologies, has also three separate contracts for "operational research" in the Latin America-Caribbean region; the Asia-Near East region; and Africa, respectively. Among the purposes of these grants is to evaluate the efficiency of family planning activities, to "identify opportunities" for work expansion, and to make recommendations (including policy changes) that would streamline family planning campaigns.[221]

Several projects are directed at the private sector, and have as a main objective changes in policy as it may affect private sector birth control distribution drives.

The "Family Planning Service Expansion and Technical Support" program, a $43 million, five-year effort, is intended to "develop innovative approaches to large scale [family planning] program expansion" and to participate in "strategic planning" of population programs in targeted countries. It operates in Africa, Asia and the Middle East, with special emphasis on Africa.[222]

A similar activity, called "Contraceptive Social Marketing," combines private sector promotion with policy analysis and propaganda. The $40 million

---

[221] See U.S. Agency for International Development Contract No. DPE-3030-Z-00-9019-00 (Latin America); U.S. Agency for International Development Contract No. DPE-3030-C-00-0022-00 (Asia and the Near East); and U.S. Agency for International Development Contract No. DPE-3030-Z-00-8065-00 (Africa).

[222] U.S. Agency for International Development Contract No. DPE-3048-Z-9011-00.

operation, like OPTIONS and RAPID, is under the direction of the Futures Group.[223]

Another "private sector" initiative, "Technical Information on Population for the Private Sector," was active between August of 1985 and August of 1990, and conducted similar promotion of birth control in the commercial arena. It also worked with large employers to help them set up birth control clinics at the workplace — a concept that has caused considerable controversy, but has been quietly continued by other contractors.[224]

An even stranger private-sector project, dubbed the "PROFIT" initiative, was launched in the waning days of the Bush administration with the intent to build a pool of corporate cash by offering tax incentives to U.S. companies located in target nations to divert some of their "blocked" assets (funds which cannot be repatriated to the U.S.) to the family planning program. The $36 million project, launched in the fall of 1991, is also intended to promote birth control schemes at the workplace and to impact on policy in ways that will reduce tariffs and otherwise facilitate the American population control program. According to the USAID contract (awarded to the accounting firm of Deloitte and Touche), there are an astounding $200 billion in blocked corporate ac-

---

[223] U.S. Agency for International Development Contracts No. CCP-3051-C-00-2016-00 and CCP-3051-Q-00-2017-00 .

[224] U.S. Agency for International Development Project No. 936-3035.01, John Short and Associates, Inc., August 29, 1985 to August 28, 1990.

counts which are at least theoretically the object of this activity.[225]

Several of USAID's family planning "service delivery" projects include limited policy work. The Pathfinder program, for instance, is designed to establish family planning associations, conduct training projects and youth programs, and mount propaganda drives directed both at leaders and potential consumers. Its budget for the 1992-1997 period is $136 million.[226]

The Association for Voluntary Surgical Contraception (formerly known as the Association for Voluntary Sterilization) operates under an $80 million grant from USAID, and runs training and counseling courses, assists in the procurement of equipment, and carries out a number of other activities and sub-projects designed to popularize both male and female sterilization.[227]

Another program works only in one narrow area of population policy planning. The University of Michigan's scholarship-for-leadership campaign (the "Michigan Fellows" project) sponsors study in the U.S. for graduate students from developing nations with special attention to "the skills required by the host country or international institution." It is

---

[225] U.S. Agency for International Development Contract No. DPE-3056-C-00-1040-00 and DPE-3056-Q-00-1041-00.

[226] U.S. Agency for International Development Contract No. CCP-3062-A-00-2025-00.

[227] U.S. Agency for International Development Contract No. DPE-3049-A-00-8041-00.

scheduled to receive more than $6 million from USAID over five years.[228]

The East-West Population Institute is one of the oldest population policy actors of all, and works mainly in the Asia-Pacific region. It is responsible for producing literature and organizing conferences for policy makers and host country researchers.[229]

---

[228] U.S. Agency for International Development Project No. 936-3054; September 1990 to September 1995.

[229] U.S. Agency for International Development Contract No. DPE-3046-A-00-8050-00.

Chapter 10

The Institutional Approach: CERPOD vs. the Sahel

Foreign investment and aid frequently do nothing to lessen the inequality within developing countries and may even add to it... In the case of population-related foreign assistance, it is clear that senior government policy makers in the United States and other guardians of American culture and interests held a worldview that was threatened by the rapid growth of the Third World...

Peter J. Donaldson, Senior Representative, The Population Council, in *Nature Against Us: The United States and the World Population Crisis, 1965-1980* (1990)[230]

We are witnessing today a revival of colonialism, albeit in a new form. It is a trend that should be encouraged, it seems to me...

Paul Johnson, *The New York Times* Sunday Magazine, April 18, 1993, at page 22[231]

---

[230] *Nature Against Us: The United States and the World Population Crisis 1965-1980* by Peter J. Donaldson, University of North Carolina, Chapel Hill, 1990, at page 174.

[231] "Colonialism's Back — and Not a Moment Too Soon," by Paul Johnson, *The New York Times* Sunday magazine, April 18, 1993, at page 22.

Given the unique ability of development banks to compel borrowing countries to accept and implement population programs (and to force them to "request" aid from bilateral donors, as well), many of the U.S. government-funded policy "information" activities like OPTIONS really serve the purpose of giving target states the opportunity to "save face" — or to make excuses for unpopular actions which lenders have required that they initiate. In other words, the incessant presentations, policy seminars and work-shops, informational booklets, statistical charts, and "awareness" crusades — sometimes directed toward governments officials at levels that seem to approach brainwashing — are primarily motivational techniques that prepare them to explain a strange reversal of government policy about population to suspicious or angry constituents.

But in other instances, the use of "policy research" may have an even more devious purpose. Such is the case with CERPOD — an acronym for *Le Centre d'Etudes et de Recherches sur la Population pour le Developpement* or, in English, the Center for Applied Research on Population and Development.

CERPOD was launched quietly in 1988. It is headquartered in Bamako, Mali, and is loosely affiliated with the Permanent Interstate Committee for Drought Control in the Sahel (CILSS). Its activities are directed toward nine West African countries: Mali, Senegal, Gambia, Niger, Cape Verde, Guinea-

Bissau, Burkina Faso, Mauritania and Chad.[232] Specifically, its purpose is "to promote the development of appropriate national population policies and programs in the nine countries of the Sahel."[233]

As has been noted, the promotion of unsolicited population policies in developing nations may call for some rather unusual steps. Besides conditionality in lending and foreign aid transactions, and in addition to the "shadow lobbyists" that pursue government officials and heads of ministries, donors have also financed quasi-governmental institutions to conduct demographic research and provide analytical material, at least in the early stages. After several years of existence — and once suspicions about their origins have subsided — these same bureaus may step in and actually take the place of legitimate government institutions in the planning, implementation and enforcement of population policies. There is much to suggest that this is meant to be the case with CERPOD.

So carefully has U.S. involvement in CERPOD been concealed that a delegate from Cameroun at the 1992 UN regional population conference in Senegal suggested that he would prefer to take the advice of "African" institutions like CERPOD, which he appar-

---

[232] Project Grant Agreement, Center for Applied Research on Population and Development (CERPOD), USAID Mali, August 12, 1988, English translation, at page 34.

[233] CERPOD Project Grant Agreement, Annex I, "Amplified Project Description," at page 43.

ently found more credible than American or European ones.[234]

In fact, however, CERPOD is an American invention. And it is American-controlled. It gets the majority of its funds from USAID — indeed, USAID *created* it.

Although the CERPOD project is given lesser amounts of money by other donors — the governments of Netherlands, France, and Italy, the United Nations Population Fund (UNFPA), UNICEF, and the Ford and Rockefeller Foundations — it is nonetheless directed by the United States through its Embassy in Mali.[235] Indeed, the language of the USAID project authorization document is so clever that one might miss the point if the text is not carefully read:

> While the management of the project is vested with CERPOD, implementation will require USAID/Bamako's supervision and assistance. The Project Liaison Officer position established under the predecessor project is critical to enabling USAID/-Bamako to carry out its project implementation responsibilities. ... REDSO [the USAID Regional Economic Development Support Office in Abidjan] is also expected to be substantially in-

---

[234] Unpublished account of floor discussion at Africa region population conference, held December 7-12 at Dakar, Senegal. Information Project For Africa, Inc.

[235] CERPOD Project Grant Agreement, at page 57.

volved in monitoring project progress
and to serve as a resource for the
project evaluation... ¶ CERPOD will
collaborate with AID-financed Cooperating Agencies (CAs) having specialized
expertise applicable to population
policy development. ... ¶ CERPOD will
collaborate with CILSS countries and
USAID missions in the CILSS constituency. In addition to implementing its
core program, CERPOD can, through
mission-financed procurement of its
services, provide additional technical
assistance and training to Sahelian
governments and institutions in population policy and program development. CERPOD will also be able to
assist USAID missions in the design
and evaluation of population projects.[236]

In other words, USAID's population policy
development contractors will be able to attribute
materials included in their lobbying presentations to
a "local" establishment, CERPOD, which participated
in the "design and evaluation" of these materials.
Moreover, the requirement that CERPOD "collaborate
with AID-financed Cooperating Agencies having
specialized expertise [in] population policy development" makes the institution a "front" for other heavy-
handed political "persuasion" projects funded by the
United States. And ultimately, responsibility for

---

[236] CERPOD Project Grant Agreement, at page 48.

implementation of CERPOD's programs is vested with USAID/Bamako.

The USAID-CERPOD funding document lists several cooperating agencies with population policy operations in the Sahel region which will be assigned to work with CERPOD. These include the OPTIONS project and a similar activity that is also conducted by the Futures Group, the RAPID program; the Demographic and Health Surveys initiative (a survey of fertility attitudes and intentions, among other things); the IMPACT project, yet another USAID lobbying effort contracted to the Washington-based Population Reference Bureau; the Demographic Data for Development program; and a census assistance activity in which the U.S. Bureau of the Census is a participant.[237] A project implementation schedule for the "mobilization phase," part of the original funding package, lists several more, including the New York-based Population Council, which does psycho-social research on family planning motivation and conducts clinical trials of new birth control methods, and the World Bank.

The CERPOD contract identifies numerous activities to be completed in the first phase of the operation, including workshops for journalists, the publication of brochures and booklets, a regular journal called *Pop-Sahel*, the preparation of fertility analysis surveys, and study tours for national leaders.[238] Worse yet, as an arm of the Permanent

---

[237] CERPOD Project Grant Agreement, at page 48.

[238] CERPOD Project Grant Agreement, at pages 50-53.

Interstate Committee for Drought Control in the Sahel, the institute is in a position to actually play a leadership role in the making of regulations and in devising strategies for carrying out population plans against the targeted peoples of the Sahel.

Given the power over host country institutions and political processes which aid donors have assumed, the content of the propaganda dispensed by institutions like CERPOD hardly seems relevant. Nonetheless, it is useful to compare the rationale for population control offered by the west — poverty alleviation, orderly development, and improved maternal and child health, for example — with opinions on the same issues as found in literature *not* explicitly prepared for "third world" consumption.

One especially important study was conducted by the National Academy of Sciences on behalf of the Agency for International Development. The Academy's review of population growth and its implications for development was published in 1986 as a paperback book, *Population Growth and Economic Development: Policy Questions.*

Regarding those areas in which population change was most likely to produce an impact — industrialization, agriculture, education, health, and environment, among other things — the Academy found that population growth would have negative consequences only for the environment. And this conclusion was mitigated by the scientists' admonition that "socially negotiated" access rules and environmental protection standards are more important than efforts to slow the rate of population growth.[239]

With regard to agriculture, the Academy found distinct advantages for more densely-populated regions. The more heavily-settled places offer infrastructural advantages "which facilitate the flow of information about new technologies and, by increasing the possibilities for marketing output, also increase the gains to, and incentives for, raising productivity," the scientists concluded. "Denser populations may also be better able to bear the fixed costs of agricultural research relevant to an area's particular conditions."[240]

Giving specific examples, the report added:

> India could support 2.5 times its expected population in 2000. Zaire has enormous agricultural potential by this calculation, able to support 62 times its expected 2000 population of 46 million with high inputs — enough to feed the entire population of Africa several times over — and 6 times its

---

[239] *Population Growth and Economic Development: Policy Questions,* National Academy of Sciences, Working Group on Population Growth and Economic Development, Committee on Population, National Academy Press, Washington, DC, 1986, at pages 38, 39.

[240] *Population Growth and Economic Development,* op. cit., at page 51.

expected population even under low inputs...[241]

Similar findings were cited regarding financial markets. At the early states of a nation's development, a country is likely to borrow to meet its growth requirements, the Academy stated, until such time as the domestic rate of return equals that of the lender. "Rapid population growth may encourage these inflows by boosting the domestic rate of return to capital, thus making investment more attractive."

Even more importantly, the developing nations have a decided advantage over other regions because of their relatively high fertility. "Whether the country can expect to raise its steady-state per capita consumption above its self-sufficient level by recourse to foreign lending or borrowing will depend, among other things, on *its rate of growth of population relative to that of the rest of the world.*"[242]

In other words, a high-fertility nation has a distinct advantage if it must borrow, in that a growing number of workers will be present to help repay the debt over the long run.

Technological innovations, too, are more feasible in regions of high population density because large populations produce economies of scale. Said the researchers,

---

[241] *Population Growth and Economic Development*, op. cit., at page 23.

[242] *Population Growth and Economic Development*, op. cit., emphasis added, at page 46.

Without a local capital goods industry, there may be less demand for locally produced technological progress. Larger economies are far more likely to support a local capital goods industry and are therefore more likely to generate indigenous technological progress. Likewise it has been argued that the rate of technological progress will be positively affected by the number of researchers, which will increase with the size of the total population.[243]

The Academy likewise observed certain benefits for the health and education sectors as a result of population growth. Although the relationship of national population growth to education was not always clear, the scientists noted that a large family may improve an individual child's chances of getting an education. Citing studies in Sierra Leone and Botswana, they remarked that, at least in those places, "children from larger families achieve higher levels of schooling." Elsewhere, said the investigators, "Parents may only have to pay for the advanced schooling of the first child, while later ones are financed by older siblings."[244]

Moreover, the scholars said, "government school expenditure per school-aged child rises when fertility

---

[243] *Population Growth and Economic Development,* op. cit., footnotes omitted, at page 48.

[244] *Population Growth and Economic Development,* op. cit., at page 55-56.

falls," meaning that education becomes more cost-effective in a high-fertility society.

The Academy also determined that...

> "...population growth may actually assist governments in achieving health objectives ... by increasing rural density. It is often alleged that, especially in Africa, the dispersed, low-density rural population is difficult to reach with government health services."[245]

Of course, none of this information will filter into the Sahel by means of CERPOD. One brochure produced by the establishment predicts — contrary to the judgment of the USAID-funded scholars at the Academy — that health care services will "worsen as the population increases," and that governments in the region will be unable to provide "housing, transportation, sanitation, water, fuel and basic public services for a much larger population."[246]

Indeed, the one real accomplishment of CERPOD in its activities to date is an "N'Djamena Plan of Action for Population and Development in the Sahel," adopted in January of 1989, that urges all states in the region to "ensure that family planning services are integrated into all maternal and child health

---

[245]*Population Growth and Economic Development*, op. cit., at page 61.

[246] *Population and Development in the Sahel: The Challenges of Rapid Population Growth*, CERPOD, Bamako (undated), at pages 13, 15.

programs," to "consider and test various alternatives for delivery of family planning services," and to "establish a supply system for contraceptives, equipment and other essential supplies in order to avoid any interruption of family planning delivery services."[247] Still worse, the N'Djamena declaration says that "member states are urged to ensure that the human and financial resources required to implement population programs are made available to the appropriate organizations," and to "create or strengthen agencies in charge of the development, implementation and evaluation of population policies and programs."[248]

And, predictably, the statement ends with a request for more population control: "Donor countries are urged to continue to increase their financial and technical contributions to population programs in Sahelian countries."[249]

---

[247] *N'Djamena Plan of Action for Population and Development in the Sahel,* the text of the 1989 declaration published as a booklet published by CERPOD, Bamako, at page 5.

[248] *N'Djamena Plan of Action,* op. cit. at page 4.

[249] *N'Djamena Plan of Action,* op. cit., at page 8.

Chapter 11

Intellectual Warfare:
University Linkage in Nigeria

If you give a man the correct information for seven years, he may believe the incorrect information on the first day of the eighth year when it is necessary, from your point of view, that he should do so. Your first job is to build the credibility and the authenticity of your propaganda, and persuade the enemy to trust you although you are his enemy.

Operations Research Office
A Psychological Warfare Casebook (1958)[250]

In the early years of the cold war, the United States recognized that it could not hope to exploit its superpower status if it were not ever vigilant of competing ideologies — taking steps to influence the thinking of intellectuals, the leanings of political leaders and potential leaders, and the attitudes of other influential segments of humanity in foreign lands thousands of miles from its shores. By the beginning of the 1950s, a rudimentary system for planning the global ideological offensive had been

---

[250] *A Psychological Warfare Casebook*, Operations Research Office, Johns Hopkins University Press, Baltimore, 1958, at page 38.

established under the name of the Psychological Strategy Board. The Psychological Strategy Board (or "PSB") consisted of a few top officials from the Department of State, the Defense Department, and the Central Intelligence Agency who were charged with making recommendations and decisions, determining policies, and evaluating the psychological warfare activities of the U.S. government.[251]

Psychological operations are more a political activity than a military one. Although short-term "psy-war" campaigns can be used to undermine morale on the battlefield, to mislead the commanders of an enemy military force, or to facilitate the surrender or defection of an opponent's troops, it is still basically a social science, one that is every bit as much applicable to influencing civilian behavior as it is to the messy details of war.

In fact, a broad-based psy-war campaign is an attack on culture as much as anything else. It seeks to change a society — the masses as well as the leaders — by targeting them, often through local communications media, with carefully-designed messages and ideas. The constant exposure of an audience to a particular set of images or beliefs is intended to produce a gradual devaluation of prevalent customs and traditional cultural patterns, so that the new opinions and ideologies can take root. As such, psy-war tactics are especially useful in pro-

---

[251] The Psychological Strategy Board was created under a directive of President Harry S. Truman on April 4, 1951. See, i.e., Memorandum for the Secretaries of the Army, Navy and Air Force, "The Establishment of the Psychological Strategy Board," April 9, 1951; U.S. Library of Congress, Declassified Documents Section.

moting the use of birth control among traditional societies where the practice is strongly resisted by a majority of the people. A cultural offensive of this kind generally involves covert propaganda — communications falsely attributed to members of the target group — to give the impression of a spontaneous change within the target population itself. This, in turn, seduces the group as a whole into changing its behavior to conform to the needs or fears imposed through the campaign. It is essential, however, that the entire operation be carefully planned so that these influences are introduced into the community without its members being aware of the existence of the program.

Col. Alfred H. Paddock, Jr., former Director of Psychological Operations in the Office of the Secretary of Defence, defines psychological warfare in the political and military context as....

> ...the planned use of communications to influence human attitudes and behavior ... conducted to create in target groups behavior, emotions, and attitudes that support the attainment of national objectives ....[252]

Another official definition of "psychological warfare" is very similar:

---

[252] Col. Alfred H. Paddock, Jr., from a paper presented at a symposium of the Georgetown University Security Studies Program, published by the U.S. Government Printing Office in 1989, as *Special Operations in U.S. Strategy*, National Defense University Press, 1984, at page 231.

> The planned use of propaganda and
> other actions designed to influence the
> opinions, emotions, attitudes, and
> behavior of enemy, neutral, and friend-
> ly foreign groups in such a way as to
> support the accomplishment of nation-
> al aims and objectives.[253]

Early in the cold war period, psychological
warfare planning was given an exceptionally high
priority by military and political leaders in Washington. In 1948, shortly after the end of World War II,
an elite academic unit was set up to do the theoreti-
cal background work and social science research
that would become the backbone of the nation's
psychological operations policy. That unit, known as
the Operations Research Office, was run by the Balti-
more-based Johns Hopkins University under contract with the U.S. Army, and it was at first so secret
that even a description of its work was confidential.[254]

Over the next several years, the Johns Hopkins
Operations Research Office prepared sophisticated
textbooks about every facet of psychological operations. One, completed in 1953, was called *The Nature
of Psychological Warfare*. It was followed by another,
*Target Analysis and Media in Propaganda to Audienc-
es Abroad*. In 1958, a third was published with the
title *A Psychological Warfare Casebook*. These, among

---

[253] *A Psychological Warfare Casebook*, op. cit., at page 2.

[254] See, i.e., *Baltimore Sun*, June 3, 1951, "Putting the OR in
Victory" by James H. Bready.

others, were became the standard texts "for use in training of personnel for psychological warfare operations" on behalf of the United States government.[255]

Psy-war is, by its very nature, directed at groups. When the goal is to affect political decisions, the psy-war effort might be directed toward heads of state, parliamentary groups, diplomats, officials of government ministries — even opposition leaders, the news media, and selected special interest groups. If the campaign is designed to influence trade and economic activities, communications might well be directed toward leaders of the business community, merchants, trade associations, or labor organizations. And if the purpose is to alter the intellectual environment in a target country or region, academic leaders and institutions would then be the object of the campaign. Indeed, one of the most important targets in any political influence program would be the universities, since opinion leaders from all walks of life tend, more and more, to come from the university-educated elite. For this reason, a study of foreign influence activities run under the guise of U.S. foreign aid would be incomplete without reference to the penetration of academia.

In an early 1993 edition, *Innovations*, a newsletter of the U.S. Agency for International Development, reported that the Agency's two-year-old "University Development Linkages Project" (UDLP) had been

---

[255] *The Nature of Psychological Warfare*, Operations Research Office, Johns Hopkins University, 1953, at preface.

expanded to 33 developing country institutions in 23 countries.[256] In fact, one of the first such "linkage" activities launched by USAID involves the same Johns Hopkins University that guided the American military psy-war program, along with three major universities in Nigeria — the Universities of Benin, Ilorin and Maiduguri. The stated objectives of the academic influence program are listed in the written contract under which the effort is funded. These include:

> Training leaders for key positions in government service... ¶ Serving as an effective link to institutions of higher education and technical organizations outside of Nigeria and through those links enhancing Nigeria's access to relevant external expertise... ¶ Working to provide critical reviews and assessments of local, state and federal programs, and; ¶ Playing a key role in the process of determining national priorities in health, population and development.[257]

In other words, the project may very well be intended to generate a Nigerian leadership class by inserting into academic courses whatever doctrines

---

[256] *Innovation*, Volume 1, No. 3, Winter/Spring 1993, at page 4.

[257] U.S. Agency for International Development, U.S.-Nigeria Collaborating Universities Program, University Development Linkages Project (UDLP Project), Executive Summary, Contract No. DAN-5062-A-00-1109-00, at page 2.

Washington may choose — or by *withholding* and even *falsifying* certain types of information. The linkage also allows the USAID contractor, Johns Hopkins, to play a part in determining the priorities of the national development and population programs — and to accomplish this feat in such a way as to give the impression that its various priorities are those of Nigerian intellectuals. Moreover, the U.S.-funded academic program is supposed to open the three Nigerian universities to additional outside influences under the pretense of "enhancing Nigeria's access to relevant external expertise."[258]

But the project is designed to do still more. At the end of the five-year program, says the USAID project description, there is expected to be established a "sustainable linkage between JHU [Johns Hopkins University] and the collaborating Nigerian Universities to support programs of research, higher education and community outreach."[259] It is likewise intended to "build local sources for education in health planning, management and health finance."[260]

Even more incredibly, the university program is calculated, in the words of the project document itself, to provide "access by U.S. investigators to programs in Nigeria," to establish a minimum of six new teaching courses at the affected schools, to facilitate five to ten "active, externally funded research collabo-

---

[258] UDLP Project, at page 2.

[259] UDLP Project, at page 3.

[260] UDLP Project, at page 3.

rations," to produce "an institutionalized communications network," and to prepare Nigerian scholars "to compete for internationally funded research."[261]

These astounding provisions seem clearly to suggest a vigorous campaign of academic surveillance that could reasonably be expected to identify (and punish) Nigerian intellectuals who hold anti-American or anti-imperialist views and to turn the three universities into recruitment centers for various "scientific" and political programs in Nigeria and elsewhere in Africa.

Another section of the "linkage" contract calls for Johns Hopkins to "increase access by U.S. investigators to populations and community based programs in Nigeria," and to initiate 20 small pilot projects costing between U.S. $10,000 and $20,000 each, with the stipulation that those funded under these programs "must express intent to use funding to develop externally funded projects." A proposal from Johns Hopkins for the Nigerian linkage grant also promises that it will "assure that the research undertaken will be relevant and can be translated into programs and policies."[262] It explains:

> The Nigerian faculty clearly bring unique insights into African culture and society as well as an understanding of local perceptions and health needs. Traditionally, they focus on

---

[261] UDLP Project, at page 3.

[262] Johns Hopkins University Institute for International Programs. UDLP Technical Proposal (undated), at page 22.

issues of relevance to their communities. This experience is vital to programs of community outreach, population-based research and policy formulation. Nigerian faculty will bring unique insights to the analysis and interpretation of research findings and will take the lead in translating research findings into policies and programs... an aspect of development assistance that JHU could not begin to undertake without this collaboration.[263]

The same proposal stresses the benefits to the United States of the university program: "It will further the internationalization endeavors of JHU by increasing access to collaborators in Nigerian universities," the document states,[264] and will, at the same time, have the effect of "enabling Nigerian researchers to be competitive in seeking international research funds."[265]

And a project description included in the funding authorization lists additional operations to be conducted under the grant, along with their intended outcomes. One activity, meant to "support the internationalization goals of the Nigerian University and the Johns Hopkins University," will produce a "mail-

---

[263] UDLP Technical Proposal, at page 22.

[264] UDLP Technical Proposal, at page 24.

[265] UDLP Technical Proposal, at page 26.

ing list of active, university-based, research educated technical experts for use by the universities, government and the donor community," says the document.[266]

Covert U.S. government involvement in academic institutions, like interference with the press, has become so routine over the years as to constitute more or less a standard operating procedure. Attempts by the CIA to influence academics involve not only foreign students in the U.S. but also domestic universities. A pamphlet produced in the early 1970s by the Africa Research Group documents the involvement in such activities of several collaborators in today's population program. It reports that...

> ...it was the CIA which played the crucial role in stimulating interest in African affairs in the United States... In 1954, it was the CIA that put the African-American Institute on a solid financial footing, in close cooperation with the American Metal Climax Corporation... In that year, when Boston University launched its own African Studies program, William O. Brown left the State Department's Bureau of Intelligence to head it up. As the nation's chief *central* intelligence agency, the CIA understood that generating information and contacts in Africa was a priority of the U.S. was to be assured access to the Continent's "emerging"

---

[266] UDLP Project. Table 4. Summary Workplan.

political leaders and economic resources... While the CIA was "inspiring" university African affairs programs, it was also getting its own African Intelligence division organized. In August, 1958, the Committee of Africanists selected by the Ford Foundation to "survey the present condition and future prospects of African Studies" had a rare direct interview with the CIA to assess its need for personnel. According to their report, the Agency said it would need "a constant staff level of something like 70 people specializing in the Africa area..." ¶ The CIA continues to shape and monitor all government sponsored research on Africa through its participation in the Foreign Area Coordination Group and its close links with the State Department [Bureau of Intelligence and Research]. It has access to all other academic output through the willing cooperation of many scholars — who register their work with the State Department — or through close and overlapping ties with such agencies as the Ford Foundation and its academic front committees. As well, many individual scholars have ties with the CIA or its front groups. L. Gray Cowan, for example, the 1969-1970 President of the African Studies Association, was known to have liaisons with one Willard Mathias, a high-level CIA functionary. Mathias was a visiting fellow in 1958-1959 at Harvard's Center of

International Affairs. His topic of study: Africa, of course. Cowan has also been a long time member of the African-American Institute's Board of Directors...[267]

Along with the Ford Foundation, the name of Rockefeller comes up frequently in connection with funding of CIA-backed operations in developing nations. Both Ford and Rockefeller have helped finance CERPOD and numerous other population projects throughout the developing world.

The CIA-funded African-American Institute (or "AAI") is another interesting case. AAI is among a large number of institutions receiving USAID support for population policy development programs. Under a $2 million agreement between AAI and USAID, signed in early 1988, the Institution agreed to participate in mass media propaganda campaigns to promote the "acceptability of smaller family norms and family planning" and to assist in the policy development process by helping to bring about "a policy climate conducive to the successful execution of a national family planning effort and to strengthen federal, state, and local government capability in strategic planning in order to efficiently mobilize and execute an effective and self-sustaining national

---

[267] *Africa Studies in America — The Extended Family — A Tribal Analysis of U.S. Africanists: Who They Are; Why to Fight Them.* The Africa Research Group; reprinted in *Dirty Work 2: The Cia in Africa,* edited by Ellen Ray, William Schaap, Karl Van Meter and Louis Wolf, Lyle Stuart, Inc., Seacaucus, NJ, 1979.

family planning program."[268] Ironically, the AAI contract, like the Johns Hopkins University linkage agreement, was applicable in one country: Nigeria.

While there is nothing concrete to suggest that the Johns Hopkins project at the three Nigerian universities has any direct financial link to the CIA, a more obvious ploy for recruiting human "assets" and spies than the Johns Hopkins-USAID University Development Linkage Program could hardly be imagined.

---

[268] USAID Contract No. 620-0001-C-00-8008-00, February 25, 1988, at page 5 ("Statement of Work"). Ironically, the President of the African American Institute at the time the population contract was signed was one Donald Easum, U.S. Embassador to Nigeria under Nixon and Ford. In fact, Easum, reportedly a close associate of Henry Kissinger, held that diplomatic post on February 13, 1976 when Nigerian nationalist leader Muritala Muhammed was assassinated. Muhammed's pro-U.S. successor in office, the Olusegun Obasanjo, remained in office as Nigeria's head of state until 1979, and is credited with keeping oil prices low for the developed world. Curiously, Obasanjo, too, has ties to the CIA, most notably his affiliation with the African-American Institute (he heads its African Leadership Forum, which has cordial working relations with the Center for Strategic and International Studies, with which Henry Kissinger is associated). Obasanjo, using his African Leadership Forum office, has made frequent pronouncements in favor of western-initiated "reforms" in Nigeria, including the population control program.

Chapter 12

Worse Than Misguided Altruism

When will there be too many white babies
for the earth to fill and hold?
When will white people submit themselves
to population control?
WHEN HELL FREEZES OVER![269]

Listervelt Middleton, 1987

For decades now, the United States has been insisting to other countries that "modern family planning" is good for people. Fewer children make healthier mothers. Smaller families enjoy better living standards. Slower population growth makes sustainable development. Fewer people will mean fewer headaches for political leaders.

But does the American government really believe any of this? It is true that incomes are vastly higher in industrial nations than in the less-developed regions where birthrates are highest. And it obvious to almost anyone that the small families in the west have better access to certain services, like higher education, for example.

But the "small-families-equal-wealth" equation is a bit too much like the old "pornography-makes-the-rapist" argument. Might it not be true that rapists tend, more than any other group of criminals,

---

[269] "When Hell Freezes Over," by Listervelt Middleton, host of "For the People," South Carolina Educational TV (SETV). Copyright 1987 Listervelt Middleton.

to be the sort of neurotic persons who are attracted to pornography, and that their taste in literature is more a symptom than a cause? And couldn't it also be true that wealth and the general lifestyle it encourages are the *cause* of low fertility in the north, and not the result?

After all, there was once a time when America was largely rural, when refrigerators were not even invented, when the overwhelming majority of families worked in the "informal" sector as farmers, crop-pickers, and small merchants — and when average completed family size ranged somewhere around five or six or seven children. And this did not prevent the United States from emerging as a "developed" country and a world power. Indeed, the population of the United States grew at phenomenal rates during its rise to power.

In the fifty years between 1790 and 1840, U.S. population increased nearly five-fold, from less than 4 million to nearly 18 million. By the year 1870 — just three decades later — the U.S. population had more than tripled again to 38.5 million. Between 1870 and 1880, there was a 37 percent increase in the nation's population to over 50 million. By the turn of the century, the United States counted more than 76 million inhabitants — fully 15 *times* the number it had a mere hundred years before. During the next four decades, population continued to grow at a rate higher than that experienced by most developing nations today, gaining a total of 56 million more people between 1900 and 1940. Growth rates in the United States during the first half of the 20th century averaged nearly 3 percent per year. And it should be remembered that this occurred at exactly the time when the United States most effectively increased its productivity and its standing in the world.[270] It is also interesting to note that a significant part of this population increase, particularly during the latter years, was the result of foreign immigration, which is more difficult for a society to absorb than is an increase in native-born population.

One of the most telling clues as to the intentions of western foreign policy planners is that population literature intended for consumption by the public (or even by parliamentary bodies like the U.S. Congress) nearly *always* makes some reference to food shortages, damage to environmental resources, and overcrowding. Documents intended only for *internal* consumption, on the other hand, almost *never* focus on this type of argument.

A top-secret memorandum of the old Operations Coordinating Board of the National Security Council with the heading "Outline Plan of Operations for Latin America" expresses the consternation of American leaders about population change: "The rapid rate of population increase and economic growth in the area, with their *implications for probable future strength and importance to the United States,* should be taken into consideration in the execution of all programs."[271] In other words, the economic growth

---

[270] Statistics from U.S. Census Department, published in *The World Almanac and Book of Facts,* 1993 edition, at pages 386-387.

[271] Operations Coordinating Board, Working Group on Latin America, January 10, 1957 Outline Plan of Operations for Latin America, at page 3.

that accompanies population increase — rather than the disadvantages that contemporary population policy propaganda portrays — is what Washington views as the real threat to its objectives in Latin America. This is a theme that runs through the entire archives of U.S. foreign affairs with reference to every developing region.

A more recent example of the same thinking regarding Latin America appears in a 1991 research paper prepared for the U.S. Army Conference on Long-Range Planning:

> Though the populations of the nine Asian countries in the sample more than tripled during this period, and the population of the six Latin American countries rose by a factor of nearly seven, per-capita output is estimated to have risen dramatically as well — by a factor of more than three for the Asian group and by nearly five for the Latin American group... Evidently, rapid population growth has not prevented major improvements in productivity in many of the societies most directly transformed by it.[272]

This is a critical revelation. *Per-capita* income in the Latin American countries under study — the ratio of money to people — increased five-fold during

---

[272] U.S. Army Conference on Long Range Planning, reprinted in *Foreign Affairs*, Summer 1991, as "Population Change and National Security," at page 117.

a period when population increased by a factor of nearly seven. This means that overall gross earnings in the region would have increased *35-fold* during the period, since each person, on the average, gained by a multiple of five and there were seven times as many people. This does not suggest the economic stagnation predicted by western policy propaganda, but rather a dramatic growth in regional wealth and prestige. Now if all the rhetoric about population growth *impeding* development were truly believed in Washington, those "benevolent" U.S. policy makers would be delighted that the Latin American nations have done so well, saving the U.S. millions, perhaps billions, in poverty-preventing contraceptive programs. But the record shows no sense of relief whatever.

> [V]irtually all current population projections anticipate comparatively slow population growth in today's more developed regions (Europe, the Soviet Union, Japan, North America and Oceania) and comparatively rapid growth for the less developed regions (the rest of the world). With variations, these projections point to a continuation of trends evident since the end of World War II. If these trends continue for another generation or two, the implications for the international polit-

ical order and the balance of world power could be enormous.[273]

Indeed, the same research paper, produced in 1991 for the U.S. Army, comes to the conclusion that...

> By these projections a very different world would seem to be emerging. Such trends speak to pressures for a systematically diminished role and status for today's industrial democracies. Even with relatively unfavorable assumptions about Third World economic growth, the share of global economic output of today's industrial democracies could decline. With a generalized and progressive industrialization of current low-income areas, the Western diminution would be all the more rapid. Thus, one can easily envision a world more unreceptive, and ultimately more threatening, to the interests of the United States and its allies. ¶ The population and economic-growth trends described could create an international environment even more menacing to the security prospects of the Western alliance than

---

[273] U.S. Army Conference on Long Range Planning, *Foreign Affairs*, op. cit., at pages 115-116.

was the Cold War for the past generation.[274]

And the 1974 National Security Council document on population control — which remains the
definitive statement of the U.S. interest in population
control — is no less blunt. It emphatically states that
the rapid growth of population is most threatening to
U.S. interests in the largest countries — those most
likely to exert their influence on others, and especially those rich in natural resources. The Egyptians, for
instance, will become more and more strategically
important as their numbers grow. "The large and
increasing size of Egypt's population is, and will
remain for many years, an important consideration
in the formulation of many foreign and domestic
policies not only of Egypt but also of neighboring
countries," says the study.[275] Brazil, too, "clearly
dominates" Latin America in demographic significance, suggesting a "growing power status for Brazil
in Latin America and on the world scene over the
next 25 years."[276] And Nigeria is in a similarly favorable situation.

> Already the most populous country on
> the continent, with an estimated 55
> million people in 1970, Nigeria's popu-

---

[274] U.S. Army Conference on Long Range Planning, *Foreign Affairs*,
op. cit., at pages 128-129.

[275] NSSM 200, op. cot., at page 22.

[276] NSSM 200, op. cit., at page 22.

lation by the end of this century is projected to number 135 million. This suggests a growing political and strategic role for Nigeria, at least in Africa south of the Sahara.[277]

References to the "danger" to U.S. pre-eminence lurking behind population growth in less-developed countries are all too frequent, too compelling these days — and entirely too consistent in claiming that developing country population growth will hurt the United States by allowing the emerging nations of the south to advance themselves politically and economically. The importance of the issue is affirmed — or at least implied — in the huge number of current texts that exist on national security and population trends in the post-cold war world order.

But on the other hand, there is the perception that global power arrangements are fixed — that nuclear weapons and other advanced technologies have undermined the significance of large populations. This may be partly true in the short term. But western leaders are far from convinced. Indeed, over a generation or two — the time frame in which the effects of population trends must be debated — the experts paint an entirely different picture. According to one frequently-quoted source,

The argument that modern weapons will soon cancel the advantages of a large population is invalid... Atomic bombs require more than knowledge

---

[277] NSSM 200, op. cit., at page 21.

for their manufacture. American's war machine is manufactured by a long list of her greatest industries. Only a great and populous nation has the kind of industrial installations required to turn out modern weapons of mass destruction... ¶ The simple fact is that, far from reducing the power of large nations with great armies, modern weapons have increased the power of large nations with large military budgets. The advancing technology of warfare has already become so frighteningly expensive that only giant nations can afford it. Few shifts are more striking than the concentration of power in the hands of a few giant nations that has marked the first half of the twentieth century.[278]

Moreover, the size and morale of combat forces has assumed no less importance in the nuclear age. The same writers contend, in fact, that the "advantage of numbers is greatest, perhaps, for peasant nations." They explain,

Who will occupy the ruins, police the survivors? And who will fight the small wars that are typical of a century in which great nations hesitate to unloose total horror? We learned, or should have learned, in Korea and Indochina that even peasant soldiers

---

[278] *Population and World Power*, op. cit., at page 17.

can put up a good fight against modern weapons. One cannot use a jet plane to stop a coolie carrying explosives on his back. One cannot use atomic bombs on every haystack that may hide a tank. ¶... The twentieth century has taught us old methods of foiling new conquerors. The peasant guerrilla who takes to the mountains, the bomb-throwing terrorist who hides in the crowd, the army that melts in the daylight, are all a part of the total war that takes new forms. A large population can mock its conquerors, who may spread their thin net of control along the highways and across the major cities but sit like trapped birds in their own net while the country heaves beneath them.[279]

A massive war machine depends on a large-scale economy, but it also requires certain raw materials, access to which may be affected by population change. Indeed, U.S. dependence on foreign sources of "strategic" minerals, including those needed for manufacture of modern weapons, has become a preoccupation among certain circles.

A 1990 National Defense University text, for instance, draws a distinction between *dependency* and *vulnerability*, explaining that, if "foreign sources were to be disrupted by ... social or political activi-

---

[279] *Population and World Power*, op. cit., at page 16.

ties, dependency could become a vulnerability."[280] It then makes a series of policy recommendations designed to "integrate strategic materials objectives with other foreign policy objectives among friends, allies, and the Third World." These, the writer continues, would "provide clear guidance to State, AID, and other internationally oriented agencies as to the nature of US strategic mineral objectives," and would "provide development assistance to Third World countries for the sole purpose of increasing the production of strategic minerals..."[281]

In the event of a "possible political or military crisis that would impinge on our access to supplies of strategic minerals abroad," the book demands that the U.S. prepare "contingency plans" and develop a "set of options for the use of covert action" to counteract interference with U.S. mineral access.[282]

This theme, too, is heard again and again. "Nonmilitary threats, such as population growth in developing countries or competition for control of natural resources, could ultimately pose profound threats to national security," says an article in the

---

[280] *Strategic Minerals: U.S. Alternatives* by Kenneth A. Kessel, National Defense University, Washington, February 1990, at page 189.

[281] *Strategic Minerals: U.S. Alternatives*, op. cit., at page 199.

[282] *Strategic Minerals: U.S. Alternatives*, op. cit., at page 200.

Spring 1993 issue of the *International Journal of Intelligence and CounterIntelligence.*[283]

And the 1974 National Security Council memorandum on population control delivered the same message. "The location of known reserves of higher-grade ores of most minerals favors increasing dependence of all industrialized regions on imports from less developed countries," it states. "The real problems of mineral supplies lie, not in basic physical sufficiency, but in the politico-economic terms for exploration and exploitation, and division of the benefits among producers, consumers, and host country governments."[284] Therefore, the secret document concluded that population control and family planning programs should be enforced in order to guard against potential interruption of supplies:

> [T]he U.S. economy will require large and increasing amounts of minerals from abroad, especially from less developed countries. That fact gives the U.S. enhanced interest in the political, economic, and social stability of the supplying countries. Wherever a lessening of population pressures through reduced birth rates can increase the

---

[283] "The International Environment and the U.S. Intelligence Community" by David D. Dabelko and Geoffrey D. Dabelko. *International Journal of Intelligence and CounterIntelligence.* Vol. 6. No. 1. at page 22.

[284] NSSM 200. op. cit., at page 37.

prospects for such stability, population policy becomes relevant to the economic interests of the United States.[285]

Clearly, there is no other issue that incites in western policy makers a sense of crisis comparable to the matter of population growth in the developing world. And no other matter intersects with virtually every element of international power — access to materials for military use, projected troop strength, relative economic advantage, political domination, racial potency, and cultural influences.

There are sure to be some population control advocates who concede that military security is an issue, but that families in developing nations will still be better off having fewer children. If they are prosperous and content, these people say, the security threat subsides. But once again, the record suggests that concern for the quality of life in the south runs pretty thin among the gurus of structural adjustment in Washington. One need only look to the example of essential medications.

A million people are thought to die in Africa each year as a result of malaria. According to the Ghana News Agency, nearly a third of all deaths in the northern region of that country between 1989 and 1993 were due to malaria, and occurred mostly in children and pregnant women.[286] Malaria can be

---

[285] NSSM 200, op. cit., at page 43.

[286] Cited in *Ghana Review*, an electronic compilation of national news reports distributed via InterNet, January 20, 1995.

cured with antibiotics costing about one American dollar. And, as noted previously, USAID's first-phase OPTIONS policy program received $23 million under the basic contract and millions more from USAID "mission offices" overseas. Thus, it is probably fair to conclude that close to $2 million, on the average, was spent on each of the 24 countries targeted. The money used up under this project in just one country, then, would seem sufficient to purchase medicine to prevent malaria deaths all over Africa for a year. The money spent on the same activity in another country could, by the same reasoning, finance the transport and distribution of these desperately-needed medications throughout the continent for the same one-year period. And the "OPTIONS" project represents only a tiny fraction — perhaps five percent or less — of USAID's yearly expenditures on "policy development." But the malaria death toll continues unchecked.

Although considered a form of "economic" aid, the policy development program brings no monetary benefit to host countries, either. In fact, the policy campaign, expressly designed to "train" foreign leaders to make political moves advantageous to the west, puts no money into the economies of the countries in which it is active, with the possible exception of payments handed over to a few selected local people to act as "in place" agents. And these payments are nearly always concealed, thus contributing to an atmosphere of political corruption, precisely because Washington understands, as one author has stated it, that visible U.S. sponsorship "would jeopardize family planning activities by opening them to political attacks."[287]

Moreover, the program, almost by definition, was created to supply information that is starkly different from the conventional wisdom of regional leaders (and, indeed, that is why the project was created). Therefore, in reality, it serves to take something away — something no less vital than the ability of national authorities to honestly evaluate the likely outcome of events and to make independent decisions that will enhance the future well-being of their own peoples.

One could say the same about population control generally. The United Nations in 1991 estimated that between $4.5 and $5 billion is spent *per year* on population control in developing nations.[288] This includes money from multilateral institutions and bilateral programs, but not the significant private financing contributed by scores of multinational corporations and "philanthropic" foundations in the west. And the amount increases substantially every year. Were just a portion of this money allocated to African schools, to road-building, energy development, agricultural modernization, and technology — under local direction and at local currency rates — the continent would be well developed in a few short years (as was Europe in the aftermath of World War II).

---

[287] Donaldson in *Nature Against Us*, op. cit., at page 26.

[288] *The State of World Population 1991*, United Nations Population Fund, New York, 1991, at page 34.

Then one must consider the "debt crisis." The World Bank alone earns a profit exceeding a billion dollars every year, with a considerable share of that profit reaped from interest on loans involving population-related activities. This is money that will have to be repaid with interest by the next generation of workers, those future farmers and laborers and teachers and soldiers whose numbers the loans are explicitly meant to reduce.

When the United States launched its diplomatic campaign to build "international" support for the annihilation of Iraq, it offered the Egyptian government the forgiveness of $7 billion in bilateral debt for its participation. The Americans, in other words, felt it was worth the money to "borrow" Arab support for the killing of other Arabs, but does not implement debt forgiveness when systems for providing free and universal education to children start to collapse, or when urban migration, inadequate irrigation, and unfavorable (man-made) market conditions turn millions of acres of arable land to desert.

As noted earlier, even the World Bank's 1990 *Development Report* acknowledges the fact that population growth stimulates development, that "an expanding economy could absorb the additional labor and may indeed depend on it."[289] And the National Academy of Sciences likewise concluded that while...

> ...population growth can exacerbate
> the ill effects of a variety of inefficient
> policies, such as urban bias in the

---

[289] *World Development Report 1990*, op. cit., at page 82.

> provision of infrastructure, direct and
> indirect food subsidies that distort
> agricultural markets, credit market
> distortions, and inadequate manage-
> ment of common property ... [the]
> fundamental solution to these prob-
> lems lies in *better policies outside the
> population arena.*[290]

Ironically, the developed countries seem quite open about accepting population growth as a benefit when it comes to themselves. A number of relatively wealthy, densely-populated nations in Western Europe have, in fact, enacted measures to increase their birthrates.

France, for example, has declared its fertility rates too low and has attempted to restructure its system of family benefit grants to be "more favorable to young and larger families," according to a UN directory of population policies.[291] The French government has also moved to create better housing for families, provided low interest loans to young couples, and enacted provisions guaranteeing parental leave during child bearing, all with the explicit intention of bringing the birthrate up to replacement level.[292]

---

[290] *Population Growth and Economic Development,* op. cit., at page 91. Emphasis added.

[291] *World Population Policies,* Vol. 1, The United Nations, 1987, at pages 218, 220.

[292] *World Population Policies,* op. cit., Vol. 1, at pages 218, 220.

Switzerland likewise has officially declared its rate of population growth to be insufficient. The Swiss government is attempting "to increase the rate of fertility indirectly by establishing an atmosphere of economic security and well-being, especially for children and families in all sectors," says the UN source book.[293] A system of family allowances is also in force, as is maternity insurance and work leave.[294]

West Germany also announced a pro-natalist policy in 1984 which was specifically intended to increase the number of German births by 200,000 per year. The policy includes tax incentives for childbearing and a $200 allowance given to every new mother until her child is a year old. A revision of the policy added parental leave provisions and an increase in the maternity bonus.[295]

Greece, too, has enacted a law against the dismissal of pregnant women from their jobs, mandates 14-weeks of maternity leave, and allocates "child welfare allowances" to large families in an attempt to raise the birthrate. Sterilization is restricted in Greece.[296] And several other European nations provide family benefits, although not as part of explicitly-stated pro-natalist schemes.

---

[293] *World Population Policies*, op. cit., Vol. 3, at page 136.

[294] *World Population Policies*, op. cit., Vol. 3, at page 136.

[295] *World Population Policies*, op. cit., Vol. 2, at page 16.

[296] *World Population Policies*, op. cit., Vol. 2, at page 24.

Efforts to encourage high birthrates among people who have no desire for large families seldom produce the hoped-for results. But pressures to prevent births among people who desire to have many children can be devastatingly effective.

It is public knowledge that the United States was a major force behind the "population emergency" declared by President Indira Ghandi of India in 1975.[297] Between the declaration of the emergency in mid-1975 and its end in 1977, an estimated 6.5 million men were given vasectomies, mostly against their will, and a total of 1,774 died as a result of the operations.[298] This is just one example of the coercive actions that have been inspired over the past three decades by desperate minds in Washington. According to one powerful population control organization, the global population "stabilization" effort has thus far reduced the population of the southern hemisphere by more than 400 million, and the same

-----

[297] See, for example, Bernard Berelson of the Population Council, *Beyond Family Planning*. In fact, World Bank President Robert McNamara, a former U.S. Secretary of Defense, reportedly took the time to visit the ministry of Health and Family Planning in November of 1976, at the height of the compulsory sterilization campaign, to congratulate the Indian government on its "political will and determination" in solving the population problem. McNamara's trip is cited in *Choices in Childbearing: When Does Family Planning Become Population Control?* by Robert Whelan, Committee on Population & The Economy, London, 1992, at page 29, and originally appeared in the *New Scientist*, May 5, 1977.

[298] Whelan, op. cit., at page 29.

group predicts that the difference made over the next century will approach 4 *billion*.[299]

Even the more subtle (less coercive) programs have stirred an enormous amount of controversy among journalists and the medical community worldwide. The Dalkon Shield, a brand of contraceptive device that causes temporary sterility when inserted into the womb, caused numerous deaths in the United States during the 1970s, and was the subject of a historic court award.[300] Yet millions of similar devices are still being exported by the United States, often distributed in developing countries without proper warnings about the dangers they pose to reluctant users.[301] Norplant, a birth control device surgically placed under the skin of a woman's arm,

---

[299] The Population Council, News Release, "Impact of Family Planning Programs in Developing Countries Is Assessed in New Study by Population Council Researchers." 24 January 1991.

[300] See, e.g., the *Washington Post* of April 9, 1985.

[301] A press release from the Agency for International Development's Office of Press Relations, prepared in 1989 and distributed at least through the early months of 1990, proclaimed proudly that USAID provides about three-fourths of all the contraceptives in use throughout the developing world, including no fewer than 50 million IUDs. In 1991, AID's Office of Population wrote a letter to the International Planned Parenthood Federation advising the group, "All too often, in our view, family planning programs impose numerous medical barriers to service which we are convinced hinder program effectiveness and impact..." The letter, quoted in the November/December issue 1991 of *Ms* magazine (page 15), includes "excessive counseling" and "conservative medical thinking" among a list of "medical barriers" that slow the pace of population control projects.

is known to cause frequent complications, and there have been consistent reports of family planning "care-takers" refusing to remove them even when clients experience debilitating side-effects.[302] Injectable, long-acting contraceptive drugs have been the subject of numerous complaints, as well, going back to the 1970s; yet today, these drugs remain a mainstay of the global "family planning" effort.[303]

And then there are a host of experimental fertility control methods, often tested in arbitrary doses on economically-disadvantaged women in the least-developed countries — those least likely to enjoy any of the legal remedies available to western women in case of negligent injury and who lack access to medical care for treatment of potentially-deadly complications. Among the new procedures subject to clinical trial are an "anti-pregnancy vaccine" that works for about a year — with still-unknown consequences — which has been used experimentally in India since about 1985.[304] Another that

---

[302] See, i.e., *Issues in Reproductive and Genetic Engineering*, Volume 4, Number 1, 1991, at pages 45-46, "The Price of Norplant is tk.2000. You Cannot Remove it: Clients are Refused Removal in Norplant Trial in Bangladesh," originally prepared by UBINIG, 5/3 Barabo Mahanpur, Ring Road, Shaymoli, Dhaka 1207, Bangladesh.

[303] See, i.e., "The Charge: Gynocide. The Accused: The U.S. Government" by Barbara Ehrenreich, Mark Dowie and Stephen Minkin, *Mother Jones*, November 1979, at pages 26-38.

[304] See, i.e., "Birth Control Vaccine is Reported in India," Associated Press, in *Boston Globe, October 10, 1992.*

has generated even greater interest is the quinacrine pellet. When inserted into a woman's uterus, quinacrine inflicts burn-like injuries, causing sufficient damage to bring about permanent infertility. Thus it promises to be the long-sought non-surgical technique for permanent sterilization, a fact which was not overlooked by writers of a 1989 commentary in the *International Journal of Gynecology and Obstetrics* who asserted that the drug could potentially increase female sterilizations in India by about a million per year.[305] Quinacrine has several known side effects — among them "toxic psychosis," which means chemically-induced insanity.[306] Other concerns raised by these new technologies include the possibility that, once they are in widespread use as population control agents, they, like the RU486 "abortion pill," could easily be used on women without their knowledge or consent. Yet most indications are that these will become the population "management" instruments of the 21st century.

This is simply not the philosophy of a government that is motivated by a desire to improve health in developing countries. And the companion theme

---

[305] See, i.e., "Prospects for Nonsurgical Female Sterilization," *International Journal of Gynecology and Obstetrics*, May 29, 1989.

[306] See "Delivery Systems for Applying Quinacrine as a Tubal Closing Agent" by Robert G. Wheeler, in *Female Transcervical Sterilization: Proceedings of an International Workshop on Non-Surgical Methods for Female Occlusion*, Chicago, Illinois, June 22-23, 1982, G. I. Zatuchni, J.D. Shelton, A. Goldsmith, and J.J. Sciarra, editors, Hagerstown, Maryland, Harper and Rowe, 1983, at pages 112-113.

so casually echoed by technical assistance professionals in the U.S. — alleviation of poverty — is equally suspect. Entirely too much evidence exists to suggest that the population program is purposely taking advantage of externally-imposed austerity plans in its rush to promote and maintain harsh population control regimes around the world. Threats to withhold food aid are just one example. It should be remembered, too, that the basic National Security Council population planning document prescribed all this rhetoric about "fundamental social and economic development" as a means to "minimize charges of an imperialist motivation" on the part of the U.S. As was once said by former President Nixon who ordered the production of the same 1974 document: "Let us remember that the main purpose of aid is not to help other nations but to help ourselves."[307]

And there is the matter of institutionalizing the concepts of population control. There is ample evidence already that some of the more authoritarian leaders in countries with long-standing population policies have started to see them as an instrument of power over their own subjects, particularly the poor. Power is the ultimate prize to the political opportunist. And what greater power is there than for one group of people to take upon themselves the role of deciding how many persons will be permitted to make up another group?

Leaders of nations that lack an independent identity on the world's political scene may indeed be

---

[307] Richard Nixon, quoted in *Lords of Poverty* by Graham Hancock, The Atlantic Monthly Press, New York, 1989, at page 71.

tempted to resort to repression (including birth limits) in order to maintain power over future generations. But, on the other hand, countries with the opportunity to emerge as rivals to the west in the foreseeable future may instead reserve such actions for their global competitors, much as the United States and Europe have done. The superpowers of today may well have created the proverbial monster that comes back to haunt them a generation or two from now.

Still more troublesome is the fact that massive increases in expenditures for population control have taken place against a backdrop of predictions about AIDS-related depopulation in the developing world. According to an official fact sheet prepared in 1989 by the Office of Press Relations at USAID, the Reagan administration allocated roughly $3 billion dollars to population control and "family planning" activities in less-developed countries, a figure several times more than all the funds spent for the same purpose during the Johnson, Nixon, Ford and Carter presidencies combined. And this occurred just as AIDS infection rates were skyrocketing — spreading so fast in parts of Asia as to constitute a "deadly attack on the economic heart of Third World countries," in the words of a report to Congress.[308] In Africa, say some publications, the disease might actually produce a decline in population. This possibility has been noted by a number of sources.

---

[308] See, e.g., "Report to the Speaker of the House of Representatives: The AIDS Epidemic in Asia," Representative Jim McDermott, Co-Chair, International AIDS Task Force, June 6, 1991.

AIDS may end Africa's population explosion, say British researchers in a study published in the magazine, *Nature*. The study says that AIDS is spreading so rapidly in Africa that the worst affected areas will show a net population loss rather than gain within a few decades.[309]

The Pentagon's 1988 demographic research paper, too, makes reference to the implications of AIDS and the folly of forecasting. "Demography, like its parent discipline economics, can be seductively misleading because it involves the manipulation of readily quantifiable — and thus presumably hard — data," says a published summary of the report. "The quality of demographic data, however, is highly variable," it continues, with AIDS representing the most obvious example of its limits.[310]

The World Health Organization estimates that 5-10 million people are infected with the virus worldwide, a count that could reach as high as 100 million by 1991. Some analysts argue that if 100 million people, or 2 percent of the world's population, were infected, total deaths from AIDS in the 1990s could be 50 million. The number infected then could double several

---

[309] From *International Dateline*, a newsletter of Population Communications International, New York, May 1992, at page 6.

[310] *Washington Quarterly*, op. cit., at page 23.

more times after that and *wipe out
some countries in 10 to 20 years.*[311]

Moreover, it has been asserted that the western
population establishment really has no truly reliable
information about population size and growth in
many of the targeted countries. According to one
scholar who has written about fertility studies in
southwestern Nigeria, "available evidence suggests
that as late as 1977, perhaps only 8 percent of births
and 2 percent of deaths were registered."[312]

In other words, those responsible for promoting
population control in the developing world admittedly
have statistics which are less than perfect about
growth rates, and they are fully conscious of the
severity of conditions (an AIDS epidemic with the
capacity to "wipe out" entire nations, to name just
one) that might reverse what they perceive as a trend
toward rapid demographic growth in the south. This
makes the scenario all the more ominous, since it
suggests that their activities, even by their own standards, are probably far in excess of what would be
required to preserve the political-demographic status
quo.

Given the dramatic increase in child mortality
that has followed structural adjustment schemes, it
may be that some African nations with the highest

---

[311] *Washington Quarterly*, op. cit., at pages 23-24. Emphasis
added.

[312] Riedmann, op. cit., at page 3.

birth and death rates will need even higher fertility just to see a moderate increase in the census.

Race is not incidental to the population control issue, either. As hundreds of broadcasts and news clips and flyers from population groups repeatedly stress, 19 out of 20 births worldwide in coming years will occur in the developing world. This could theoretically determine the ethnic-racial makeup of the entire next generation: five young people of European heritage on the one hand, and *ninety-five* Arabs, Africans, Asians, and Latin Americans on the other. Present demographic trends, as one commentator has stated it (or perhaps understated it), "promise to have a material effect on the general complexion of the world over the next two decades."[313] And though this may not always be openly discussed, it is of profound importance to western policy makers, as is revealed in the following analysis of the fall of apartheid:

> In 1951, as the laws and practices of 'Grand Apartheid' were being formalized, South Africa's whites accounted for slightly more than one-fifth of the country's enumerated population. By the early 1980s whites accounted for less than a seventh of the population within the country's 1951 boundaries. By 2020, according to official government projections, the white population would amount to no more than a ninth of the total population, barring

---

[313] *Washington Quarterly,* op. cit., at page 5.

massive net migration of whites from abroad. Adjusting the projections to 1951 borders, whites might comprise less than one-eleventh of the country's total. South Africa's current liberalizations may not have been motivated by these trends, but they are surely informed by them.[314]

Simply stated — and assuming both the accuracy of the predictions about regional growth and at least a partial failure of the population program — the world of tomorrow will be one in which people of color have a far greater voice. And this clearly is a situation that Washington is not prepared to face. As the 1991 Army study pointed out, "Imagine a world, indeed, very much like the United Nations today, but with rhetoric in the General Assembly informing policy on a global scale, directing actions affecting the lives of millions of people on a daily basis ... this world could be a very dangerous and confused place."[315]

It would be patently absurd to expect, in light of history and what is obvious about foreign affairs, that the rich countries will voluntarily surrender power to the emerging states of the south. Thus, it is at least logical to conclude that population growth offers some of the least-advantaged nations their

---

[314] U.S. Army Conference on Long Range Planning, op. cit., at page 121.

[315] U.S. Army Conference on Long Range Planning, op. cit., at page 129.

greatest opportunity — if not their only chance — to break the bonds of imperial domination and dependency. According to at least one scholar, social organization is one of the benefits of population growth, and one that will be especially useful in developing societies.

> [A] reason for the apparent passivity of the masses in traditional society is their inability to articulate their grievances. Indeed, even in industrialized societies one of the functions of labor leadership is to give expression to dissatisfactions which workers have not effectively formulated for themselves.. ¶ ...[I]ncreasing population density, by impelling changes in social organization, itself encourages a greater diversity of organized activity, which is important as a breeding ground for new classes and new leaders.[316]

This, too, is consistent with theories about population growth and economic development. Certainly the era that saw such explosive demographic and economic growth in Europe and North America was also the time when domestic *social* institutions matured to the point that these nations acquired the collective will to become world leaders. It could also be argued that as population growth slowed and eventually came to a halt in the same areas, social deterioration set in. The prevalence of crime, urban

---

[316] *Beyond Malthus: Population and Power*, op. cit., at pages 51-52.

poverty, family instability, drug dependency, and other societal problems unquestionably assumed epidemic proportions during this phase of history, although the cause-effect relationship is surely more complex.

Then there is the ever-present "gender issue." If ministries of planning and development are hesitant to adopt birthrate reduction targets on the basis of "over-population," then health officials are incessantly told that contraceptives must be made available to women to "empower" them to make choices. After all, if the "choice" of limiting one's offspring is exercised frequently and effectively by a sufficient number of women, population control objectives will still be realized in the absence of specific population policies. But again, the record suggests that the rights of women are not high on the population agenda. Consider the following personal stories of three women who "took advantage" of the model sterilization program in Bangladesh:

> Inside the operation room ... I was supposed to sleep but I could not. ...I was not unconscious at all. As I was afraid, I requested them not to operate upon me... I was still conscious and could see and feel everything. I told them to give more anesthesia, so that I would become unconscious... The doctor did not listen to my request at all. I could see that they started operating upon my lower abdomen. My tubes were brought outside and were cut. I screamed in pain. The doctor did not stop. And finally he said, the oper-

ation was finished... They wanted me to walk down and lie on the floor.... I passed the entire night in pain and distress... I am still suffering from various complications. I am suffering from severe bleeding...

I went to have a ligation operation [sterilization] with a village midwife called Rabeya... This was about 12 years ago. My youngest child was only 2 years old. I did not want to have the operation so early. But my husband told me if I had another child he would send me out for begging. So I was forced to accept his decision. My husband arranged my trip to Dhaka along with my youngest child... On the table, they gave me an injection and a pill to swallow. It did not have any effect on me... On the table, I enquired about my child. They did not answer my question. I was covered with a white sheet. I do not know what happened afterwards... I gained consciousness at 5 p.m.... I could not eat. I only asked about my son. ... My son was kept in another room. He was very scared, and was crying all the time. Next day, I came back home. My son became very sick. My son died later on. I started suffering from various side-effects... After the operation they gave me a card to receive soap (2), oil and wheat per month. In the first month, they gave me biscuits as well. But it was given only once. That's all. I received no more of these.

When my youngest son was six months, the family planning worker, Kulsum, came to persuade me for operation. My husband was a day laborer, his earnings were not enough for maintaining the family... The family planning worker told me that she would arrange a ration card for wheat so that I get wheat every month. One day, she took me to Pakulla hospital... I saw that the women ... were screaming out of fear. I also found that the doctor was very angry at these women; he even slapped at the face of one of those women. I told the doctor that I would only agree for operation if I was made fully unconscious. I threatened them that if I was treated [like] these other women then I would go back to the village and tell everybody what I had seen on that day... Next morning, I regained consciousness. I heard my son crying. I enquired whether he had taken food since last night. Actually they did not give him any food... After ten days, I went for stitch cutting. But there was infection on the stitches... After one month, there were bad smell from the operation site... I suffered a lot. It looked like a hole. Nine years have passed since I had the operation. I had been suffering from various complications. I regret now for taking the decision for sterilization. I did it mostly

> because Kulsum told me that she
> would be able to give wheat if I showed
> the certificate of sterilization. I kept
> the certificate for a long time, but
> never got any wheat.[317]

As the above suggests, human rights are the first thing to crumble under a population policy. The World Bank, as was noted earlier, grudgingly accepts that procreation is a human right, but then says this "does not mean that the government can never infringe it." How would Americans feel if *their* government told *them* how many children to produce? Worse yet, how would they feel if a foreign power — say an Indonesia or an India with designs on becoming the dominant force on the planet — should intervene on American soil to influence this most private of human decisions?

And last — but perhaps most important for the future — is the question of religion. As national boundaries become less important in world affairs and ideological alignments take center stage, the west will have to contend with challenges that are quite different from the east-west conflict of the cold war. As one influential academic has predicted, "The great divisions among mankind and the dominating source of conflict will be cultural. Nation states will remain the most powerful actors in world affairs, but

---

[317] Stories of the women in Bangladesh are taken from women's experiences with family planning clinics in Bangladesh, transcribed verbatim, and published as *Violence of Population Control* by Narigrantha Prabartana, the Feminist Bookstore, Dhaka, Bangladesh, September 1994.

the principal conflicts of global politics will occur between nations and groups of different civilizations. The clash of civilizations will dominate global politics."[318]

The amount of literature available in the United States to illustrate western paranoia about the rise of Islam as a global power is literally incredible. "We continue to experience a threat that is not politically or economically motivated but is based in the radical Islamic fundamentalist movement, which is largely anti-United States and committed to expansion in the Middle East and Africa," says one report prepared for a conference on "Worldwide Threats."[319] Thousands of similar reports, news features, and political commentaries from every imaginable source offer a perspective that is almost identical. And these assertions are heard on both sides of the globe. Says one Muslim activist from India, the next confrontation to western powers "is definitely going to from the Muslim world. It is in the sweep of the Islamic nations from the Mahgreb to Pakistan that the struggle for a new world order will begin."[320]

Here, the enormous implications of demographic change are most apparent, quietly but irreversibly working its process of political evolution within na-

---

[318] "The Clash of Civilizations" by Samuel P. Huntington, *Foreign Affairs*, Summer 1993, at page 22.

[319] GAO, *Papers Prepared for GAO Conference on Worldwide Threats*, op. cit., at page 133.

[320] M. J. Akbar, quoted in "The Clash of Civilizations," op. cit., at page 32.

tions and around the world. Between one-third and one-fourth of the population in the Middle East and southern Asia is "in the politically volatile 15 to 24 age group, a consequence of high population growth rates during the 1950s and 1960s," says a confidential intelligence assessment prepared by the CIA in February of 1984 which, to date, has only been partially de-classified. These youths, it adds, "will be ready recruits for opposition causes [such as] Islamic fundamentalism, which currently offers the principal ideological haven for Muslim youth..."[321]

The image of a slippery world that could be yanked right out of American hands at any minute is reinforced over and over by political commentators in the west. As one prominent Arab-bashing columnist has written, "one big victory" for the Islamists — "the fall of Egypt," for example — will mean an unravelling of American influences throughout the region.[322]

Moreover, Islamic teaching against western birth control means that the Muslim peoples of the world will continue to become more numerous, and also makes intervention to promote population "stabilization" all the more difficult and risky.

The matter of north-south cultural and religious differences is made even more meaningful by the fact that a second major religious group, consisting both

---

[321] CIA. *Middle East-South Asia: Population Problems and Political Stability*, February 1984, at page 3.

[322] "Iran: Orchestrator of Disorder" by Charles Krauthammer. *The Washington Post*, January 1, 1993 at page A19.

of Roman Catholics and Eastern Orthodox Christians, holds the same view about the use of artificial fertility control. While this might have a small impact on allocations of population control money from the European nations (and to a lesser extent the U.S.), it will almost certainly have its greatest impact in the countries targeted for these birth-reduction schemes. Already, fully half of the world's Roman Catholics reside in Latin America. The African Catholic Church is the fastest growing in the world, and Africa is expected to have a larger Catholic population than Europe in the very near future.

The Catholic Church, despite accusations to the contrary by professional critics, has never been as politically involved as have Muslim leaders. Technically, there is no such thing in the modern world (even in Northern Ireland) as "Catholic nationalism." But there are signs that the Catholic hierarchy may be willing in the future to work more closely with Islamic leaders on the politics of what both consider "demographic imperialism." In fact, with more and more of the Church's people residing in developing countries, it will likely be imperative that they do.

At the time of the UN's 1994 international population conference in Cairo, *Time* reported on what it called "an unusual convergence of interests" on the part of Rome and Islam. "[T]he International Conference on Population and Development ... was in danger of falling apart before it even got started," began the article. "An unusual convergence of interests between Roman Catholic and Muslim leaders put the organizers of the United Nations-sponsored conference on the defensive..."[323] A tactical alliance between the world's two billion Catholics and Muslims, in which both groups act in defense of mutual interests, would indeed present a formidable obstacle to population control. And it is at least theoretically possible.

This puts western population programs in a difficult situation. The right to freely exercise one's religion is part of international law. "Freedom to manifest one's religion or beliefs may be subject only to such limitations as are prescribed by law and are necessary to protect public safety, order, health, or morals or the fundamental rights and freedoms of others," says the Declaration on the Elimination of All Forms of Intolerance and of Discrimination Based on Religion or Belief, enacted by the UN General Assembly on November 25, 1981.[324]

For that matter, the sovereignty of nations — including Islamic ones — is protected against the arbitrary population policies which western leaders seek to impose. Says a December 1966 UN General Resolution, "the sovereignty of nations in formulating and promoting their own population policies [must include] due regard to the principle that the size of

---

[323] "Clash of Wills in Cairo" by Christian Gorman, *Time* magazine, September 12, 1994, at page 56.

[324] Declaration on the Elimination of All Forms of Intolerance and of Discrimination Based on Religion or Belief, UN General Assembly Resolution 36/55, November 25, 1981.

the family should be the free choice of each individual family."[325]

And there are other bothersome matters which may at some point pose barriers to the population control establishment. Although it would appear that political leaders have enjoyed little success to date in fending off obligatory population policies defined for them by aid donors, they may still attempt to evade complicity in these plans by citing an even more pertinent international treaty, the 1948 Genocide pact, formally known as the Convention on the Prevention and Punishment of the Crime of Genocide.

The Convention makes genocide a crime against humanity which is punishable under international law, and it expressly forbids, not only acts of genocide, but also complicity in genocide, incitement of others to commit genocide, and even conspiracy to engage in genocide. Genocide is defined under the convention to include "acts committed with the intent to destroy, in whole or in part, a national, ethnical, racial or religious group," which may, in the words of Article II of the Convention, include killing members of a group, causing serious bodily or mental harm to persons belonging to the group, inflicting on the group conditions meant to destroy it in whole or in part, forcibly transferring children from the group to another group, or "*imposing*

---

[325] General Assembly Resolution 2211 (XXI), December 17, 1966.

measures intended to prevent births within the group."[326]

It would be naive, of course, to suggest that U.S. leaders would bow to this kind of criticism. Powerful western nations have never felt constrained by international law, and even less so by the notion of fairness. Thus, while the United States and its allies continue to hold on to monumental arsenals of nuclear weapons, they recoil in horror — and expect the rest of the world to do the same — at the mere thought of such capability in the hands of the North Koreans, the Pakistanis, or the Iraqis.

In the final analysis, population control is about power. It is not negotiable. And it seems fair to say that the response to the issue of population growth overseas is comparable to the mobilization of resources to counter communism at the start of the cold war. But the extreme urgency with which population control programs have been launched in the past decade or so also reveals an apparently genuine concern that efforts to curb the "third world" birthrate might very well fail if not implemented quickly.

It has been half a century since French demographer Alfred Sauvy warned that malthusian propaganda might backfire. His position was that the grotesque images of "over-population" generated in low-birthrate societies might have far greater effect at home than abroad, thereby producing a result quite

---

[326] United Nations. Convention on the Prevention and Punishment of the Crime of Genocide. General Assembly. December 9, 1948. Emphasis added.

the opposite of what had been planned. According to his now-famous thesis:

> The fear of seeing others multiply thus leads to a diminishing vitality, to a recrudescence of Malthusian attitudes in populations already sapped by demographic aging. At the same time, the populations that elicited those fears remain unaffected... The usual perils of preachers who address only the already-converted are therefore compounded by the risk of reducing their very numbers from one generation to the next. Thus the spread in the levels of fertility between countries, regions, and social classes, and so on, is further extended, even though the goal was to narrow the gaps.[327]

In other words, despite the enormous surge in population control commitments (by virtually every state in the industrial world), and despite the coercive aspects of development lending and aid, the success of the population plan is by no means assured.

A more commentary on the global future states:

> The transition from unipolarity to multipolarity will challenge the United

---

[327] Alfred Sauvy in "*Le faux probleme de la population mondiale,*" in *Population,* Volume 4, Number 3, July-September 1949, reprinted in English in *Population and Development Review,* December 1990, at page 765.

States to devise a policy that will arrest its relative decline while minimizing the chances that other states will be provoked into balancing against the United States. Relative decline has internal and external causes. Relative decline can be addressed by policies that focus on either or both of these causes. It would be counterproductive for the United States to attempt to maintain its relative power position by attempting to suppress the emergence of new great powers. This approach would heighten others' concerns about the malignant effects of unchecked American power, which probably would accelerate the rise of new great powers....[328]

The question, then, is not, "why population control?" — but rather whether it will produce the intended impact within a short enough time to avert the rise to power of the "new" states. And even more essential is another question: What will happen if the population control mission fails to stem the tide, succeeding only in creating ill will and resentment?

---

[328] "The Unipolar Illusion: Why New Great Powers Will Rise" *International Security*, op. cit., at page 45.

Appendix A

OPTIONS FOR POPULATION POLICY I
FINAL REPORT

The following is a reprint of the OPTIONS Population Policy project, Final Report, Country Activities section (Appendix A in original), consisting of the full text of the section as presented in writing to the U.S. Agency for International Development by the contractor, the Futures Group, May 15, 1992.

Country Project Activities

AFRICAN LEADERSHIP

Activities and Results

Activities under the Africa Leadership program were scheduled for approximately two years duration, with projected completion by the first quarter of 1991. Each country program was uniquely and independently designed to meet country-specific requirements to increase leadership commitment to population activities in both the public and private sectors.

The results of the African Leadership program were as follows:

Madagascar — The results of the OPTIONS Madagascar program were encouraging, particularly African Leadership activities. Since an assessment trip in December 1988, OPTIONS developed a microcomputer-based graphics presentation on "Child Survival Maternal Health and Fertility", and under the auspices of the Prime Minister, conducted very successful seminars for key religious, intellectual, and women's leaders, Parliamentarians are utilizing the microcomputer system provided by OPTIONS to write and revise legislation that currently Limits family planning activities, such as restrictions on advertising contraceptives. The Parliamentarians are also using the microcomputer system to develop awareness raising materials and disseminate information on population policy. Most significantly, OPTIONS activities have culminated in the formulation of a population policy for Madagascar, which is currently' being reviewed by the President. Because African leadership activities were so successful, USAID/Antananarivo provided OPTIONS with a $200,000 buy-in. This buy-in enabled OPTIONS to continue policy work in Madagascar well into the implementation planning phase.

Zambia — Outputs from OPTIONS African Leadership program for Zambia Include the following: 1) sponsored The National Population Conference and ITCP Seminar from May 17-19, 1989 to announce the enactment of the National Population Policy; 2) developed a computer-based, graphics presentation on the NPP, which will be used to conduct nationwide awareness raising campaigns for provincial and district level policy-makers; 3) conducted a target analysis and training to help the Zambians envisage family planning program needs to achieve the nation's stated fertility objectives: 4) developed a detailed planning guide to design a national family planning program; 5) sponsored the "Third Policy Implementation Workshop of the ITCP from March 26-30, 1990 to analyze and determine strategies for family planning service delivery; and 5) established linkages with other donors, including the Population Council, to provide follow-on assistance to conduct operations research for pilot family planning programs.

Togo — OPTIONS collaborated with USAID/Lome and the University of Benin's Demographic Research Unit (URD) to conduct the National Conference on Population and Family Planning, which was held March 19-23, 1990. For the conference, OPTIONS mobilized African Leadership support to develop a microcomputer-based presentation which combined the essential elements of the RAPID/Togo model and the draft national population policy. A conference outcome was the call for the draft Population Policy's revision and adoption.

In May 1990, OPTIONS funded a three-day national level conference for the National Union of Togolese Women (UNFT). At that conference, the two OPTIONS presentation policy tools were again applied.

Also in collaboration with UNFT, OPTIONS co-sponsored a National Information and Awareness Raising Seminar on Family Planning and Family Welfare from August 16-18, 1990. The 60 participants were drawn from local and regional sections of the UNFT and various ministries concerned with maternal and child health, family planning and development.

As a follow-up to the March 1990 National Conference on Population and Family Planning, OPTIONS collaborated with URD to conduct further analyses of the DHS data. The results were synthesized in a booklet, "Family Planning and the Health of Mothers and Children in Togo." The analyses also formed the basis for three presentations: I) unmet need in family planning; 2) determination of family planning needs by area of residence; and 3) relations of contraceptive practice and use of health services, which were used at a seminar for high-level government policymakers on December 4, 1990.

Sudan — The extenuating circumstances in Sudan resulted in a modification to OPTIONS original program for the Africa Leadership fund. OPTIONS efforts on behalf of the National Population Commission have resulted in a series of successful awareness raising activities with national and regional leaders. The investment has been rewarded by the official adoption of the National Population Policy in September 1990. The policy was adopted by both the Revolutionary Command Council and the Council of Ministers. Workshops for the uniformed services, initiated under the African Leadership program, have continued and received strong support from the civil police, the game warden, the fire brigades, and the prison administration.

Liberia — OPTIONS had originally intended to co-sponsor a series of workshops to assist Liberian task forces to develop sectoral action plans to implement Liberia's National Population Policy (promulgated July 1988); however, on March 19, 1989 USAID/Monrovia announced an overall policy to stop provision of donor assistance to the Liberian public sector. Prior to the cessation of transfers to the government, OPTIONS mobilized resources, through the African Leadership program, to enable the Liberians to complete the task of developing the sectoral action plans. These plans constituted deliverables in an OPTIONS subcontract, which was negotiated prior to USAID's disengagement. Funding from the African Leadership project enabled the Liberian task forces to complete the development of sectoral action plans for population policy implementation.

Cameroon — The nascent African Leadership activities in Cameroon resulted in a plan and subcontract to build broad-based support for the draft national population policy from local to national levels, including government, non-government, religious, intellectual and private sector leaders. OPTIONS anticipates further results to include the formulation of a draft national population policy document, which is supported throughout all levels of the Cameroonian government.

Outcomes

African Leadership activities resulted in the following:

- Increased support of population policies by specific leadership groups;

- Increased participation of local and/or new leadership groups in policy development;

- Adoption or reform of population policies, and

- Improved institutional capacity to coordinate and implement population policies and programs.

African Development Bank

Activities and Results

OPTIONS supported the ADB in its efforts to educate its staff about population issues, to integrate population variables into its planning process, and to begin planning for the ADB to respond to requests from member countries for population projects. The goal of the OPTIONS assistance to the ADB was to encourage the ADB to actively solicit requests for loans for population projects from the member countries and, ultimately, for the ADB to become a significant financier of population projects in Africa.

The Seminar on Population and Development in Africa was held as scheduled in 1987. Approximately 65 people attended; they included ADB senior professional staff and resource persons from selected foreign national and international organizations. The summary report of that seminar took note of the pronounced shift from negative to positive attitudes by African governments about the importance of the population factor in development. The report also affirmed the African Development Bank's commitment to support population-related activities and detailed the measures the Bank intended to undertake.

Specific actions directly attributable to the Seminar included:

- Preliminary design of in-house technical training on how to integrate population factors in development projects;

- Recruitment of a population specialist to assist ADB field missions in compiling, analyzing and applying country population data to various development sectors; and

- Reservation of a monthly meeting of the ADB'S Board of Directors to sensitize Directors to the importance of the population factor and acquaint them with management's plans.

Due to the difficulty of reserving a Board meeting exclusively for a discussion of population issues, the monthly Development Policy Seminar, which is attended by both professional staff and Directors, was selected as the venue. It was for this Policy Seminar that OPTIONS provided two resource persons on October 5. 1988.

Attendance at the Policy Development Seminar was by approximately 41 Bank staff. Although only the Director representing the U.S. attended, the seminar was another step in the process of preparing the ADB for active involvement in population activities. Specific results directly attributable to the 1988 Seminar included:

- ADB request for consultants for the development of procedures for identifying and preparing population projects, training in the use of population information and assistance in the development of the first ADB population project.

- Request for training of ADB staff (up to 150 people) in demographic analysis.

Outcomes

The desired outcome for OPTIONS work with the African Development Bank was a substantial, measurable increase in ADB financing of population activities. Towards this end, The Futures Group was retained under a separate contract by the ADB to provide technical assistance that will allow the Bank to expand its population portfolio. A number of ADB personnel were trained in incorporating demographic factors into rural and agricultural project design.

Bolivia

Activities and Results

In keeping with GOB policy, OPTIONS provided assistance in the context of reproductive health: increasing access to and use of voluntary family planning services and methods for the purpose of reducing maternal and infant mortality. To turn this new policy into practice, OPTIONS introduced the tools and procedures needed to initiate and sustain the policy implementation process.

OPTIONS also initiated the coordinating process needed to plan, implement and evaluate the Reproductive Health Project among the various public and private implementing institutions: the Ministry of Health, the Bolivian Social Security institute (CNS), and approximately six PVOs.

An analysis of the population policy environment was undertaken and OPTIONS country strategy prepared. The strategy was designed to support the GOB's new initiative to greatly expand the availability of the family planning services in Bolivia through an integrated program of reproductive health.

Implementation of the OPTIONS country strategy began with the installation of the Quipus performance monitoring and evaluation and logistics management modules in the Ministry of Health, the Social Security Institute and six PVOs.

As a result of the activities undertaken, the implementing institutions have opted for standardizing the collection and analysis of commodity distribution and service delivery statistics as a basis for monitoring and evaluating the performance of the family planning component of the national program. In the future, this information will also be used, in part, to coordinate planning and budgeting among the various public and private sector institutions.

Technical assistance using this data will be continued under OPTIONS II.

Outcomes

The outcomes of OPTIONS assistance include the capability of the implementing institutions, under the leadership of the Ministry of Health, to develop detailed, coordinated national plans for expanding family planning services and allocating resources on an annual basis.

BOTSWANA

Activities and Results

OPTIONS activities in Botswana were focused on facilitating the implementation of the Botswana Population Sector Program Assistance Agreement (BOTSPA).

The first visit to Botswana in July 1988 resulted in OPTIONS being identified as a primary source of assistance in the effort to develop a national population policy and an organization structure for policy implementation. An October 1988 trip was devoted to encouraging the Government to meet the Conditions Precedent of BOTSPA (Particularly the establishment of a population unit and a technical committee to coordinate population activities) and identification of awareness raising activities that should be undertaken.

In 1989 activities focused on formulating a policy development program to be financed under BOTSPA. Results included:

1. An annual workplan and five year plan were jointly developed with the Interministerial Programme Steering Committee on Population and Development (IPSCPD) and the Population Unit indicating activities needed to develop and effectively implement a national population policy.

2. Representatives of 6 organizations were contacted to assist the IPSCPD in expanding its membership to include non-government organizations and commercial private sector institutions.

3. OPTIONS assisted the Population Unit and the IPSCPD in drafting its First Annual Progress Report. The report, required under the BOTSPA

agreement, outlined the achievements of the IPSCPD and GOB during the project's first year.

4. OPTIONS assisted IPSCPD in designing a study on attitudes towards population and development issues in rural areas that was administered in five districts of the country.

5. In Dec. 1989, OPTIONS assisted the Population Secretariat in integrating population issues into key sectors in the forthcoming 7th National Development Plan. Staff also reviewed the separate population policy section that will be included in the national development plan.

In 1990 a number of activities were undertaken to promote the expansion of family planning programs.

1. OPTIONS staff with assistance from the executive committee of IPSCPD, developed the framework for a national 6 year population work plan that consists of three components: a. family planning service delivery, b. the promotion of family life, and c. policy development and coordination. The first two components were written by the Ministry of Health. OPTIONS staff developed the framework for the policy section which was expanded by the Ministry of Finance and Development Planning. The policy component consists of six sections — 1. consensus building activities; 2. the integration of population into the 7th National Development Plan; 3. policy drafting and consultations; 4. program implementation, management and coordination; 5. legal constraints, and 6. monitoring and evaluation.

2. OPTIONS staff assisted with the final revisions of the District level reports and suggested ways to disseminate different aspects of the data to a wide audience.

3. Staff assisted the executive committee of IPSCPD with revisions of the Population Progress Report of the National Parliamentary Council on Population and Development. The report was designed to brief all members of Parliament on population activities undertaken by the Council. The report consists of 5 sections: 1) the formation of the

National Parliamentary Council on Population and Development; 2) achievements of the Council and its technical committee; 3) the new 6 year work plan on population and development; 4) constraints on plan implementation; and 5) concluding remarks.

4. To monitor population and health services, the Ministry of Health is designing a "sentinel" or periodic brief survey to detect changes in the use of health and family planning services. OPTIONS staff provided a prototype family planning questionnaire that will assist the Ministry in monitoring family planning services.

Outcomes

Outcomes resulting from OPTIONS activities include:

• The formulation and adoption of a national population policy;

• Increased support for the implementation of population policies among key constituencies;

• Improved institutional capacity to coordinate and implement population policies and programs; and

• Increased private sector investments in family planning services.

BURKINA FASO

Activities and Results

All but two of the original activities proposed in 1988 were accomplished. Due to the DPD's extremely heavy schedule, the DPD requested that the observational travel for two Burkinabe policy makers and technical assistance during the UNFPA-sponsored workshop on the integration of demographic variables be postponed.

In 1988 Burkinabe representatives participated in the CERPOD regional policy conference. Recommendations of that conference (N'Djamena Program of

Action) were passed on to the CILSS Council of Ministers for consideration at their meeting in January 1989. The Council of Ministers of the Intergovernmental Committee for Combatting Drought in the Sahel (CILSS), which includes Burkina Faso, adopted the N'Djamena Program of Action. This action established a framework for population policy development for governments throughout the Sahel.

In March, 1989 OPTIONS visited Burkina Faso to review with GOBF officials the elements of population policy as found in the N'Djamena Program. During the visit a calendar of activities leading to the drafting of a national population policy was developed.

During the second and third quarters of 1989 OPTIONS provided training in the RAPID/Burkina model, sponsored Burkinabe participation in the regional economic-demographic modeling workshop and provided technical documentation to the committee charged with drafting the national population policy.

In January 1990 a multisectoral committee completed a draft population policy. Resource materials provided by OPTIONS, including the N'Djamena Action Program, were used to draft the document.

In Mach 1990 OPTIONS met with USAID representatives and the DPD's population unit to discuss technical assistance activities as a follow up to the drafting of the policy. Proposed activities included:

•   assisting the DPD and Technical Committee in developing a methodology for planning the implementation of the family planning and IEC strategies outlined in the policy; and

•   assisting the DPD with the dissemination of policy information in order to gain the support and participation of several key constituencies including politicians, planners, technicians and program directors.

During the first general assembly of the National Population Council (NPC), held in April 1990, the draft policy declaration was reviewed and subsequently revised. The revised policy was submitted to the Executive Council of the Popular Front in June. While final approval and adoption is pending, the DPD received authorization to draft the Population Priority Action Program (PPAP). The PPAP was to have been finalized in time for it to be integrated into the second five year National Development Plan (1991-1995), with implementation to begin January 1991.

OPTIONS and CERPOD made a joint visit to Burkina Faso in August-September 1990 to assist the DPD in planning priority policy dissemination efforts. During the visit, OPTIONS accomplished the following:

(1)   provided technical assistance to the Ministry of Plan and Cooperation/Direction of Planning and Development's (DPD) population unit on dissemination of the National Population Policy and related action program;

(2)   negotiated a subcontract with the DPD to support policy dissemination through: 1) the purchase of visual equipment for policy presentations; 2) development and reproduction of a summary of the policy and action plan for broad distribution; 3) policy presentations to technical personnel and political leaders; and 4) a policy workshop for the Burkinabe private sector;

(3)   trained MOH personnel in the use of the TARGET Model; and,

(4)   provided the DPD and MOH with sample action plans for family planning and IEC. These sample plans are designed to provide guidelines in the development of sectoral action plans.

Outcomes

Burkina Faso adopted a national population policy in 1991.

CAMEROON

Activities and Results

The primary goals of the OPTIONS subcontract with the Ministry of Planning (MINPAT) (beginning in September, 1990) were achieved. The objectives of

OPTIONS initiatives were threefold: 1) fund a seminar for five Cameroonian provinces in which at least 120 regional leaders, both government and non-government, would provide feedback on the National Population Policy draft document; and 2) sponsor a national seminar to consolidate regional inputs and to complete the policy document; and 3) support a meeting of the National Commission on Population to review, approve and submit the National Population Policy document to the executive and legislative branches of the government for approval.

The National Seminar on the Cameroonian Family sponsored by RAPID II in March, 1988 was successful in moving the nation towards development of a national population policy. The USAID Mission considered the seminar "a major achievement in reporting on population matters in Cameroon." The presentations of the OPTIONS policy tools "The Cameroonian Family in the Year 2000 and Demographic Perspectives for the 21st Century," "The Cameroonian Family Research Methodology" and "Responsible Parenthood" helped Seminar participants to become more aware of the implications of current demographic trends.

During a planning visit in May 1988, an OPTIONS I strategy was developed which spanned two years and budgeted approximately $300,000. The strategy built upon past RAPID II efforts and had as objectives the development of 1) a national population policy, 2) the institutional capabilities to implement it, and 3) a national awareness and support for the policy. The strategy was supported by the Mission with a $75,000 buy-in.

In December OPTIONS began implementation of the strategy. A subcontract with a specific program of activities was negotiated with the Ministry of Plan and Regional Development. OPTIONS and the UNFPA expected to coordinate the long term population policy efforts. Further, OPTIONS planned to support its Cameroon efforts with $70,000 of African Leadership funds. Unfortunately program momentum was lost due to an inability to visit the country at the time.

The National Population Seminar took place from March 12-14, 1991. Participants included representatives from the provincial seminars. An inter-ministerial technical committee meeting held in April, 1991, provided a final technical review of the National Population Policy, and established the agenda for the meeting of the National Population Commission which will ratify the draft Population Policy before transmittal to the presidency for signature.

In May, 1991, a computer system was transferred to the Ministry of Plan and Regional Development.

Outcomes

The principal expected outcome of OPTIONS activities in Cameroon will be a national population policy. This national population policy will evolve from a series of local and national level leadership seminars.

CERPOD

Activities and Results

OPTIONS was identified in the Population Policy and Program Development paper as one of the principal coordinating agencies to offer assistance to CERPOD. The task falling to OPTIONS was to develop, with CERPOD staff, an appropriate framework for population policy development in the Sahel and to assist in country applications of that framework.

During visits in September and October, 1988, OPTIONS devised a strategy for its collaboration with CERPOD. The strategy has two essential elements: development and adoption by CILSS of a regional population program of action and implementation of policy development programs in four Sahelian nations.

In December, 1988, OPTIONS provided assistance for a CERPOD population policy conference in N'Djamena, Chad. In particular OPTIONS provided two policy tools: "Materials for Preparing National Population Policies in African Countries" and "Population Policy in Sub-Saharan Africa." Conference participants adopted the "N'Djamena Program of Action on Population and Development in the Sahel" which calls on member states to act on a number of important population policy issues. The "N'Djamena Program of Action" was formally adopted in January, 1989, by the Council of Ministers of the

Intergovernmental Committee for Combatting Drought in the Sahel (CILSS). This adoption adds to the list of multi-governmental declarations on population policy including the "Mexico City Declaration" and "Kilimanjaro Programme of Action."

The regional conference was held as planned December 5-9, 1988 in N'Djamena, Chad. The conference brought together representatives from seven Sahelian nations. The conference's recommendations as embodied in the N'Djamena Program of Action were adopted by the CILSS Council of Ministers in January 1989.

With the Program of Action officially adopted as CILSS policy, one of the four principal objectives of OPTIONS/CERPOD collaboration was achieved. Also as a result of the CILSS action, significant progress was observed in the achievement of the remaining objectives as well:

- Leaders and key constituencies gained familiarity with population policies and strategies.

- CILSS participants represented ministerial level recognition from the 9 member nations.

- Conference recommendations were widely distributed.

- Adoption and implementation of population policies in four member states were encourages.

The adoption of the N'Djamena Program of Action by the CILSS member countries presented CERPOD with the need to assess and develop its capabilities to assist the Sahel countries in the adoption and implementation of population policies conforming to the principles and strategies put forth in the document. With this in mind, CERPOD organized a retreat in December 1989. The goal of the retreat, to which all CERPOD professional staff were invited, was to reflect on the best way of attacking this issue given the resources available. OPTIONS was invited to help CERPOD start to develop its strategy of fostering policy activities in the Sahel. At the retreat CERPOD decided it needed to come up with a methodology for evaluating the status of population policy and programs in a given country and for recommending CERPOD interventions based on the needs of the country.

OPTIONS and CERPOD worked jointly on developing the methodology. This methodology was tested in two countries, Guinea-Bissau and Niger. OPTIONS was part of the Guinea-Bissau team. After producing preliminary reports on these two countries, the staff of OPTIONS and CERPOD most involved in the development of the canvas met to discuss and critique it.

Based on these discussions, the methodology (especially the part dealing with recommendations and policy tools) was included as one of the major issues at the December 1990 retreat (Selingue II). Other issues discussed at Selingue II include:

1.   Schedule of future CERPOD activities in the policy arena; and

2.   Discussion on how recommendations stemming from the policy analyses will be incorporated into CERPOD's activities.

Selingue II was held Dec. 17-20, 1990. The OPTIONS team participated fully in the presentations and discussions. As the goal of the seminar was to move toward better defining CERPOD's interventions in the CILSS member states in the area of population policy, OPTIONS presented its methodology for defining its interventions. OPTIONS insisted on the need to set objectives, identify target groups and then define activities and tools to be used to achieve stated objectives. The various policy tools available were also discussed.

Following the retreat, the OPTIONS team met with the CERPOD division heads to discuss future collaboration with CERPOD under the OPTIONS II project. In April, 1991, an OPTIONS II team travelled to Mali to develop a strategy for continued policy activities with CERPOD under the OPTIONS II project.

Population policy development programs were continued in Niger under the aegis of the CERPOD/OPTIONS regional population policy development strategy.

Outcomes

The CILSS adoption of the N'Djamena Program of Action marks the achievement of the fist OPTIONS outcome. Other expected outcomes include population policy adoption by the governments of Burkina Faso and Niger. OPTIONS also encouraged more narrowly defined policy reforms that facilitate implementation of population programs and access to family planning services; see, for example, the program designed for Niger.

CHAD

Activities and Results

In October 1988, OPTIONS provided financial and technical assistance to the First Chadian Conference on Family Planning. The Conference was attended by approximately 150 Chadians and international delegations from 13 countries. This Conference resulted in the following initiatives being recommended:

- Development of a national population policy;

- Establishment of a national family planning program;

- Abrogation and repeal of Chad's 1965 anti-contraceptive law;

- Collaboration between the public and private sectors to ensure the development of a family planning program and the creation of a family planning association.

OPTIONS utilized the RAPID model for Chad at the Conference as a policy tool to increase awareness and understanding of the relationship between population growth and economic development. Other responsibilities included planning, monitoring and overall coordination of the conference with USAID/N'Djamena and the Chadian Conference Organizing Committee.

In conjunction with the OPTIONS and CERPOD collaborative program of activities, another conference was held in N'Djamena during December. At that conference the N'Djamena Program of Action on Population and Development in the Sahel was developed and approved by representatives from 7 member states, including Chad.

Regarding the legal review, OPTIONS visited Chad in March of 1987 and prepared the document "Proposed Contraceptive Legislation to Replace Article 98 of the Law of Chad." The document proved useful to USAID/N'Djamena in preparing a new discussion paper with draft legislation for the Ministry of Public Health.

Outcomes

The conference clearly achieved its principal objectives by enhancing support for family planning and population programs among national leaders. The impetus provided by the conference facilitated the inauguration of a national family health and child-spacing program and the adoption of a national population policy statement. The Conference participants fully endorsed recommendations which resulted in these outcomes. During the CERPOD conference held in Chad in December, the N'Djamena Program of Action (see CERPOD) was adopted by representatives from seven member states, including Chad. This evidence suggests that a consensus among key Chadian leaders has developed which is supportive of family planning service delivery.

OPTIONS also provided the needed technical inputs for developing legislation supportive of family planning.

COTE D'IVOIRE

Activities and Results

OPTIONS was invited to provide assistance by REDSO/WCA to extend the audience reached by the RAPID modeling efforts to a broader spectrum of actions important to the policy development process.

In 1987, OPTIONS successfully completed work on two national conferences on population and development. In November 1987, OPTIONS assisted the

Ministry of Labor in organizing and conducting a conference on Population Growth, Urbanization and Employment.

The National Seminar for Parliamentarians, sponsored by AIBEF, was held November 23-26, 1987. The Ministry of Labor conference was held November 30-December 4, 1987. OPTIONS provided technical and financial assistance to both conferences. The technical assistance for each conference included two staff members who: 1) trained group facilitators prior to the events; 2) assisted the sponsors in the organization, logistics and monitoring of the conferences; and 3) applied the RAPID model as a policy tools for participants.

Indicators of success of the conferences include:

- REDSO comments that momentum was generated by the two highly successful and visible population conference and, as a result, a softening of the pronatalist positions in the Cote d'Ivoire is perceptible; and

- Wide and in-depth media coverage of both conferences which fueled a national debate on population issues.

Some Ivoirien leaders still hold that no serious population problem exists, and that once the current economic crisis passes, an expanding economy will accommodate the nation's growing population. Development of strong population policies and programs in the short run appear tenuous. Nonetheless, due to the OPTIONS work with labor and parliamentarians, a strong advocacy group for family planning exists.

Outcomes

The anticipated outcomes for OPTIONS activities were successfully achieved. The two conferences resulted in a substantially increased awareness by Ivoirien leaders of the relationships between population and development; in both conferences significant policy recommendations were produced.

ECUADOR

Activities and Results

OPTIONS visited Ecuador in May and July 1987 to work with Consejo Nacional de Desarollo (CONADE) through Centro de Estudios para la Paternidad Responsable (DEPAR) on the development of a project strategy that would promote formation of a population policy that would strengthen private and public family planing programs. During trips in September and October 1987, OPTIONS aimed at institution building and review of the policy formation process by CONADE. These efforts came to fruition with Ecuador's adoption of a national population policy in October, 1987.

OPTIONS presented the Technical Information on Population for the Private Sector Cost-Benefit Model to IESS in an effort to increase budget allocations to public family planning services and delivery. Such growth in spending would be particularly important to expansion of the rural delivery system.

Following the adoption of the official National Population Policy on October 26, 1987, OPTIONS made a trip to Ecuador to provide technical assistance to two successful CONADE-RAPID conferences.

In September 1990 OPTIONS visited with USAID/Quito and Ecuadorean officials. Interest was expressed in further OPTIONS activities; however, the limited availability of bilateral funds is constraining the involvement of OPTIONS II.

Outcomes

A National Population Policy for Ecuador was approved by CONADE on October 26, 1987 along with an implementation plan that includes an operational tracking system. The CONADE/RAPID Conference subsequently held, were successful in raising awareness among high-level policy makers and officials.

Although the Social Security Institute expressed interest in application of the OPTIONS TIPPS Cost/Benefit Model in its budget, progress was limited due to IESS reluctance because of the sensitivity of the family planning issues within IESS and the public sector in general. IESS, however, increased its allocation for family planning services.

The "Family Planning Service Statistics Program" has been instituted in CONADE and other institutions to provide an effective uniform system to collect and analyze information on family planning statistics as part of its responsibility to develop and coordinate population policy implementation plans.

EGYPT

Activities and Results

The OPTIONS objectives in Egypt were to revise the National Population Policy (NPP) and to prepare a 2-Year Population Plan/Program (originally a 5-Year Plan). These goals were successfully accomplished. The National Population Policy and 2-Year Population Plan were widely reviewed and cleared among the Egyptian Ministries.

OPTIONS role in the Egyptian Population Policy development process included technical assistance to the National Population Council through the Interdepartmental Task Force. Though meetings with members of the Task Force and implementing ministries, and in review of previous Task Force documents, OPTIONS assisted in identifying population policy issues, and assisted in the development of a process to guide Task Force activities. Technical assistance also included drafting a National Population Strategy and an outline of a 5-Year Plan including the implementation plans for the current Five Year National Economic Plan.

The Egyptian members of the Task Force drafted segments of a National Population Policy based on the existing NPP, the World Population Plan of Action, the Recommendations of the Mexico City International Conference on Population (which Egypt attended), and other policy guidelines, OPTIONS reviewed the draft and suggested revisions which were ultimately incorporated.

APPENDIX A
USAID OPTIONS PROJECT, FINAL REPORT, COUNTRY ACTIVITIES

During a workshop designed to discuss the NPP and the 2-Year Action Plan, OPTIONS assisted in making final modifications to the documents before they were circulated among high GOE officials for review and comment.

OPTIONS staff visited Egypt in October, 1990, and carried out two major projects:

1) Technical backup on the first Population Dynamics and Target Setting Course for the Governorates. Beginning in 1989 a major purpose of the Egyptian National Population Council was to decentralize the planning and administrative activities for family planning services to the Governorates. After OPTIONS successful work with the NPC in 1989, the NPC specifically requested a return visit to Egypt to initiate this process, with training of officials of the governorates. Nineteen senior representatives from 7 governorates, plus 4 participants from the NPC, were trained. The NPC training team, including some young specialists, performed well and their participation should institutionalize the capacity of the NPC to give the course in future years.

2) Technical assistance in planning was also provided. OPTIONS, with the NPC staff, drafted a schedule of activities covering November 1990 to June 1991 to prepare the Plan. These include technical assistance to be sure that target setting, planning and management skills are integrated in the process; targeting setting by the governorate offices based on local needs and resources; coordination of all programs in the governorate, both public and private, to meet the targets; development of ongoing mechanisms for program monitoring and coordination; training of the NPC in how to ask outside help for resources needed for the governorate projects.

A comprehensive mechanism for coordinating between central level delivery programs and governorate NPC offices, particularly to incorporate governorate targets and capabilities into national planning is especially needed. The national population program worked concertedly to reach the goal of including a viable population component in the next National Five Year Plan.

Paralleling this work in target setting and planning, OPTIONS also started the development of a new high-level presentation. OPTIONS staff concluded that although the Egyptians were making good progress in family planning and in increasing the prevalence level and reducing the TFR, they were in danger of unmanageable future population growth unless they strengthened their action program. Consequently, OPTIONS illustrated 1) the desirability, in view of the geography and climate of the country, of determining to reach a replacement level of fertility at the earliest practicable time, and 2) the low costs of such an effort to the very high ratio of benefits. OPTIONS staff drafted a presentation in a form similar to a RAPID analysis before leaving Cairo in mid-December 1989 and began the necessary demographic projections.

At the end of OPTIONS I the presentation was in completed draft form; the presentation was made to the Prime Minister and six Ministers under OPTIONS II in February 1992.

Outcomes

OPTIONS work in Egypt advanced the tasks of developing: 1) a greatly expanded National Population Policy, providing more guidance to implementing ministries and agencies; 2) a National Population Action Plan, incorporating population activities into the current and future 5-Year National Economic Plans; and 3) a detailed set of projects and programs for each implementing agency/ministry. It also set up the conditions for utilization (under OPTIONS II) of present economic and cost/benefit information to present government officials with the rewards of increased public investment in the National Population Action Program.

HAITI

Activities and Results

The goal of OPTIONS activities in Haiti were to strengthen the public and private sector environments for family planning service delivery as well as to enhance the role of the public and private sectors in supporting the formulation of a national population policy.

Prior to the revision of the strategy in Haiti, most of OPTIONS activities focused on the National Population Council (CONAPO). CONAPO was established in 1986 as an interministerial commission for population policy development. OPTIONS activities included the development of a policy tool "Haitian Population and Development" (POPDEV) Model, provision of staff training for analytical and management purposes (including observational travel), and provision of equipment (computer, video projector) and materials for information dissemination.

After an initial assessment trip in February, 1987, OPTIONS activities began with Observational Travel by Dr. Emmanuel Adé, head of the CONAPO Secretariat in June, 1987. During the Observational Travel, Dr. Adé went to Guadeloupe, where he worked with Dr. Jean-Pierre Guengant of the Caribbean Family Planning Association on computer modeling, and to St. Kitts to attend the Caribbean Family Planning Association Conference. There he was able to compare Haiti's population policy progression with those of 17 other Caribbean nations. The Observational Travel proved most useful for Dr. Adé in the areas of increased demographic skills and an awareness and understanding of larger Caribbean population policy issues.

Political conditions forced a hiatus in OPTIONS activities between June, 1987 and April, 1988. Nonetheless, OPTIONS was able to complete the POPDEV Model. Presentations of the model to a wide array of public and private sector leaders were conducted during visits in June, 1987, three visits in 1988 (July, August and December) and in February and June, 1989. OPTIONS provided training to the Haitian Child Institute in the use of the model. The POPDEV Model has been a very important instrument in raising awareness. Significantly, OPTIONS presented the model to President Avril in June, 1989. OPTIONS has also developed a Population Strategy for USAID/PAP that will help guide Mission investment in this sector. This paper was developed during several visits over the course of 1988 and was presented to the Mission in December, 1988. The paper was reviewed with the Haitian population community during a February, 1989 visit.

Furthermore, both the UNFPA and the World Bank reacted favorably to the conclusions of the Strategy Paper. As a result, the World Bank has requested OPTIONS assistance in the preparation of its first Health Loan in Haiti (this was carried out in June, 1989) as well as OPTIONS participation in the 1990 Country Economic Memorandum for Haiti (population sector review). Moreover, UNFPA began to support CONAPO activities in the field of population policy formulation.

Concurrent with the development of the Population Strategy, OPTIONS developed national contraceptive prevalence targets using the Target Model. The target setting exercise capitalized on new population projections developed by OPTIONS staff. Later efforts focused on the development of prevalence targets disaggregated by region and source of supply, including a detailed analysis of the potential demand and the actual supply of family planning services in Haiti.

OPTIONS collaborated with the Haitian Child Institute in organizing several meetings of private family planning organizations. The objective was to promote better coordination of efforts among the numerous service providers. Ultimately, the goal was to promote the development of a "population lobby" that could serve as an effective advocate for population policy in Haiti.

Private sector support for family planning was also supported through a joint OPTIONS/TIPPS activity that yielded application of the TIPPS Benefit-Cost Model to several important private sector employers.

In June 1989 a visit was made by OPTIONS in order to prepare a comprehensive assessment of population policy needs in Haiti. OPTIONS team also participated in two presentations of the POPDEV Model, including a successful presentation to General Prosper Avril, President of the Military Government, during the first National Seminar organized by CONAPO and the Demographic Analysis Research Division (DARD). Another presentation of the POPDEV Model was made to the Haitian American Chamber of Commerce (HAM-CHAM). In addition,k staff worked with the World Bank Staff Appraisal Mission to help design a family planning component within the first International Development Association (IDA) Health Loan to Haiti.

In August 1989 OPTIONS returned to undertake steps to better disseminate the POPDEV analysis, such as the preparation of the next series of POPDEV presentations to key constituencies and the initial drafting of scientific papers aimed at wider recognition of the validity of the POPDEV analysis. In addition, coordination of USAID- and UNFPA-sponsored population policy activities was thoroughly discussed, especially with CONAPO staff.

OPTIONS returned in September to continue the implementation of the Target Model. The purpose of the visit was to initiate disaggregation of the National prevalence targets, estimated as part of the Population Strategy Paper (1989), also prepared by OPTIONS, and thereby provide a framework for program planning.

In January 1990 OPTIONS participated in the Population and Development Seminar organized by CONAPO and the DARD of the Haitian Institute of Statistics and Data Processing. The seminar's purpose was to review materials prepared by the DARD and the Inter-Sectoral Committee (which is coordinated by CONAPO). The materials were used in preliminary activities toward preparation of a national population policy and include sectoral papers and population projections prepared by DARD, which were discussed along with papers on various aspects of the Haitian demographic situation.

During an OPTIONS visit in April 1990 a presentation on contraceptive target setting was made in collaboration with CONAPO. In attendance were the major Haitian actors in the fields of public health and family planning service delivery. Data collection to compute sub-national targets was completed during the visit. Separate meetings with Private Voluntary Organizations focused on the potential donor support required to expand family planning service delivery.

Finally, during an OPTIONS visit in February-March, 1991, OPTIONS monitored the population policy dialogue process after the democratic elections which took place in December 1990 and the appointment of the new government in February 1991. During the same visit, the microcomputer tools for the demand and supply analysis of family planning service delivery were transferred to the Haitian institutions involved in population policy and service delivery, namely the CONAPO and the Planning Unit for Priority Programs (UCPP) at the Ministry of Public Health and Population.

APPENDIX A
USAID OPTIONS PROJECT, FINAL REPORT, COUNTRY ACTIVITIES

OPTIONS visited Haiti again in July, 1991, to formulate a general assessment of the situation there and to follow through on three proposed activities. The first was to build support for the National Population Policy. The second was to develop national plans to expand family planning services. The third and final goal was to promote greater expansion of the commercial private sector role in the financing and delivery of family planning services.

Unfortunately, in September 1991, a political coup in Haiti led to the termination of AID support there, and OPTIONS activities in Haiti currently remain dormant. The team hopes to continue work there under OPTIONS II when the political situation stabilizes.

Outcomes

The OPTIONS program in Haiti yielded a Population Strategy for USAID/-PAP, increased awareness of population growth impacts among Haitian leaders (including a former President of Haiti), prevalence targets to guide program planning, and demand and supply analysis of family planning service delivery at the sub-national level. If political conditions allow, OPTIONS II will strengthen the role of the public and private sectors through the mapping of disaggregated prevalence targets that can guide the planning of individual organizations, improved coordination among public and private sector family planning organizations and increased support for family planning from other international donors as well as private employers.

INDONESIA

Activities and Results

OPTIONS provided assistance in evaluation of the legal and regulatory constraints in Indonesia as part of an OPTIONS/SOMARC team which was requested to assist USAID/JAKARTA and BKKBN, the Indonesian Family Planning Board. This information was necessary for BKKBN leadership in understanding the policy/regulatory constraints that would have to be overcome for any such expansion in the private sector to be successful, and in deciding which of the two plans would best serve the needs of an expanding social marketing program.

APPENDIX A
USAID OPTIONS PROJECT, FINAL REPORT, COUNTRY ACTIVITIES

A joint OPTIONS and SOMARC consultant team traveled to Indonesia in February of 1988. OPTIONS investigated the following:

- Regulations governing doctors and midwives dispensing contraceptives within their practice.

- Regulations which currently dictate the distribution relationship between manufacturers, wholesalers and retailers.

- Regulations regarding the listing of contraceptives as an ethical product.

- The impact of changes in these regulations on sales and distribution of contraceptives.

The draft report was presented by the consultant team in a briefing to the BKKBN and USAID on February 12, 1988 and based on this information the following decisions were made by those agencies:

- Plan A (see Outcomes) was selected as the implementation plan for the expanded social marketing program

- Only one product per category (i.e., market leaders) is to be the "official" designated products of the expanded social marketing program. Currently, these products appear to be Microgynon 30, low-dose pill; Depo-Provera, injectable; and CUT, IUD. Later, Norplant, a contraceptive implant, is to be added.

- The BKKBN organized a small group responsible for developing a plan for resolution or modification of the policy constraints to the expanded social marketing program.

- Continued USAID funding of the expanded social marketing program is contingent upon development by the BKKBN of an acceptable plan for resolution or modification of the policy costraints mentioned above.

Outcomes

Based on the final report produced by the OPTIONS/SOMARC consultant, the BKKBN decided to adopt proposed Plan A to expand social marketing efforts in the private sector and increase low- to medium- priced FP services and commodities to the public.

Plan A relieved the BKKBN of being a contraceptive provider and encouraged pharmaceutical manufacturers to sell currently available commercial brands at new, lower prices. Product distribution was implemented by commercial distributors, and a private sector body, under the policy guidance of an advisory council (BKKBN), was responsible for overall program operation (including advertising and research).

LIBERIA

Activities and Results

The OPTIONS role in Liberia was a continuation of technical assistance for population policy development begun under the RAPID II project in March 1983.

OPTIONS official began Liberian activities through its collaboration with Pathfinder in Observational Travel for five Liberians to Jamaica in May, 1988. OPTIONS role was to accompany the Liberians (representing the Population Commission and the Population Technical Committee) and examine Jamaica's policy implementation efforts. The Observational Travel was valuable in helping the Liberians think through the immediate stages of policy implementation, especially the institutional arrangements for policy implementation, the design of sectoral Action Plans and alternative strategies for reaching youth through population programs. During the week-long visit the potential for OPTIONS assistance was explored.

The Observational Travel led to an invitation to OPTIONS to visit Liberia in July, 1988. At that time discussions begun in Jamaica were continued. The Population Commission and the Population Technical Committee were planning population awareness activities and designing plans to implement the national population policy. The visit resulted in a contract with the Ministry of Planning and Economic Affairs on behalf of the Population Commission. Through the contract OPTIONS would provide financial and technical assistance for a number of activities during and around the Second Annual Population Awareness Week and for the activities of the task forces responsible for developing the seven Action Plans for implementation of the national population policy.

The Awareness Week activities (November 21-25, 1988) consisted of broadcast messages and dramas on population, a lecture series in 3 urban centers and distribution of 500 Commission Newsletters. The opening program was attended by about 400 people including Ministry-level representatives from Planning, Internal Affairs, Education, Information and Justice; the population Commission;p the private sector; and the donor community. While the Awareness Week overlapped with the Ministry of Health's Immunization Campaign, participation levels indicated that the Commission was able to reach the target audiences in order to sensitize them to population issues and their impact on socio-economic development.

In December, 1988 OPTIONS visited Liberia to discuss development of Action Plans to implement the national population policy. In particular, the Orientation Workshop for task force members was discussed in terms of the purpose and content of the Action Plans, priority areas or strategies, the staging of the seven plans and suitable task force members.

In March 1989, members of seven task forces met for three days in an OPTIONS-supported Orientation Workshop. The task forces are responsible for developing action plans for seven areas in the national population policy. The workshop gave an overview of the process for Action Plan development including program planning and budgeting as well as systems for monitoring and evaluation.

Outcomes

Although the recent events in Liberia have drastically changed the political landscape, a number of OPTIONS outcomes prior to the upheaval are noteworthy:

- The national Population Policy was passed by the legislature and approved by the President.

- Awareness of population issues was widespread.

- The Population Commission had developed the independent capacity to carry out awareness raising activities.

- The development of plans for the implementation of the National Population Policy had been initiated.

- One and five-year plans for implementation of each sector of the Policy were to be developed by the seven task forces charged with that task.

- UNFPA agreement to support future population activities had been secured.

MADAGASCAR

Activities and Results

Since an assessment trip in December 1988, OPTIONS developed a microcomputer-based graphics presentation on "child Survival, Maternal Health and Fertility," and, under the auspices of the Prime Minister, conducted very successful seminars for key religious, intellectual, and women's leaders.

The legal and regulatory analysis of the potential legislative barriers to population policy implementation has been completed Parliamentarians are utilizing this analysis and the microcomputer system provided by OPTIONS to write and revise legislation that currently limits family planing activities, such as restrictions on advertising contraceptives. The Parliamentarians are also using the microcomputer system to develop awareness raising materials and disseminate information on population policy.

Previous constituency building efforts have been successful and have significantly defused potential criticism of the population policy. The GDRM is already taking steps to increase access to family planning. As a result of the ongoing policy developments, several institutions have been established and/or strengthened (CIT, GNPPD, UPD, MOPSCYS, FISA, MOH) to play an important role during policy implementation.

The cumulative effect of previously reached objectives resulted in the proclamation of the population policy as national law. The fact that it became a law includes it de facto in the national budget. It is not likely that a large budget will be allocated for the policy implementation, but the GOM may at least provide minimal resources.

The computer model on population and environment has bene instrumental in demonstrating the systemic relationship between the two parameters. This resulted in the request for further development of the model toward a more detailed policy tool.

OPTIONS also worked closely with the National Parliamentarians Group on Population and other key sectors to secure passage of the national population policy. The policy was passed by the Parliament and signed by the President on December 19, 1990.

OPTIONS also worked towards the development of a strategy for policy implementation. A first step was accomplished by completing preparations for an April 1991 study tour for senior officials to Indonesia, Mauritius, and Thailand.

During the period from May 1991-February 1992, Madagascar experienced several large scale events:

- Challenge to the President and his Government by the Opposition.

- Seven months of almost constant general strike by civil servants and in some cases the private sector.

- Changes of successive governments.

Outcomes

The main outcome of the OPTIONS work in Madagascar is the adoption of the National Population and Development Policy, the creation of a political environment conducive to population programs, and the initiation of planning for expanded service delivery.

MOROCCO

Activities and Results

The OPTIONS program for Morocco consisted of economic and demographic analyses that were designed to resolve the problems identified in the mid-term evaluation of the Moroccan Population and Family Planning Support Project.

Draft reports on the time use and cost survey were completed in October, 1991, and presented to key Ministry of Public Health (MOPH) officials in November. Comments were incorporated into a final report, which was translated into French and transmitted to MOPH and to USAID. MOPH has requested that another report be prepared on the cost effectiveness of family planning, which will be suitable for a broad dissemination. This report is currently being prepared as a policy tool under OPTIONS II.

The greatest pay-off from the OPTIONS work in Morocco has been an enhanced awareness within the MOPH of the need to address the future resource needs of the family planning program. MOPH has begun building support for the program through a series of computer-assisted presentations of DHS data and FP services statistics on the past accomplishments of the program and plans for its future expansion. These presentations, which build on earlier OPTIONS presentations, have been made to a wide range of audiences in recent months, and support has been provided under the RAPID III project to prepare an Arabic-language version of these presentations for the Parliament and for several Arabized ministries (e.g., the Ministry of Religion). In addition, it is expected that MOPH will utilize the results of the OPTIONS time use and cost survey to improve the efficiency of its existing resources.

The result of OPTIONS-supported analysis of existing survey data were also used in the design of a more effective IEC program. The findings of the OPTIONS contraceptive market model were useful in gaining MOPH acceptance and support for the social marketing of oral contraceptives.

Outcomes

The outcomes of the Moroccan activities include an increase in public and private sector investment in family planning and population programs, improved allocation of resources between alternative service delivery strategies, lessening of constraints to efficiency in the contraceptive market and increased use of extant data to evaluate and modify family planning programs.

Support for the OPTIONS program in Morocco was provided through a $416,000 buy-in from USAID/Rabat.

NIGER

Activities and Results

The goal of OPTIONS was to help the Directorate of Statistics (DSD) to prepare and present a draft population policy to the government for approval, and to help DSD carry out activities which will result in widespread support for population programs in Niger.

OPTIONS assistance was instrumental in keeping population high on the policy agenda in Niger. Through its assistance to Unité d'Etudes Démographiques at de la Développement (UEDD), which acts as the secretariat for the Interministerial Technical Committee (CTIP), OPTIONS has enabled the development of the National Population Policy. Furthermore, by association CERPOD staff in all of its Niger activities, OPTIONS was able to increase CERPOD's role as a leader in population policy development in the Sahel (see CERPOD).

The long-term advisor played in a key role in the overall OPTIONS strategy, particularly in moving the USAID/Niger population program forward. She played a very important role in coordinating the various centrally funded activities underway in Niger and was instrumental in maintaining the progress of the bilateral population project, which was signed by the Government in August, 1988.

In August, October and December 1989, joint OPTIONS/CERPOD teams visited Niger to help organize a workshop on the integration of population into development planning. Apart from assistance in the logistics of the seminar, OPTIONS/CERPOD staff helped UEDD staff undertake the analysis (based on the INTEGRA model developed under the RAPID III project), which formed the basis of the seminar.

The journalist seminar provided for under the subcontract took place March 26-April 3, 1990. Georges Collinet of the Voice of America acted as a consultant to OPTIONS to be the principal trainer for the conference. CERPOD also supplied trainers for the conference. Eighteen communication technicians participated in the seminar and after receiving information on population and development, produced a song, a video and a radio spot on population issues. The first population and development bulletin, which UEDD is calling "POP-INFO," was also produced. The second, third, and fourth issues of POP-INFO were developed with assistance (in the form of training) from OPTIONS. They were produced and distributed to key officials nationwide.

The closing ceremonies of the journalist seminar were used to launch the CTIP: the members were announced, and they were given the charge to produce a draft population policy. UEDD acted as the secretariat for the CTIP and OPTIONS provided them with technical assistance to that end.

A joint OPTIONS/CERPOD mission in September 1990 helped develop a series of activities and a schedule for the CTIP to accomplish its mission. The proposal was accepted by the CTIP.

Following the OPTIONS visits in September, the organization of a national conference on population policy was substituted by the organization of two retreats allowing the CTIP to draft the population policy document. UNFPA funded the national population policy conference at which the document was to be presented.

A "storyboard" presentation to be used in awareness raising activities aimed at garnering support for population policy activities in Niger was developed during the November 1990 OPTIONS mission. The presentation, which covers population and development links in Niger and the need for population policy, is based on the 10% results of the census, the INTEGRA study, and the documents developed during the first CTIP seminar. It has been widely used to develop support for the population policy both among GON officials and among donors, including USAID/Niger.

The draft population policy was developed during the second CTIP retreat held in Maradi February 11-15, 1991. The draft policy was presented to the Secretaries General and the Directors of the various Ministries in Niamey, and then presented at the National Conference held in Niamey March 25-27, 1991. "Population Policies in Africa" developed by OPTIONS was also presented during the conference. The conference recommended that the government incorporate demographic variables into the planning process, and that the draft policy be submitted to the government for adoption.

Due to political events in Niger, the policy was not adopted in 1991, but adoption of a population policy was recognized in the National Conference as a priority for the Transitional Government. Population was added as an attribution of the former Ministry of Social affairs and Promotion of Women, which became the Ministry of Social Development, Population and Promotion of Women (MSDPPW).

Outcomes

The outcomes of OPTIONS activities in Niger were (a) drafting of a national population policy; (b) development of a constituency supportive of the policy; and (c) expansion of service delivery through the technical and management support offered to the USAID/Niger and the government.

NIGERIA

Activities and Results

The A.I.D. Affairs Office (AAO) requested OPTIONS assistance to design a single, comprehensive Family Health Services Project for the implementation of the National Population Policy. The OPTIONS project has successfully completed its program for Nigeria, whose strategy was largely defined by AAO's requested to design the "policy component" of the FHS project. After designing the "policy components," the AAO provided OPTIONS with a $60,000 buy-in to extend ongoing policy activities until the FHS contracting process could be resolved. In particular, the buy-in supported activities with the National Council for Population Activities (NCPA), state family planning coordinators, local government authorities, Federal Office of Statistics and the National Population Commission.

OPTIONS provided a highly diversified set of services that facilitated implementation of the national population policy and prepared Nigeria for the policy component of the bilateral population project financed by A.I.D.

Outcomes

Subtasks/Accomplishments

1.   Training

Enhanced skills in management, organizational development, computer use, fund-raising and workshop planning/logistics during five weeks of U.S.-based training.

2.   Financial & Infrastructure Support

Provided funding for three Full Time Equivalent staff salaries for six months. Extended loan of two computers, one printer, video equipment and peripheral equipment.

3.   Business Leaders Conference

In preparation for the BLC, OPTIONS arranged for cosponsorship between NCPA and Arthur Young & Co., adapted the storyboard policy presentation, established a Conference framework, developed a preliminary agenda, initiated a call for papers, identified potential key speakers and drafted a list of candidate organizations to attend.

4.   Awareness Raising Seminars

OPTIONS TA enabled the NCPA to conduct policy-awareness dissemination activities, build consensus, and expand its membership and resource base. Toward this end, OPTIONS built the seminar mechanism; developed a computerized graphic policy tool and script; and identified, scheduled and supported, both financially and technically, NCPA's participation in the Annual State FP Coordinators Workshop, Oyo State Local Government Area Workshop. NCPA has conducted an additional 2-4 seminars throughout Nigeria for public and private organizations.

NIGERIAN INSTITUTE FOR SOCIAL AND ECONOMIC RESEARCH (NISER)

1.   Training

Provided training to assure continuation of computer-based presentation to disseminate the National Population Policy.

STRATEGIC PLANNING

1.   Policy Monitoring System (PMS)

Sponsored and conducted a two-week, U.S.-based computer training course for the FMOH to learn how to develop information systems. Provided training on information systems methodology. Designed a two-part conceptual framework for the PMS, including (1) quantitative indicators and (2) activity tracking. Modified the annual state family planning coordinator questionnaire to collect policy information for use in future planning. Implemented the annual survey and analyzed the results for state and national leaders.

2.   Contraceptive Forecasting

As directed by AAO, conducted preliminary contraceptive forecasting exercise for 22 states and armed forces divisions, interviewed over 500 state coordinators and deputies to collect qualitative data on programmatic issues, trained coordinators on use of hand calculators and basic mathematical equations, and adapted existing forecasting methodology using Lotus 1-2-3 to project method-specific commodity requirements for 1989.

3.   State Family Planning Coordinators Workshop

A.   Port Harcourt 1987

Provided TA to develop workshop agenda, conducted a presentation on the role of the private sector in population activities, and led the strategic planning session.

B.   Ibadan

Provided TA to develop workshop agenda; provided financial and technical assistance to NCPA to deliver the policy presentation "A Vision for the Future," provided financial and technical assistance to FMOH to process, analyze and present results from the coordinator's survey; and conducted preliminary contraceptive forecasting exercise for each of the 22 states and armed forces divisions.

4.   State Local Government Area (LGA) Workshops

A.   Kwara State 1987

Assisted in the substantive organization of the Workshop, developed model LGA implementation plans and provided financial support. Played key roles in presenting methodology, guiding small group discussions, and assisted in the development of 14 LGA plans.

B.   Oyo State 1988

Provided background materials, assisted in the development of the agenda and development of 22 LGA plans. Sponsored FMOH staff participation in conducting training on contraceptive forecasting and instruction on meeting the requirements for the family planning management information system.

EVALUATION/POLICY FEEDBACK

1.   Pilot Sentinel System (PSS)

Developed a statistical model to determine sample size and observation period requirements to detect changes in fertility over time; designed and printed completed set of questionnaires (8 separate forms) to collect reproductive status data on 2,000 women for 12 months; wrote handbook describing the flow of information within the project; how to conduct the survey and complete all forms within the project; trained state officers (and their assistants) from 4 states on the conduct of the sentinel system; recruited and trained 28 interviewers; selected and redrew maps of 20 enumeration areas; conducted a baseline survey in 4 states and set up record system to follow changes in reproductive status and contraceptive use for a 12-month period; designed and tested data entry program for the baseline survey; entered and edited data for 3 sites; monthly reporting began for 3 sites; first quarterly interviews conducted in the same 3 sites, and inconsistencies between quarterly and monthly data were followed up; and forms for the first quarter from 3 sites were sent to Lagos for data entry.

2.   General Household Survey

Provided extensive TA to conceptualize and evaluate relevance to policy and planning. Designed a new one-page questionnaire insert dealing with contraceptive prevalence and supported one FMOH staff person to monitor Federal Office of Statistics (FOS) household survey activities and to liaise with OPTIONS and FOS staff.

3.   EPI Evaluation System

Initiated the establishment of an evaluation system. Developed and field tested a prototype questionnaire to utilize existing data collection system to provide demographic information to decision makers.

PAPUA NEW GUINEA

Activities and Results

OPTIONS provided support to Papua New Guinea in the development of a national population policy. An awareness raising activity was conducted in order to increase the awareness of PNG officials of the importance of addressing the problem of population growth. Support for policy development was also provided, including a policy conference which produced guidelines for a national policy.

OPTIONS laid the groundwork for future activities in May 1987 with a trip that assessed the population policy needs of PNG and designed an assistance strategy. Demographic data and background information were collected in preparation for the development of a RAPID-model presentation to the Parliament on the effects of population growth in PNG.

OPTIONS provided extensive technical assistance in the preparation, implementation and follow-up of the National Advisory Council on Population Policy (NACPP) workshop in April 1988. Activities associated with the workshop included:

1) Organizational and logistical support for carrying out the workshop;

2) Two major presentations including a presentation of the RAPID model and the accompanying paper developed by OPTIONS, "The Effects of Population Growth on Social and Economic Development in Papua New Guinea" and presentation and discussion of the OPTIONS guide "Background Materials for Use in Drafting a National Population Policy for Papua New Guinea," which addresses principles embodied in recent international population conferences (Mexico City, 1984 and the Third Asian and Pacific Population Conference at Colombo, 1982), and the

content of recently adopted National Population Policy statements (Nigeria 1985, Zaire 1986, and Liberia 1987).

3)   Technical assistance to the NACPP in drafting the report of the workshop.

OPTIONS recommended and the NACPP unanimously agreed to establish a coordinating unit within the Department of Finance & Planning to develop an action plan and designate departmental responsibilities for its implementation. An ad hoc three-person coordinating unit has been set up while also working through official bureaucratic channels to formally recognize this population body.

The instability of the Papua New Guinea government and personnel changes within the Department of Finance and Planning slowed down the process towards adoption of a National Population Policy. However, PNG used the guidelines to form the basis of a national population policy that was finally adopted in June 1991. The policy is contained in the document An Integrated National Population Policy for Progress and Development, Department of Finance and Planning, June 5, 1991.

Outcomes

The principal outcomes of the OPTIONS program in Papua New Guinea include:

- Increased awareness among senior officials of a broad range of Ministries of the effects of rapid population growth;

- Increased understanding among these same officials of the elements and goals of population policy;

- Inauguration of the activities of the NACPP, which was created shortly before the Workshop, and strengthening of the NACPP's capacity to undertake policy formulation; and

- Promulgation of a national population policy in June 1991.

PERU

Activities and Results

By September, 1990, OPTIONS had completed its activities in Peru, including the installation of the programming and budgeting, performance monitoring and evaluation, and logistics management components of the Quipus Model in the National Family Planning Program Division of the Ministry of Health. A new opposition party (Cambio 90) had won that summer's national elections adn taken office. The new govenrment fully adopted the Quipus Model. For two years, 1991 and 1992, the new leadership has continues to use Quipus to plan and coordinate the activities of the National Family Planning Program without OPTIONS assistance.

The GOP's support for family planning activities in Peru is strong. In September, 1991, at the closing ceremony of a three-day meeting on family planning service delivery sponsored by INPPARES, the local IPPF affiliate, President Fujimore delivered an address that was widely covered in the media in which he forcefully reaffirmed his govenrment's support for Peru's population policy and its emphasis no expanding the availability of family planning services. In that speech he declared the 1990s to be the "decade of family planning."

Brook amendment sanctions have brought A.I.D. support to the public sector to a virtual standstill. The sanctions are likely to be lifted during the first quarter of 1992. Peru also qualifies as a BIG country under the Office of Population's new worldwide BIG Country Strategy.

In anticipation of these changes, the GOP has requested OPTIONS II assistance to complete the job begun under the OPTIONS I project; namely, to train program officials in the use of Quipus to coordinate the planning and delivery of family planning services among private and public sector institutions at the national and subnational, i.e., regional levels. Training was not included in the original USAID buy-in to the OPTIONS I project because of budgetary constraints at the time of the buy-in.

RWANDA

Activities and Results

OPTIONS was requested by USAID/Rwanda through a $50,000 buy-in to undertake studies in support of the Rwanda Family Planning II Project which followed up on FP activities initially established under the first USAID project.

In February of 1988, OPTIONS traveled to Rwanda to conduct an assessment of the institutional framework, the legal/regulatory environment, and private sector involvement regarding population activities. This research was the groundwork for "Diagnostic Studies of Family Planning Activities in Rwanda" in preparation for a new project aimed at increasing support and expansion of the FP activities established under the first AID project.

OPTIONS also produced a separate document "Lois, Réglements et Directives se rapportant à la Planification Familiale au Rwanda" that addressed the legal and regulatory situation within the country.

Outcomes

The two documents prepared by the OPTIONS team were presented to AID/Kigali and officials from various Rwandan Ministries, and a strategy for a continuing project was drafted.

"Diagnostic Studies of Family Planning Activities in Rwanda" and "Lois, Réglements et Directives se rapportant à la Planification Familiale au Rwanda" were prepared by OPTIONS staff and used as tools in assessing the population environment and framework of Rwanda.

SENEGAL

Activities and Results

OPTIONS provided technical assistance in Senegal which led to the adoption of a National Population Policy.

OPTIONS assistance included: financing three Senegalese consultants to the Ministry of Planning and Cooperation (MOPC) for a period of six months to help draft a NPP; observational travel for four Senegalese to Nigeria and Zaire; providing background documents for population policy development; support for RAPID presentations in each of Senegal's regions in connection with the dissemination of the draft national policy; and providing direct short-term technical assistance during the policy development process, as needed.

A study tour to Zaire was successfully conducted during November 1987 (a planned trip to Nigeria was canceled due to time constraints). The Senegalese delegation met with the Government of Zaire and officials of international agencies and benefitted from well-planned presentations on the substance and sequence of steps entailed in the recent formulation of Zaire's national population policy.

In April 1988 a Workshop on the draft National Population Policy was held by the Government of Senegal. OPTIONS provided technical assistance to the workshop.

Outcomes

On April 28, 1988, the Government of Senegal (GOS) formally adopted a National Population Policy, thereby realizing the intended outcome of OPTIONS activities in Senegal.

SOCIAL SECURITY SYSTEMS IN LATIN AMERICA

Activities and Results

The purpose of OPTIONS work with Social Security Systems in Latin America was to share different approaches to establishing successful family planning service delivery by the Latin American region's Social Security Institutes.

After the success OPTIONS experienced with the Peruvian Institution for Social Security, preparations were made to participate in the 1989 Regional Social Security Conference in Costa Rice. The Conference proved to be an excellent forum to discuss the different approaches to family planning service delivery.

Interest generated by the 1989 Conference led OPTIONS to finance and organize with the Centro Interamericano de Seguridad Social (CISS) at its facilities in Mexico City. Participating in the seminar were Cabinet members, Medical Directors and technicians from Social Security Institutes representing nine countries. While Social Security coverage of the national population varies greatly country to country, health represents the largest portion of most Latin American Social Security budgets.

The content of the seminar focused around three subject areas: 1) health and financial benefits of family planning — as favorably shown by the benefit/cost studies of Peru, Mexico and Bolivia; 2) the exchange of information between countries on their respective programs; and 3) policy analysis and implementation tools which employ computerized approaches, such as the TIPPS and Quipas models.

The results of the seminar were quite satisfying. A framework incorporating family planning into overall reproductive health was adopted which supersedes the long standing regional reluctance to discuss demographic objectives. A general consensus was achieved on the need for Social Security Institutes to provide family planing services. The participants felt it would be extremely valuable to meet on an annual basis. Concrete requests for technical assistance have bene received.

Outcomes

The outcome has been to encourage Latin American Social Security Institutes to expand the delivery of family planning services.

SUDAN

Activities and Results

OPTIONS project work began in Sudan in March 1987 in support of the efforts of the Sudan National Population Committee (NPC) to promote the development of a national population policy. In particular, the NPC organized the Third National Population Conference in October 1987. The NPC is a committee under the authority of the National Research Council and is composed of representatives of various government Ministries and private organizations. NPC previously had only a part-time Secretary General, and for the implementation of the Third National Population Conference, the organization established an Operations Secretariat consisting of three professionals plus supporting staff. Throughout and after the period of OPTIONS assistance, the NPC has grown in both size and influence. It now has multiple departments, a staff of over thirty, regional affiliates, and has begun to be the implementing agency for a number of donor projects (UNFPA, Dutch, Japanese).

The Policy Conference, held October 10-14, 1987, was a major success. Prime Minister Sadiq El Mahdi opened the Conference with a strong statement endorsing the development of a national population policy for Sudan. The Conference issued a lengthy set of recommendations that serves as the interim population policy for Sudan. The policy recommendations concluded that high birth rates, high death rates and excessive migration are key factors that inhibit Sudan's development effort and harm the health of its people. In particular, the document called for policies to:

1. Provide family planning services and information to all Sudanese couples;

2. Expand programs to improve infant and child health, promote child survival and ensure safe motherhood; and

3. develop programs to improve rural services and economic opportunities to reduce levels of internal migration.

The Prime Minister and the Minister of Finance and Economic Planning both charged NPC to continue its policy development work.

OPTIONS staff helped the NPC develop a proposal for continued policy activities to be submitted to the Ministry of Finance and Economic Planning (MFEP) for funding through the local currency budget of USAID/Khartoum.

MFEP eventually approved the project and funded it at 1.7 million Sudanese pounds. The 18-month program was to cover May 1, 1988 until October 21, 1989, but was extended until December 31, 1989 to take into consideration delays due to floods and the change in government.

In July 1989 after USAID/Khartoum was notified to begin a phase-out of all activities, OPTIONS staff worked closely with NPC, Mission and UNFPA to develop a five-year plan for continued NPC activities, which would be supported under AID local currency and by UNFPA for external costs. OPTIONS also worked with the NPC and USAID/K to revise the NPC workplan to take into account the change in government. The NPC continues to be financed under the AID local currency agreement, but UNFPA support for core population policy activities was delayed until 1992, creating difficulties in obtaining computer supplies, etc. which require hard currency. The recent devaluation of the Sudanese pound (from 4.5:$1 to 90:$1) also means that the local funds provided for the 1990-1995 period under the USAID/Khartoum arrangement will not be sufficient to meet operating expenses. The NPC is currently negotiating with the Dutch government for additional funding.

The NPC program included several key components: (1) organization of population policy workshops in the many diverse regions of Sudan; (2) development of ministerial action plans so that key ministries could move toward organization and expansion of programs for population policy implementation; and (3) organization of three special seminars: the first to consider private-sector initiatives in family planing service delivery, the second to look at migration issues, and the third to address leaders in the military, the prisons, game wardens, fire brigades and policy. Since the military coup, the NPC canceled activities with the military, but continues to work successfully with the other services.

The official GOS adoption of a National Population Policy in September 1990 marked the final achievement of OPTIONS activities in Sudan, but OPTIONS team members have continued working with the NPC (through UNFPA support) and maintain close contact with NPC staff. If (or when) the conditions change in the country, enabling USAID support to resume, the NPC is eager to work with OPTIONS II.

Outcomes

The following outcomes were achieved despite extraordinarily difficult economic and political circumstances:

- An interim national population policy in the form of recommendations from the Third National Population Conference.

- High successful regional workshops in Kordofan, Central, Northern and Eastern regions, including strong statements of support from regional political and religious leaders and creation of regional affiliates of the NPC.

- Workplans and follow-up activities in the Ministries of Health, Education, Social Affairs and Zakat, Religious Affairs, and Information.

- Commitment from the Ministry of Religious Affairs and regional religious leaders to support the activities of NPC.

- Organization of an Advisory Committee to help the MOH expand its service delivery program.

- A successful workshop on private-sector initiatives in family planning service delivery that concluded with strong recommendations for establishment of a national contraceptive social marketing program. (This has been put on hold under the current regime which is reorganizing the national financial system.)

- Formulation of three active task forces on migration, one of which has completed, with UNFPA support, a baseline demographic survey of the capital area for use in urban planning and service delivery.

- Organization of IEC activities in close cooperation with the Population Education (MOE) and Information (MOI) programs, including design and production of population television spots on family planning, AIDS, female circumcision, and oral rehydration.

- Inclusion of contraceptives on the Essential Drugs List to facilitate their importation.

- Adoption of a National Population Policy by the Revolutionary Command Council and the Council of Ministers.

- Institutionalization of the National Population Committee along with increasing government financial and other material support.

Because of continuing war and financial crises, as well as radically changed political, ideological, and security emphases, the new government commitment to population policy implementation has been weak. However, the NPC has been strengthened tremendously and has become a respected national institution which plays a part in many Ministry decisions, consequently influencing those new policy makers who might have been antagonistic to population issues. Despite the massive purges in the government and academia during the current regime, and the regressive social policies adopted (particularly in women's rights), the NPC has survived and continued to expand its activities and push its message. The strategy of the NPC leadership — to work with a wide variety of groups both in and outside of government — has been successful thus far and the institution has been able to adroitly navigate the successive waves of political purges and repression, despite the loss of some valued staff who have been detained or are in exile. The extremely difficult political conditions in the country are well known. The fact that the NPC has continued to function and has expanded its activities in so many areas is a tribute to the dedication of the staff and to the building of a professional and sturdy institution, in which the OPTIONS project played a critical role.

TOGO

Activities and Results

The OPTIONS strategy for Togo emphasized the following elements: constituency building in support of the national population policy; encouraging the government to formally adopt the policy; and building the institutional capacity within the Ministry of Plan and Mines to oversee policy implementation and development of a policy implementation plan.

A number of accomplishments related to overall OPTIONS goals can be noted:

1)   Two presentations made to President Eyadema;

2)   The National Population Policy in Togo was drafted, revised and distributed to relevant GOT and Togolese NGO program planners and directors;

3)   An executive summary of the report of the National Conference on Population and Development, held in 1987, was prepared and distributed on a limited basis;

4)   A microcomputer was installed at the Population Coordination Office and computer training provided to the staff; and

5)   The Chief of the Population Coordination Office participated in observational travel to Zaire.

In addition, an 11 point program for developing a population policy implementation plan was developed in collaboration with the Ministry of Plan and Mines. The essential elements of this program recommend: 1) development of an institutional structure for policy implementation (Population Unit in the Ministry of Plan and Mines and National Technical Committee) by MOPM; 2) training for key technical staff, 3) awareness raising activities among important constituencies; 4) analysis of relevant legislation; and 5) development of detailed plans for policy implementation.

During August 1989 meetings were held during an OPTIONS visit with the Ministry of Plan, USAID and the INTRAH Africa Regional Director. As a consequence of those discussions, OPTIONS and USAID decided to refocus remaining resources on activities that would educate and inform Togolese officials in 3 areas:

1.   Components of the Togolese Draft National Population Policy;

2.   The Relationships between Family Planning and Maternal Child Health; and

3.   Family Planning and Standards.

OPTIONS agreed to develop presentation policy tools on the above topics and support dissemination efforts to public and private decision makers. The following two presentation tools have successfully been developed:

1.   A presentation that combines the essential elements of the RAPID/Togo model and the draft national population policy; and

2.   A presentation that draws upon the Demographic and Health Survey data and demonstrates the impact of high fertility on maternal and child health; this presentation has also incorporated elements of the newly drafted Family Planning Program Standards.

In pursuit of the policy presentation objectives, OPTIONS collaborated with USAID/Lome in the support of the University of Benin's Demographic Research Unit (URD) organization of the National Conference on Population and Family Planning held 19-23 March 1990. At the Conference OPTIONS presented the two presentation policy tools to 39 technical representatives from the private sector and various government ministries.

A conference outcome was the call for a draft Population Policy's revision and adoption. A booklet summarizing the key points of the maternal child health presentation was prepared for wide dissemination.

During May 1990 OPTIONS funded a three day national level conference for the National Union of Togolese Women. At that conference the two OPTIONS presentation policy tools were again applied. The Union further disseminated the information presented to representatives at all levels of the organization.

As a follow-up to the March 1990 National Conference on Population and Family Planning, OPTIONS collaborated with URD to conduct further analyses of the DHS data. The results were synthesized in a booklet "Family Planning and the Health of Mothers and Children in Togo." The analyses also formed the basis for three presentations: 1) unmet need in family planning; 2) determination of family planning needs by area of residence; and 3) relations of contraceptive practice and use of health services. In October, OPTIONS staff traveled to Togo to work with counterparts at URD to finalize a draft of the family planning unmet need presentation. A preliminary presentation was held with over 40 persons from national and international agencies. Modifications to the presentation were made based on the suggestions received during the preliminary presentation. In November Dr. Assogba of URD worked with OPTIONS in Washington to make adjustments to the presentation and to deliver the presentation to AID/Washington staff. Upon Dr. Assogba's return to Togo, the presentations were used at a seminar for high-level government policymakers on December 4, 1990. A written report of the family planning unmet need presentation was prepared and disseminated widely in Togo.

OPTIONS also worked with the National Union of Togolese Women to support their efforts to disseminate information on population policy, maternal child health and family planning to its membership nationwide.

Outcomes

The outcome of the OPTIONS program in Togo was increased support for a National Population Policy and the national family planning program.

ZAIRE

Activities and Results

The ultimate OPTIONS goal for Zaire was the formal adoption of a National Population Policy and the development of plans for implementation.

A National Population Policy was drafted in January 1986 and accepted by the National Population Committee (CONAPO) in June 1987. Early OPTIONS activities focused on the development of the current 21 task program.

The first major task was implemented in June 1987 with OPTIONS support for a national seminar officially inaugurating CONAPO, as well as the Coordinating Committee (CECAP) and the Interministerial Technical Committee (CTIP).

CECAP is pivotal to the GOZ effort through its mandate to coordinate all activities related to population. Therefore, OPTIONS provided substantial technical assistance as well as office equipment, supplies and a vehicle.

During the period from October 1987 to March 1988, OPTIONS traveled to Zaire on four occasions. During the first three visits, a series of training activities were launched to address needs of CECAP's staff and the Interministerial Technical Committee. During the fourth visit, the OPTIONS team participated in two workshops:

1. A National Workshop to draft full and comprehensive budgets and plans for each of the 9 sectors of the Policy; and

2. A Workshop for Consolidation of Sectorial Plans into an overall national action plan.

These two workshops led to the development of a national action plan to implement the NPP. This document was the first step toward developing a cross-sectoral planning and resource allocations tool.

In the second quarter of 1989 the OPTIONS resident advisor began his 1 year assignment. His responsibilities were two-fold:

1. As a population policy advisor, he assisted CECAP in:

    •   planning the implementation of the policy through the application of programming and budgeting tools; and

    •   decentralizing the planning and implementation of the policy through the establishment of regional committees on population.

2. As a family planning management advisor, he assisted the GOZ family planning project in:

    •   improving the quality of existing services;

    •   expanding the range of services made available to the acceptors;

- decentralizing FP services operations to the regional level; and,

- strengthening the projects management information system.

In Zaire, any document to be presented to the GOZ must be reviewed by two preparatory committees, the Comité Economique et Financier and the Comité Restreint, before it reaches the government itself for final approval. These committees are subcommittees within the Executive Council of Ministers. The NPP was reviewed by the Comité Economique et Financier in May 1990. A series of questions were raised regarding implementation costs which were answered by the Department of Plan (DOP) and its population policy planning unit, the Cellule des Etudes et de la Coordination des Activités en Matière de Population (CECAP) and the OPTIONS advisor. The NPP did not pass through the Comité Restreint, which return the NPP to CECAP with detailed comments and questions.

In response to questions raised by the Comité Economique et Financier:

The DOP/CECAP and the OPTIONS advisor determined the total cost of nation-wide, sector-wide implementation of the NPP.

Several other macroeconomic analyses and program management points were informally discussed with the COP senior officials, and the analyses convinced them to present the NPP and its action plan to the Comité Restreint.

In response to the Comité Restreint:

CECAP/OPTIONS prepared appropriate answers as well as developed a series of presentations for the GOZ. A presentation was developed that can be used to raise awareness among leaders and key constituencies as to the contents and rationale of the NPP. Plans were discussed for a schedule of presentations and target audiences.

Agreement was reached with the Secretary General to call a meeting of CONAPO in October. However, a new Secretary General was appointed. Consequently, preparatory actions for the meeting of the CONAPO are suspended for the moment.

CECAP is a unit created by ministerial directive and is directly attached to the Secretary General's office within the DOP. CECAP has not been able to acquire the breadth and depth of staff, the authority or the institution vigor originally envisaged. OPTIONS staff discussed the possibility of transforming CECAP into a directorate and investing it with the resources needed to lead a broad-based population program.

In other activities during the period October 1989-September 1990, a computer system and supplies were installed and training began, and the DOP/CECAP and OPTIONS began planning for awareness activities to answer questions raised.

Now, at the conclusion of OPTIONS assistance, the principal goal of an official population policy has not yet been accomplished. The obstacles to a satisfactory outcome are in two main areas:

1.   Numerous changes in government personnel. Eight different Commis-saires d'Etat au Plan resulted in continuity problems.

2.   Educational and awareness-building activities designed to promote the NPP did not overcome unfamiliarity with population issues among Zaire policy makers. Resistance to dealing with population issues and implementing relevant programs is still prevalent among national leaders.

OPTIONS, however, was instrumental in having the National Policy Develop-ment designated as an official Government of Zaire working document to be used by all national and international agencies involved in population issues. It is hoped that the April election will result in the installation of a new government that will be in a better position to adopt the policy as a law subsequent to passage by the newly elected parliament.

With assistance from OPTIONS, CECAP revised its policy awareness program to target the main national leadership groups. OPTIONS provided technical and financial support to the implementation of the policy awareness program. The updated plan called for five policy workshops conducted by CECAP in collaboration with representatives of the National Assembly, religious, business and media leaders; and the new executive council.

OPTIONS activities in Zaire were stopped as a result of the Congressional restrictions on transfers of funds and other resources to the Government of Zaire.

The social and political situation in Zaire has gotten worse since the OPTIONS visit in that country in December 1991. The then transition government has been changed, civil servants went on strike, successive governments were dismissed, riots took place and the present situation does not provide any optimistic outlook for the near future. In this context, the USAID Mission ceased its collaboration work in the country and had to evacuate its direct hire staff and layoff its locally-hired employees. At this point, no foreseeable visit to Zaire is planned by OPTIONS.

Outcomes

Adoption of a National Population Policy.

Establishment of institutions capable of implementing the National Policy, particularly with regard to the decentralization of the policy implementation through regional committees on population. This includes establishment and training of CONAPO, CECAP, and CTIP; and

Development of detailed action plans.

APPENDIX A
USAID OPTIONS PROJECT, FINAL REPORT, COUNTRY ACTIVITIES

ZAMBIA

Activities and Results

The principal objectives of the OPTIONS strategy for Zambia were:

- Generate broad-based political support through disssemination of the National Population Policy at a conference for 200 national, provincial and district level policy-makers;

- Conduct a "target Model" analysis to assit GRZ in estimating contraceptive prevalence required to achieve the NPP fertility target;

- Develop a microcomputer-based, graphics presentation to disseminate the NPP;

- Support preparation of sectoral action plans to implement the National Population Policy through a series of workshops and seminars; and

- Strengthen National Commission for Development Planning (NCDP) capability to coordinate Zambia's population activities through the transfer of computer equipment essential for NCDP's awareness raising and implementation planning activities.

OPTIONS achieved the following results:

- Developed and built consensus for a national population program;

- Assisted the Zambia Mission in the development of a technical workplan for $102,947;

- Negotiated a subcontract with the NCDP to fund the National Population Conference and Interagency Seminar;

- Co-sponsored the May 1989 "National Population Conference and Interagency Seminar" to disseminate the NPP throughout the public

policy making community and to initiate dialogue on policy implementation;

• Held coordination meetings with the UN/ILO, Population Council,
Enterprise Program, and SEATS Projects;

• Designed a computer-based, graphic presentation on the National
Population Policy, for use in nationwide awareness raising campaigns
for provincial and district level policy-makers;

• Participated in the UNFPA/NCDP National Workshop on Population
Project Management;

• Developed consensus of approach to prioritize policy actions sectors for
implementation planning, beginning with fmaily planning;

• Conducted an illustrative Target Analysis to help the Zambians envisage
requirements for family planning program expansion to achieve the
nation's stated fertility objectives and transferred the technology;

• Developed a detailed outline for the design of a national family
planning program;

• Sponsored the "Thrid Policy Implementation Workshop of the IFCP"
from March 26-30, 1990 to analyze and determine strategies for family
planning service delivery; and

• Established linkages with other donors, including the Population
Council, to provide follow-on assistance to conduct operations research
pilot family planning programs.

Outcomes

The outcomes of OPTIONS activities in Zambia include:

• Evidence of nationwide support for ppulatino policy;

- Establishment of institutional capacity to implement the National Population Policy; and

- Formulation of a National Plan of Action including sector specific policy implementation plans.

ZIMBABWE

Activities and Results

The primary objective of OPTIONS was to join a forum of international experts and local leaders assembled by the Minister of Health to advise him on a comprehensive plan to formulate a national policy on population and development, action plans for policy implementation, and an organizational structure to carry out policy-related activities.

The second objective was to discuss with concerned Ministries, the Parliamentarian Group on Population and Development, private sector organizations, USAID Mission and the US Ambassador the expansion of support for future population-related activities and to build consensus for the steps necessary to continue with the policy development process.

OPTIONS participated in the two-day forum (October 24-25, 1988) and subsequent debriefing sessions. OPTIONS also assisted Dr. Boohene in designing and conducting a computerized graphics visual aid, which complemented the presentation of her paper "The Establishment of a Population Policy Secretariat." The expert group substantially endorsed Dr. Boohene's plan. They recommended that Zimbabwe formulate a national population policy; make plans for its implementation; and establish the necessary organizational structure.

The experts presented their recommendations to the Minister of Health, who accepted it, expressed appreciation and encouraged continued commitment to Zimbabwe's policy development process, Dr. Muchemwa expressed his intent to immediately seek the approval of President Mugabe to proceed with carrying out the recommendations.

Outcomes

The principle outcome was the formulation of a draft national population policy, action plans and organizational structure.

Appendix B

Compilation of Population
Policy Development Projects

Explanation of Terms

The phrase, "to assist a ministry," often is used to describe pressure applied to public officials to follow through on a donor-required activity. In other cases, it may refer to a project in which the USAID field operative takes responsibility for an activity which is too controversial to be entrusted to local staff. To "improve the capacity" of an indigenous institution to conduct a particular task often refers to a similar situation in which host country officials need some "encouragement" (or donor-supplied personnel) in order to meet program obligations. A "growing demand" for services or supplies (birth control in particular) is often cited in USAID literature to imply a spontaneous surge of interest in western contraceptives, while, in reality, the term may suggest a target number of contraceptive users the activity is expected to recruit. "Information, education and communication" refers to propaganda campaigns in a variety of media, and usually designed to create a psycho-social climate conducive to fertility decline. Host country subcontractors and collaborators are sometimes called "indigenous" organizations even when they are organized and funded by aid donor nations. The term "voluntary" is likewise used loosely. When program goals are to reduce population growth rates or to boost the number of modern contraceptive users (the "contraceptive prevalence rate"), the objective is generally to have a specific minimum number of persons adopt a family planning method through some form of persuasion short of absolute force. "Target setting" is done either by calculating the initial "contraceptive prevalence" rate that must be achieved to produce a particular demographic objective or to establish a time frame for the escalation of a project. In some cases, however, "targets" refers to audiences for whom certain propaganda messages or "constituency building" actions are intended. "Motivators" are persons assigned to encourage certain practices (i.e., birth control) that the subjects would not otherwise be inclined to adopt — generally through personal contact with members of the target group. And the term "motivational exercise" describes a series of events, announcements, rewards, or punishments designed to stimulate the same response. "Extension workers" are usually non-professional staff charged with some aspect of motivational work. In the context of this database, "research" may refer to scientific study, or it may simply be meant to imply the existence of such study. Some program descriptions, for instance, cite the dissemination of "research findings" to policy makers when the information actually provided to local officials is in no way the product of a real inquiry, but rather data carefully arranged in such a way as to justify its own conclusion. Permanent sexual sterilization is sometimes called "surgical contraception." In recent years, some "surgical" birth control specialists have tried to broaden the definition (for legal reasons) by insisting that it include long-term contraceptive implants. To "institutionalize" a program or to make it "sustainable" is the language used by donor agencies when a program has become established and the new goal is to get the host country to actively support it. At this stage, "operational research" (or "operations research") may be done investigate steps that might be taken to make a program "self-sustaining." Perhaps the most frequently and dangerously misused term of all is "requests for assistance." This phrase is habitually used by sponsors of population projects to make them appear to be "cooperative" efforts between donor and host country leaders. Many requests for assistance from within a country actually originate with oversight personnel at U.S. Embassies, and are accurately described as such in contracts and program descriptions. However, "requests for assistance" from host country personnel may also be the result of negotiations in which the aid recipient had no desire for the "help" but was either (a) obliged to seek it under an agreement in which something of value was at stake or (b) permitted the solicitation to be made by "advisors" on the donor-government payroll in the name of the host country.

CURRENT POLICY DEVELOPMENT CONTRACTS
From USAID Programs Computer Database
Current to end of 1993

Title: Population Project / Family Planning II
AID Project No: 2630144
Program Area: Egypt
FY Year Begin: 1983
FY Year End: 1993
Total Cost: 117600000 (US dollars)
Status: ACTIVE

Project to support the Government of Egypt's (GOE) family planning (FP) program. The project, which includes contraceptive procurement and distribution/promotion, FP statistics/policy, and technology transfer activities, will be primarily implemented by the Ministry of Health (MOH). The project has seven components. (1) The GOE's FP program will receive an adequate supply of contraceptives as well as medical equipment (mainly IUD insertion kits) for physicians and nurses. (2) To improve private/commercial contraceptive distribution and promotion, the Family of the Future contraceptive marketing program will be expanded in cities and

suburbs and into Upper Egypt, with a mass media campaign, 12-14 additional clinics, and an expanded product line. The Egyptian Pharmaceutical Trading Company, a GOE contraceptive distribution agency, may also be supported. (3) To upgrade community-level activities of the Population and FP Board's Population and Development Project (PDP) in rural areas, support will be provided, inter alia, to improve the performance of PDP female extension workers and to upgrade clinics in conjunction with project component (4) - to support a MOH campaign, to be undertaken in rural areas of 20 governorates (initially the 12 where the PDP operates), to promote contraceptives on a health basis and provide them in connection with clinic maternal/child health care. (5) The State Information Service's mass media FP information, education, and communication (IEC) program will be improved through greater private sector involvement; targets include FP materials for illiterates, a standard FP manual for physicians, and feedback bulletins for FP workers. Also, support will be provided to IEC activities of the Ministry of Education's Office of Population and Environmental Education. (6) To improve population planning and policy, the capability of the Central Agency for Public Mobilization and Statistics will be upgraded in regard to data collection, analysis, and processing, vital statistics, and census operations and cartography, in part through overseas and in-country training. The Population and FP Board will help to clarify and coordinate GOE policy by conducting FP studies and disseminating results to decisionmakers. (7) Finally, support will be provided to low-cost technology transfer activities by population intermediaries such as Pathfinder and the American Public Health Association, as well as by indigenous FP organizations such as the Institute for Research and Training in FP, which will train 310 women leaders to promote FP in their communities. Amendment of 6/20/87 extends project to 5/31/93 at no extra cost. Emphasis will shift from supportive activities such as IEC and school population curricula to direct public and private FP and contraceptive delivery systems.
< Goal > To reduce the rate of population growth in accordance with the Government of Egypt's national 5-Year plan and strategy program.
< Purpose > To increase family planning practice among Egyptian couples of reproductive age. Subpurpose. To strengthen and expand Egypt's population/family planning activities.
< Outputs > 1. Availability of an adequate supply of appropriate contraceptive materials and commodities to meet the growing demand. 2. Improved distribution and promotion of contraceptive services by means of the private and commercial sector. 3. Improved family planning management within the Ministry of Health. 4. Improved delivery of public sector family planning services. 5. Expansion and institutionalization of community based population/development programs. 6.

Trained family planning service providers. 7. Effective dissemination of population/family planning information, education, and communication. 8. Institutional capability to carry out applied research. 9. Reliable statistics and analytical capabilities. 10. Clinic renovation. 11. School renovation. 12. Series of population policy studies.
< Inputs > 1. A.I.D.: funds; technical assistance; census and survey expertise; commodities; operational support; and fellowships. 2. A.I.D. direct hire technical assistance estimated to consist of 36 person-months per year. 3. GOE: staff; facilities (clinics); local funds; commodities; logistics; and operating costs and maintenance.

Title: Population Welfare Planning
AID Project No: 3910469
Program Area: Pakistan
Year Begin: 1982
FY Year End: 1991
Total Cost: 77650000 (US dollars)
Status: ACTIVE

Project to support the Government of Pakistan's Population Welfare Program in four areas: management information and demographic research and evaluation; logistics and contraceptive supplies; bio- and sociomedical research; and professional motivation. The Population Welfare Division (PWD) will implement the project.
The project will support the following activities for PWD's research and data processing unit, the Population Development Center (PDC): (1) surveys on contraceptive use, vital statistics, male attitudes, and types of evaluations; (2) seminars and workshops in data presentation/use, self-evaluation, target setting, population policy, and population-development interface; (3) in-country and overseas training of junior PDC staff, along with internships at local universities in data collection, processing and analysis, and research administration; (4) staff and commodity support for publications activities; (5) institution building through short-term TA and creation of a visiting scholars program (to assist in training, data analysis, and publication) and of service statistics, feedback/evaluation, and data processing systems. Logistics will be improved by building a warehouse for contraceptives; upgrading PWD's supply management system through field trials, a supply procedures manual, training of district-level staff in service delivery, and evaluating the system's impact and its training program; and by providing condoms, orals, and other contraceptives (excluding IUD's). Bio- and sociomedical research of the National Institute of Technical Research (NITR) will be supported by: two

M.S. degrees along with short-term U.S. training for NITR staff and of short-term TA; creation of an NITR condom testing unit; and construction of a building to house NITR's offices, laboratories, and conference rooms. Promotional/motivational activities will include 50 short-term training/observation visits to the United States or Third World countries by key public and private individuals and 15 short-term visits to Pakistan by U.S. experts.

Amendment (3/85) adds $14.4 million in funding to meet substantially increased demand for contraceptives. Amendment (6/86) extends project 2 years to 9/89, increases funding, and places greater emphasis on institutional strengthening and technology transfer. The amended project consists of 7 components: program monitoring, research, and evaluation; contraceptive supplies and logistic support; voluntary surgical contraception; support to nongovernmental organizations and to district-level operations; a mass media campaign; and mid-level management training.

< Goal > To reduce the rate of natural population increase as part of the goal of achieving national social and economic development.

< Purpose > To strengthen the Government of Pakistan's population planning, evaluation, research, motivational, and logistic capabilities and performance.

< Outputs > 1. Management information, demographic research, and evaluation: a. national Contraceptive Prevalence Surveys (CPS); b. smaller scale evaluation surveys; c. data processing capability; d. seminars and workshops; e. publications; f. trained personnel; g. provincial research capability. 2. Logistics systems and contraceptive supplies: a. warehouse constructed and equipped; b. supply procedures designed and tested; c. supply manual developed; d. trained personnel; e. continuing contraceptive availability. 3. Bio-medical and socio-medical research: a. trained personnel; b. facility constructed; c. improved contraceptive testing capability. 4. Professional and personal motivation: a. trained program personnel; b. motivated government officials and prominent citizens.

< Inputs > 1. A.I.D. funding for: a. technical assistance; b. commodities: i. contraceptives, ii. other; c. training; d. local currency costs; e. construction. 2. Government of Pakistan funding in cash or in kind for: a. salaries and benefits; b. operating expenses; c. land used for program facilities.

Title: Family Planning Outreach
AID Project No: 5210124
Program Area: Haiti
FY Year Begin: 1981
FY Year End: 1989
Total Cost: 13948000 (US dollars)
Status: <u>ACTIVE</u>

Project to help the Government of Haiti (GOH) establish a national family planning (FP) program. The Department of Public Health and Population (DSPP) and its Division of Public Hygiene (DHF) will be the primary implementors. To strengthen FP program management, consultants will upgrade DSPP's use of service statistics, streamline its decisionmaking structure, and provide in-service staff training. FP management training (brief U.S. courses and 15 in-country seminars) will be held for key staff. To upgrade maternal/child health and FP services, the project will (1) increase from 123 to 235 the number of DSPP facilities providing FP counseling and services and from 9 to 30 the number providing sterilization (10 will be equipped to use laprocators); (2) train 80% of DSPP health professionals in FP counseling and services; (3) establish 3 rural nurse/auxiliary training centers and hold 2 annual workshops for nurses and auxiliaries; (4) provide FP orientation to medical students; (5) develop information, education, and communications (IEC) materials for use by health workers and traditional midwives; and (6) fund 4 small operations studies each year. To support FP services by private groups, local workshops will be held, IEC materials developed, and contraceptives provided as needed. Efforts will be made to increase private physicians' knowledge of FP and to train military doctors in FP techniques and provide courses for military staff. A national contraceptive retail sales program will ensure alternative access to reasonably priced contraceptives. Community and private support for FP will be expanded. Urban efforts will include encouraging factory workers to participate in the GOH's mobile clinic program; encouraging FP seminars for youth organizations; and strengthening media coverage of FP. In rural areas, efforts will be made undertake "mini" IEC efforts through 1,000 Community Action Councils. Finally, population policy seminars will be held, GOH participation at international population policy meetings funded, and U.S. graduate training in demography provided to 5 persons.
Amendment of 3/31/87 extends PACD 2 years. Activities are to: add a national FP coordinator; improve public sector FP management; upgrade at least one central referral clinic in each of the 15 public health districts; support IEC; and fund technical and managerial training and policy and medical studies.
< Goal > To improve health and social/economic welfare of poor Haitians.

< **Purpose** > To assist the Haitian Government (GOH) to establish a cost-effective national family planning program by: 1. improving program management; 2. improving quality/quantity of maternal child health/family planning (MCH/FP) services available; 3. expanding community support of and participation in MCH/FP by enlisting private, voluntary, and non-health sector agencies and groups; 4. increasing commercial availability of contraceptives at reasonable prices; 5. designing and articulating appropriate population/FP policies and programs.

< **Outputs** > 1. Health staff trained in FP. 2. FP services available in all Department of Public Health and Hygiene (DSPP) facilities; contraceptives available at community level; manuals and service guides updated. 3. Prenatal/postnatal counseling in FP. 4. Improved management/program surveillance system in place; key personnel trained in management. 5. Small operations research studies completed. 6. Commercial sales plan developed and implemented. 7. Information/ education program designed and implemented. 8. Private groups and community councils recruited and participate in program; community volunteers trained; community outreach mini grants system developed and tested. 9. Population impact analyses completed; leadership seminars; population addressed in GOH planning documents. 10. Strengthening of logistical system. 11. Demography trainees return and are engaged in population policy studies.

< **Inputs** > A. U.S. Contributions. 1. Medical supplies. 2. Equipment/ renovation. 3. Training. 4. Short-term consultants. 5. Services contracts. 6. Evaluations/operations research. 7. Local salaries. 8. Transport/per diem. 9. Allowances/fees. 10. Contraceptives. 11. Contingency funds. B. GOH Contributions. 1. DSPP. a. Direct salaries. b. Operating expenses. c. DSPP in-kind. 2. Other in-kind. C. Other Donors (U.N. Fund for Population Activities). 1. Contraceptives. 2. Equipment/drugs. 3. Training in-country. 4. Foreign training. 5. Salary support. 6. Operating expenses. 7. Information, education, and communications.

Title: Private Sector Family Planning
AID Project No: 5210189
Program Area: Haiti
FY Year Begin: 1986
FY Year End: 1991
Total Cost: 16660000 (US dollars)
Status: ACTIVE

Project to expand the delivery of family planning (FP) services by Haitian PVO's. The project will be managed by a U.S. nonprofit institution and implemented by four Haitian NGO's - L'Association pour la Promotion de la Familie Haitienne (PROFAMIL), Association des Oeuvres Privees de Sante (AOPS), the Haitian

APPENDIX B
POPULATION POLICY PROJECTS DATABASE

Community Health Institute (INHSAC), and the Child Health Institute (CHI). INHSAC will develop training courses in FP counseling; contraceptive methods; information, education, and communication (IEC); program management; record-keeping; and clinical contraceptive techniques (e.g., IUD or NORPLANT insertion and removal, pill evaluation, etc.) for physicians, auxiliary nurses, and record-keepers from 65 PVO's affiliated with either AOPS or PROFAMIL. One member of the INHSAC staff will attend a year-long training of trainers course at a U.S. university, and 3 others will attend short courses. INHSAC (with TA from Johns Hopkins) will also develop IEC materials (e.g., posters, radio spots, videos) for use by AOPS and PROFAMIL. IEC will include a series of PROFAMIL-sponsored seminars for Haitian health professionals and leaders. FP service delivery will be provided by PROFAMIL, AOPS, and their affiliates. About 45 PVO's working in fixed centers will receive sub-grants of $6,750 each; another 20 AOPS-member PVO's currently offering health outreach services will participate in FP training activities. Community collaborators will be used to provide door-to-door contraceptive distribution and to make follow-up visits to acceptors. In areas where only Catholic PVO's operate, PROFAMIL will consider providing training in natural FP for these PVO personnel. PROFAMIL will also identify alternative FP service mechanisms, such as affiliations with private physicians. Other delivery methods will include factory-based programs and PROFAMIL model FP clinics. The project aims for a contraceptive acceptance rate of 12.5%. Finally, CHI will conduct operations research, coordinate TA (2 long-term advisors and 20 months of consultancies) for the project, collect service statistics, and carry out monitoring and evaluation. Amendment of 8/24/88 extends PACD 18 months to 3/91, increases the number of participating major Haitian PVO's to 10, and expands the project's scope. Major changes will be to: expand PVO training and FP service delivery through PVO's, as well as activities relating to model clinics and factory- and community-based contraceptive distribution; pilot test a commercial retail sales program and a collaborating network of private physicians; and add a voluntary surgical contraception (VSC) component and incorporate a NORPLANT research/implementation activity previously funded under a public sector FP project. Amendment of 7/17/90 doubles funding and extends PACD to 6/92. The major new activity will be assistance to the public sector to allow the Ministry of Public Health and Population (MPHP) to revitalize its FP program (following a period of civil unrest) and, to a lesser extent, to develop a national population program. Funds will be channeled mostly through the International Planned Parenthood Federation (for PVO's) and the Pan American Health Organization (for MPHP). MPHP will provide FP services in 252 facilities, with focus on long-term clinical methods such as NORPLANT; 14 medical centers and 7 mobile teams will specialize in VSC for men and women, while MPHP outreach workers will provide temporary methods.

< Goal > To reduce the population growth rate in Haiti.

< Purpose > To increase the availability and effectiveness of family planning service delivery. < Outputs > (1) PVO's more capable of offering family planning services (2) PROFAMIL fully established and operating model clinics (3) INHSAC family planning training program functioning (4) IEC materials prepared and utilized (5) CHI population unit operational

< Inputs > Technical assistance. U.S. Institution costs. Commodities. Sub-grants. IEC. Training. Evaluation/audit. Operations research. Construction renovation. Other local costs.

Title: Private Sector Family Planning

AID Project No:	5270269
Program Area:	Peru
FY Year Begin:	1986
FY Year End:	1987
Total Cost:	13000000 (US dollars)
Status:	**ACTIVE**

Project to strengthen the capabilities of at least 16 Peruvian private family planning (FP) agencies (including one training institute) and the National Population Council (CNP) to increase contraceptive coverage, influence population policy, and improve private sector FP coordination and financial self-sufficiency. A nonprofit organization will be selected to implement the project. To increase contraceptive coverage by 400,000, the project will help participating agencies: (1) upgrade management (planning, accounting, evaluation, logistic, and data collection and reporting) systems; (2) train new personnel (including 200 managers and administrators, 650 medical and 1,000 non-medical service delivery personnel) and provide annual refresher training to 90% of the community-based distribution (CBD) supervisors and promoters; (3) develop a culturally appropriate, mass media FP information, education, and communication campaign for rural and urban areas; and (4) add 65 new FP clinics and 40 new CBD sites and improve and expand services in 90% of existing clinical and CBD sites. Continuous TA is a feature of this component, which will also provide participating agencies with sub-grants for particular activities and help them secure other funding. The population policy component will strengthen the capabilities of CNP, two research agencies (AMIDEP and INANDEP), and, possibly, a third research agency (IEP). In each, the project will train new staff in planning, management, and data analysis skills and upgrade computer hardware and software. Participating agencies will jointly develop a yearly research needs plan, 4 policy-related and 10 operational studies, and a strategy to disseminate FP information, through publications, seminars, and personal contacts, to legislators and other policymakers. The project will create a Peruvian Coordinating Agency (PCA) to represent private FP agencies and increase FP collaboration within the private and between the public and private sectors. This component will also promote private sector financial self-sufficiency through, e.g., income generation training for the PCA and participating agencies; fundraising; increased sale of services; increased use of volunteer services and of lower cost CBD and social marketing methods; and use of excess U.S. government property where available.

< Goal > To assist Peru in lowering the population growth rate in order to reduce its negative impact on social and economic development.

< Purpose > 1. To expand and increase the capability of Peruvian private sector family planning (FP) agencies to increase cost-effective contraceptive coverage. 2. To strengthen the capacity of these same agencies and of the National Population Council (CNP) to influence, improve, and strengthen population policy as it relates to the private sector. 3. To strengthen coordination among the private sector agencies through the creation of the Peruvian Coordinating Agency (PCA) representing private sector FP agencies.

< Outputs > A. Purpose One. 1. Number of women in union of fertile age (MWFA) receiving services increased. 2. Number of new FP clinical delivery sites and community-based distribution (CBD) sites increased and existing ones improved/expanded. 3. Availability of culturally appropriate FP information increased. 4. Number of trained FP personnel increased. 5. Management systems in private sector FP agencies improved. B. Purpose Two. 1. Survey and research capability enhanced. 2. Private sector ability to influence policy increased. B. Purpose Three. 1. Collaboration among currently identified and additional private sector FP institutions increased. 2. Ability of PCA and participating member agencies to become more financially self-sufficient increased.

APPENDIX B
POPULATION POLICY PROJECTS DATABASE

Title: Population and Family Planning Services
AID Project No: 5320069
Program Area: Jamaica
FY Year Begin: 1982
FY Year End: 1992
Total Cost: 10711000 (US dollars)
Status: <u>ACTIVE</u>

Project to increase the coverage and improve the effectiveness of contraceptive services delivery in Jamaica. The National Family Planning Board (NFPB) will coordinate implementation of the project through seven public and four private sector agencies. The project's major focus will be on strengthening and expanding the physical delivery system. Relevant public sector activities will include providing technical assistance to improve the effectiveness of the NFPB, the Ministry of Health (MOH), and other agencies; designing and developing specific programs (e.g., voluntary sterilization and male motivation); training MOH and other health workers in contraceptive technology and family planning extension techniques; and providing contraceptive supplies and related equipment. Within the private sector, A.I.D. will provide supplies and logistical support for the NFPB's commercial retail sales of contraceptives program and will assist the Jamaican Family Planning Association (JFPA), the YWCA, and Operation Friendship to carry out community-based adolescent fertility programs. In regard to developing an institutional capability in population planning and policymaking, the project will establish Population Units within the National Planning Agency and the Department of Statistics; provide long-term technical assistance to the Population Council to aid development of population policy and to the University of the West Indies to support its Population Policy Coordinating, Committee, its demographic studies program, and its fertility-related research; and support the national vital registration system of the Registrar General's Department. Expanding family planning motivational and educational networks will entail supporting research on the socio-cultural determinants of fertility; training health and family planning workers and extensionists in the proper methods of family planning counseling; expanding large-scale mass media information and education programs; supporting the community outreach efforts of the NFPB, the JFPA, and Operation Friendship; developing and disseminating client-oriented educational materials; and conducting seminars for schools principals, social workers, and similar professionals. In sum, the project will provide contraceptives, sterilizations, counseling, research, information and commodities, as well as the training for 13,000 workers, managers, and educators.

Amendment of 7/29/86 extends project to 3/31/91. Activities for the remainder of the project will be: support for provision of FP education and services by the MOH and the NFBP; voluntary surgical contraception; and commercial distribution of contraceptives.

< Goal > To improve the health, social, and economic status of the Jamaican people, and to reduce the crude birth rate over the next 20 years.
< Purpose > To expand the coverage and increase the effectiveness of contraceptive services delivery. < Outputs > 1. Trained indigenous staff functioning at all levels of the family planning delivery system. 2. Increased availability of family planning services through the MOH and NFPB clinics and through the commercial distribution contraceptive program. 3. Research carried out on determinants of fertility, migration, and contraceptive prevalence. 4. Population policies adopted at both the national and sectoral levels and policy, planning, and monitoring apparatus established.
<Inputs > Technical assistance: A. Population policy development; B. Registration and vital statistics; C. Development and coordination of training programs; D. Family planning management; E. Program development and evaluation. Training: A. U.S. and other overseas participant training; B. Local training and agency orientation in all aspects of family planning program development, management, and implementation. Commodities: A. Centrally-procured condoms and oral contraceptives; B. Other contraceptive supplies, medical equipment, and vehicles. Other: Salaries, local consultant services, research costs, per diem, and other local costs of special projects of NFPB, MOH, MYCD, YWCA, MOA, JFPA, NPA, DOS, UWI, RGD, ACOSTRAD, Women's Center, and Operation Friendship.

Title: Population and Development
AID Project No:	5380039
Program Area:	Other West Indies-Eastern Caribbean Reg
FY Year Begin:	1982
FY Year End:	1992
Total Cost:	8477000 (US dollars)
Status:	ACTIVE

Project to reduce fertility in the Eastern Caribbean by helping: the Caribbean Community Secretariat (CARICOM) to instruct national leaders and medical personnel in population issues; and the International Planned Parenthood Federation (IPPF) to improve family planning (FP) services, especially for adolescents.
CARICOM will create task forces in up to 8 countries to promote the formation of national population policies and will fund country reports summarizing population trends and projections. A regional awareness conference and RAPID presentations

will highlight for ministerial officials the impact of overpopulation, and some 20 mid/upper-level demographic statisticians will receive 2 weeks of U.S. Census Bureau training. CARICOM will also review medical policies and practices and hold a regional seminar for up to 20 doctors on these issues, followed by 20 national seminars. Observational training in modern contraception will be held for select persons at the University of the West Indies (UWI). IPPF will train 8 government physicians in surgical sterilization; contract UWI to provide on-site training to 70 government physicians in reversible contraception; and hold refresher seminars for 100 doctors. IFFP will train 2 nurses from each country as trainers for an on-site nurses training course to be developed with the help of UWI and of 14 additional nurses who will receive advanced training in fertility management at UWI. IFFP will also provide training for 400 allied health and community workers, seminars for 140 pharmacists, and short courses at UWI for 5 FP administrators. To combat high adolescent fertility, up to 7 lecturers from teacher training colleges will attend a 2-week family life education course with a strong sex education (SE)/FP component, and 280 teachers from the region will attend in-country SE seminars; SE teaching materials will be developed. IFFP will also improve government FP supply systems, develop a commercial retail sales and 5 community-based delivery programs, provide management TA to public health services and commodity assistance to 60 FP clinics, and establish 8 adolescent and 10 youth outreach clinics.

Amendment of 6/26/87 extends PACD 2 years to 12/31/90 and adds 4 activities to be implemented by the Caribbean FP Affiliation (CFPA): (1) training and TA in program management, information systems, revenue generation, and contraceptive supply logistics for CFPA and affiliated FP Associations; (2) IEC (formerly funded under 5380116); (3) clinics or counseling at 5 industrial/manufacturing sites; and (4) coordinated regional training of trainers and establishment of a CFPA training clearinghouse. Amendment of 8/31/89 to the Cooperative Agreement with CFPA adds an FP clinic/counselling services and day care center at Frequent Park Center, Grenada.

< Purpose > To reduce the number of unwanted pregnancies in the Eastern Caribbean.

< Outputs > 1. Revitalize regional and national demographic and medical policies as the outcome of increased awareness of population problems. 2. Increased FP service availability and use through public, private, and commercial sectors: a. Training provided to doctors, nurses, allied health workers. b. Commodity supply and distribution improved in government, commercial, and community sectors. c. Improvement of clinic services. d. Adolescent services expanded.

Title: Planning, Management and Research
AID Project No: 6250929
Program Area: Sahel Regional
FY Year Begin: 1983
FY Year End: 1990
Total Cost: 37783000 (US dollars)
Status: <u>ACTIVE</u>

Project to support the planning, management, and research activities of the various working teams and commissions of the Club du Sahel and the design of U.S. programs and projects relating to the Sahel Development Program (SDP). The project has two major goals: to support the research and analysis necessary for long-term planning in crop production, water resources development, livestock and fish production, economic analysis, health, demography, and education; and to design all A.I.D. projects financed by the Sahel Development Program.

The eight Sahelian states (Cape Verde, Chad, The Gambia, Mali, Mauritania, Senegal, Niger, and Upper Volta) will provide their own technicians and local support to many of the activities financed under this project. A number of activities will be jointly financed with other donors such as the United Nations Development Program (UNDP), the World Bank, the Food and Agricultural Organization (FAO), and bilateral donors such as Canada, France, and the Netherlands. (CP81, p.168)

Title: Promoting Population Policy Development
AID Project No: 6250978
Program Area: Sahel Regional
Year Begin: 1988
FY Year End: 1994
Total Cost: 8000000 (US dollars)
Status: <u>ACTIVE</u>

Grant to develop the capacity of the Center for Applied Research on Population and Development (CERPOD) to promote the development of appropriate population policies in the nine member countries of the Permanent Interstate Committee for Drought Control in the Sahel (CILSS). CERPOD will implement the project, which consists of activities in two areas: CERPOD institutional development, and outreach services to CILSS nations. Under the institution-building component, A.I.D. will provide TA, training, and equipment to expand CERPOD's: (1) leadership base and its staff competencies in population policy development and related analytic methodologies and techniques; (2) data bank, data base, and microcomputer ability; and (3) capacities in planning, monitoring, and evaluation, as well as in resource management. Outreach services to CILSS member countries will include: (1) research and analysis (preferably using existing data collections) on population-development linkages, maternal/child health, child survival, and family planning; (2) training, including two conferences annually for Sahelian and international experts on subjects related to population policy, the integration of demographic variables into national development plans, and demographic and health research methodologies) as well as long-term degree training of eight persons from CILSS member states, and ten seminars, workshops, and study tours to facilitate information dissemination and networking; and (3) financing of a variety of publications, including <<Pop Sahel>>, the CERPOD journal.

Title: Population Sector Assistance
AID Project   No: 6330249
Program Area: Botswana
Year Begin: 1988
FY Year End: 1993
Total Cost: 5000000 (US dollars)
Status: ACTIVE

Sector program to strengthen the Government of Botswana's (GOB's) population and family planning (P/FP) programs through a process of policy reform and implementation. A.I.D. will provide conditional dollar assistance to the GOB under 633T601 (local currency proceeds of which will be used mostly or entirely in the P/FP sector) and will under 6330249 directly finance TA, training, and other support. An inter-ministerial steering committee will implement the program. Outputs will be in seven areas. (1) The GOB will prepare, officially adopt, publicize, and begin implementing a national population policy. (2) The GOB will establish or designate a government office responsible for coordinating GOB institutions dealing with P/FP programs. (3) A written plan will be prepared and procedures established for procurement and distribution of contraceptives by the Central Medical Stores (CMS). The CMS will begin implementing this plan. (4) The GOB will assign an official counterpart to the A.I.D.-funded long-term advisor for information, communication, and education (IEC) and will prepare and begin implementing a written plan to expand the provision of IEC services by the Health Education Unit and by district health education teams. (5-6) The GOB will prepare and begin implementing written plans to: improve the quality and effectiveness of existing maternal/child health (MCH)/FP clinical services and expand the number of service delivery points; and expand the participation of nongovernmental organizations and the private sector in P/FP programs. (7) The GOB will increase the number of trained staff for P/FP programs - with the help of A.I.D.-funded long- and short-term participant training - and will also increase its financing for the P/FP sector, particularly for contraceptive procurement. In addition to participant training and a long-term IEC advisor, A.I.D. will fund short-term TA in contraceptives logistics, natural family planning, IEC, and MCH/FP service delivery. No commodities will be funded by A.I.D.

Title: Chad Child Survival
AID Project No: 6770064
Program Area: Chad
FY Year Begin: 1989
FY Year End: 1994
Total Cost: 8500000 (US dollars)
Status: ACTIVE

Project to help Chad's Ministry of Public Health (MOPH) to establish a Maternal Child Health/Family Planning Unit and to initiate pilot MCH/FP service delivery programs in two prefectures, first Moyen-Chari and later Salamat. The new MCH/FP unit will develop Chad's first national MCH/FP program. The project will provide TA, both to the new unit and to four other MOPH elements which are fundamental to the success of the MCH/FP program. (1) It will help the <<Bureau de la Statistique, de la Planification et des Etudes>> operate the national health information system and incorporate an MCH/FP data and analysis capability into the system. (2) It will help formulate national population policies and strategies. (3) It will upgrade the MCH/FP skills of MOPH and Ministry of Social Affairs and Women's Welfare (MSAWW) personnel by developing two MCH/FP preservice curricula at the <<Ecole Nationale de Sante Publique et de Service Social>>, developing in-service training curricula for health and social workers, and developing a training of trainers program in MCH/FP at both the national and prefecture levels. (4) Lastly, the project will help the MOPH to develop an MCH/FP information, education, and communications (IEC) program, produce audiovisual materials, and develop an IEC preservice curriculum for ENSPSS. The pilot service delivery component will consist of implementing three MCH/FP services in the prefectures of Moyen-Chari and Salamat: (1) dietary management of diarrheal disease, including use of oral rehydration therapy; (2) prenatal care, including risk assessment and referral; and (3) family planning. To this end, the project will upgrade about 20 and equip about 30 MOPH or MSAWW facilities, including IEC and demonstration centers. In addition, project-trained personnel will train some 200 health and social service workers in MCH/FP. Other activities will include a variety of IEC efforts, training of two field supervisors, and development of a pilot cost-recovery program based on the sale of essential drugs in five health units.

Title: Niger Health Sector Support
AID Project No: 6830254
Program Area: Niger
Year Begin: 1986
FY Year End: 1992
Total Cost: 23693000 (US dollars)
Status: ACTIVE

Program to help the Government of Niger's (GON's) Ministry of Health (MOH) implement health and population policy and institutional reforms by providing: (1) conditional budgetary resources for selected programs; and (2) TA and training. The MOH and the Ministry of Plan are the major implementing entities. Dollar disbursements to the GON will be made in tranches upon satisfaction of conditions precedent which consist of specific policy and institutional reforms. The program's main policy aims are to: (1) increase cost recovery for curative services; (2) control unit costs in hospital and pharmaceutical supply services; (3) allow increased spending on primary and secondary services and on consumables; (4) improve personnel and supply management and upgrade the MOH's capacity to plan and manage health programs and services, including preventive and promotive health services (particularly for child survival); and (5) promote development of national population policies and increase access to family planning services. Upon receipt of dollar funds, the GON will make an equivalent amount of local currency available for joint GON/A.I.D. programming for activities that contribute to the program's policy reforms and institutional strengthening aims. Criteria for local currency use will also encourage financing of child survival programs and pilot programs. A.I.D. will retain 8% of the local currency funds for use in activities to be identified by A.I.D. in Program Implementation Letters. The program's TA component will provide long-term TA (12 person-years) in health planning and policy monitoring and short-term TA (40 person-months) in support of policy and institutional reforms in health planning, health economics, financial management, child survival technologies, and other areas. Policy studies are planned in cooperation with a complementary World Bank health project, the results of which will be used by the GON to design and institute new policies and practices in such areas as cost recovery and personnel supervision. Long- and short-term training as well as in-service training in the above areas will also be provided. Amendment of 3/2/90 provides funds for additional TA/training in child survival and policy reform areas. The amendment changes conditionality for tranches 2-5, extending the timetable for meeting many of the conditions precedent, but generally strengthening the policy measures to be undertaken.

< Goal > 1. To assist the Government of Niger (GON) in the provision of health care which will help avert premature (i.e. preventable) death and reduce the extent and severity of illness and malnutrition. 2. To assist the GON effort to slow the rate of population growth.

< Purpose > 1. To facilitate policy and institutional reforms which will contribute to: a. increased long-term sustainability of primary and preventive health care (particularly child survival programs), and b. structural adjustment in the health sector and improved management. 2. To provide conditional budgetary resources for support of local currency requirements for local and recurrent costs of selected health and population programs.

< Outputs > Policy and institutional reforms: 1. Health services recover and retain portion of costs in order to increase sustainability of programs and beneficiary participation. 2. Containing costs to improve financial viability of the health systems. 3. More equitable financial resource allocation improves viability of primary health care, increases material supplies in services. 4. Improved resources management strengthens health service capacity. 5. Increasing institutional capacity in policy analysis, health investment planning, project monitoring, information management, and financial management. 6. Adopting a clear statement of population policy backed by plan of action and necessary legislative action.

< Inputs > 1. Dollar disbursements. 2. Technical assistance (long-term, short-term). 3. Policy studies, seminars, workshops, in-service training. 4. Long-term training. 5. Evaluation/audit. 6. Contingency/inflation.

Title: Maternal Child Health / Family Planning
AID Project No: 6960113
Program Area: Rwanda
FY Year Begin: 1984
FY Year End: 1990
Total Cost: 7715000 (US dollars)
Status: <u>ACTIVE</u>

Project to assist Rwanda's National Office of Population (ONAPO) to develop and carry out research and education programs aimed at increasing demand for and political support of family planning (FP) services and to introduce FP services, linked to expanded maternal child health (MCH) services, within the Ministries of Health and Social Affairs. ONAPO will design an MCH/FP service delivery system which will include client record-keeping, a supply system, and patient education. By project end, MCH/FP services will be available at 153 health facilities and MCH/FP education and information will be available at 150 nutrition and community development centers. ONAPO will train more than 500 nurses, nutrition monitrices, and social workers to provide MCH/FP services and education; 32 doctors and nurses will be trained as supervisors. ONAPO's capacity to collect demographic data, conduct population research, and disseminate findings to policy planners will be developed. An ONAPO demographer and ten hospital statisticians will receive U.S. or third country training. ONAPO staff will participate in 25-35 project-funded research and survey activities. ONAPO's information, education, and communication (IE&C) capability will also be developed. An ONAPO IE&C expert and a graphic artist will receive long-term training in communication theory and techniques, ONAPO technicians will be trained in audiovisual equipment maintenance, and up to 30 Rwandan officials will receive short-term training in MCH/FP communications. ONAPO will develop a resource center, a newsletter, group training materials, and client education materials and in coordination with other Government units will broadcast and publish mass media MCH/FP information. MCH/FP training will be integrated into the curricula of Rwandan health and social training institutions. In addition to training, the project will provide ONAPO with 5 person-years of long-term technical assistance (TA) in health education and curriculum development and 36 person-months of short term TA; fund the construction of four health centers, two nutrition centers, and an ONAPO training center (including a graphic arts workshop); and fund necessary contraceptive and medical supplies, IE&C supplies and equipment, FP vehicles, and printing costs.

< Goal > To complement agricultural, energy, and other development projects, to help bring the demographic situation in Rwanda into balance with development

potential, and to effect a general improvement in the status of health of the Rwandan population.

<Purpose > To improve the capacity of the Rwandan government (GOR) to deliver (MCH/FP) information and services to the population and to assist the GOR in creating an awareness among individual Rwandans and GOR planners of the relationship between population growth, health, and development.

< Outputs > 1. Training capability in MCH/FP information and education. 2. Trained providers in MCH/FP information and education: a. Nutrition, CCDFP, and health staff trained in MCH/FP information and education; b. Medical assistants and nurses trained in service delivery; c. Health staff trained in service delivery and supervision. 3. Operating service delivery system to include: client record-keeping and information system; supply system for materials and equipment; patient education program; supervision. 4. Data collection, research, and evaluation capability. 5. Mass media communication capability. 6. Facility training center construction.

Title: Maternal Child Health / Family Planning II
AID Project No: 6960128
Program Area: Rwanda
FY Year Begin: 1989
FY Year End: 1994
Total Cost: 9000000 (US dollars)
Status: ACTIVE

Project, follow-on to project -0013, to improve and expand the delivery and use of family planning (FP) information and services in Rwanda through the public and private sectors. The project, to be implemented by the National Population Office (ONAPO), the Ministry of Health (MINISANTE), and various private institutions, will have four components -- policy analysis, FP service delivery, IEC, and institutional development. The project will support policy analysis efforts by ONAPO and MINISANTE and provide their staff short-term TA/training in operations research and study design. The two agencies will evaluate the impact of public sector FP activities, define and target high-risk groups, and identify con- straints to FP service delivery. ONAPO will conduct a demographic and health survey with help from project 9363023. Three seminars will be held for public and private leaders and decisionmakers to discuss research findings. The project will improve and expand FP service delivery by both the public and private sectors. MINISANTE will integrate FP with maternal/child health care in each of its health centers, and will receive TA/training to improve the quality and supervision of its FP services, integrate FP into the health information system, and modify the logistics system for distributing contraceptives and medical equipment. The project will also provide grants to private sector entities for FP programs and will initiate community-based distribution and contraceptive social marketing programs. In regard to IEC, public and private sector promoters will receive training which focuses on the National Population Program and the availability of FP services. The project will also provide TA/training and distribute IEC materials to: village-level FP promoters, Village Community Development Centers, MRNP (a national political organization), the Rwandan Women's Association for Development, the Ministry of Youth and Cooperative Movement, MINISANTE and PVO health educators, and agricultural extensionists. The project will improve academic IEC activities by refining and integrating FP curricula into primary, secondary, university-level, and Rural Artisan Training Center curricula. IEC efforts will target groups most in need of FP information, particularly young people. To improve the management capacity of the implementing institutions, the project will supplement the participant training component of project -0013 by providing MINISANTE and ONAPO with on-the-job training in financial management and administration. It will also provide TA to various PVO's in FP service delivery. Private agencies possibly participating in the project include the National Secretariat for Family Action, CARE, and AFRICARE. Amendment of 8/25/91 finances TA, training, equipment, and supplies to assist MINISANTE in offering surgical methods of contraception, including tubal ligation, vasectomy, and surgical implants, on a pilot basis, with subsequent expansion of these activities nationwide at selected health facilities.

< Goal > To reduce fertility rates in Rwanda.

< Purpose > To expand and improve the delivery and use of family planning (FP) information and services through both the public and private sector.

< Outputs > 1. Improved Government of Rwanda (GOR) research, evaluation coordination, and policy analysis capability. 2. Improved delivery of FP services in public and private sectors. 3. Improved dissemination of FP information. 4. Effective financial and management systems in place for FP programs.

< Inputs > A.I.D.: 1. Long- and short-term TA. 2. Training (long- and short-term, in-country, participant). 3. Commodities. 4. Other costs. GOR: 1. Personnel. 2. Health facilities/offices. 3. Operational costs.

Title: Family Health Initiatives II
AID Project No: 6980462
Program Area: Africa Regional
FY Year Begin: 1987
FY Year End: 1994
Total Cost: 35599000 (US dollars)
Status: ACTIVE

Umbrella project, follow-on to project 6980662, to increase the acceptability and availability of affordable family planning (FP) information and services in Africa Bureau countries. The project, in accordance with A.I.D.'s four priority emphases, will: (1) promote policy dialogue aimed at formulating or strengthening host country population policies and at reviewing laws and directives affecting FP service delivery; (2) build indigenous capacities by providing management-oriented long- and short-term TA and training to public and private sector development planners and service delivery managers and by supplying basic equipment and supplies such as examining tables and contraceptives; (3) transfer technology through population and FP information, training, and operational program review by direct hire and cooperating agency advisors; and (4) study ways to stimulate use of the private sector to increase the delivery of contraceptives. Proposals for individual subprojects (SP's), which will have a funding limit of $3 million, will be accepted from host country government agencies, universities, statistical institutions, research centers, and other public and private institutions or companies, and from international PVO's working in the country. Priority will be given to countries which have a high overall priority for A.I.D., have large populations and high population growth rates, are in the early stage of population program development, lack a bilateral program, are ready to make a significant gain in policy development and service commitment, and have good absorptive capacity. SP selection will also depend in part on the stage of A.I.D. programming in candidate countries. SP content will depend on the status of a country's population policy development. All SP's will take into consideration what other donors and centrally funded cooperating agencies are doing, as well as the potential for programmatic impact, replication, and cost-effectiveness. It is expected that SP's will be allocated as follows: policy development, 10%; information/education, 15%; training and personnel development, 20%; public and private sector service delivery, including contraceptive commodities, 50%; operations research, and data collection, analysis, and dissemination, 5%. Some 3-4 major SP's per year are anticipated; provision is also made for grants, not classified as SP's, to satisfy small, ad hoc targets of opportunity.

Title: Nigeria - Family Planning (subproject of: Family Health Initiatives II)

AID Project No:	698046201
Program Area:	Africa Regional
FY Year Begin:	1987
FY Year End:	1994
Total Cost:	35599000
Status:	ACTIVE

Project Note: Approved under Project No. 698046220. Please see that record. Subproject to increase the acceptability and availability of affordable family planning services and information in the private and public sectors throughout Nigeria. The project's 4 functional components (policy development; information, education, and communication; and private and public sector service delivery) will be supported by TA, extensive training, and commodities and implemented through a collaborative assistance approach by 5 primary contract implementors (one per component, plus a fifth for logistics). By project end, an expected 15% of eligible couples (vs. the current 3%) nationwide will be using a modern contraceptive method.

Title: Family Health Initiatives II — Niger (subproject of: Family Health Initiatives II)

AID Project No:	698046283
Program Area:	Africa Regional
FY Year Begin:	1987
FY Year End:	1994
Total Cost:	35599000
Status:	ACTIVE

Subproject to provide TA in support of the Government of Niger's (GON) family planning program. The subproject will provide an advisor to serve as Population Program Coordinator and assist the GON in: (1) formulating a national population policy; (2) planning and implementing an expanded family planning program; (3) designing and implementing a demographic research program; and (4) managing AIDS prevention activities.

Title: Rwanda Family Health Initiatives (subproject of: Family Health Initiatives)
AID Project No: 698066201
Program Area: Africa Regional
FY Year Begin: 1980
FY Year End: 1989
Total Cost: 22500000
Status: ACTIVE

Grant is provided to the Government of Rwanda (GOR) to train the health professionals and government officials necessary to establish a nationwide delivery system of family planning (FP) and mother/child health (MCH) services. Implementation will be by the Rwandan Central Population Office, the Ministry of Health Prefecture Hospitals, and the commune-level Development Councils. The subproject will be implemented in conjunction with the Pathfinder Fund pilot project as part of A.I.D.'s regional Family Health Initiatives Project. A total of three regional and seven prefecture hospitals will be staffed with trained, indigenous health teams, composed of 14 nurses and medical assistants, and 14 social assistants, to provide MCH and FP services. USAID will contract a consultant to train physicians and assist with other aspects of the subproject. The three regional teams will serve in the Pathfinder pilot project. Community health motivators (CHMs) will be trained and installed in each of 143 communes. The 300 CHMs will work with local Development Councils and will perform outreach education and health motivation services for each commune's 34,000 members. The prefecture teams will supervise all CHM activities. A national plan for complete MCH/FP coverage will be drawn up by the consultant as a blueprint for Phase Two of the Rwandan Family Planning Program. A Central Population Office (CPO) will be created to administer the plan and will be staffed with 13 government officials. A short-term observation tour in the U.S. will be provided to three GOR leaders, and long-term training given to ten professionals. Each of the three regional teams and the central staff team will also receive a vehicle to facilitate outreach programs to the communes and to assist in supervising the prefecture teams.

< Problem > The rapid population growth rate in Rwanda, one of the world's five poorest countries, is straining the country's agricultural system to the point where famine before the year 2000 is a likelihood. Lowered food production from diminishing land resources adds to the population problem and contributes to widespread malnutrition and disease, especially among mothers and children. Rwandan government agencies have insufficient technical and financial resources to adequately cope with these severe health problems.

< Strategy > Two-year subproject consists of grant for technical assistance, training and commodities to the Government of Rwanda for a national mother/child health

and family planning program. Host country will provide salaried staff. Other donors include the Pathfinder Fund, a U.S. PVO.

< Goal > Improved maternal and child health, and reduced population growth rate.

< Purpose > Establish trained human resources infrastructure for nationwide availability of Mother/Child Health and Family Planning (MCH/FP) services.

< Outputs > 1. National plan for complete MCH/FP service coverage. 2. Staff for Kigali-based central population office oriented/trained. 3. Seven non-pilot prefecture hospitals have trained core MCH/FP staff. 4. Three pilot prefecture teams and central unit staff mobile for upcountry work and supervision. 5. Trained community health motivators in place. 6. Project evaluations.

< Inputs > 1. Observation tour. 2. Central office staff: A. Training. B. Salaries after training. 3. Prefecture team: A. Training. B. Salaries after training. 4. Community Health Motivators: A. Training. B. Salaries after training. 5. Team to assist national plan formulated. 6. Vehicles. 7. Evaluation. 8. Miscellaneous/Other.

Title: Reproductive Health Surveys (Contraceptive Prevalence Studies)
(subproject of: Family Health Initiatives)

AID Project No:	698066219
Program Area:	Africa Regional
FY Year Begin:	1980
FY Year End:	1989
Total Cost:	22500000
Status:	ACTIVE

Subproject to conduct two population-based sample surveys - one in Nigeria and the other in Zimbabwe, Botswana, or the Gambia - concerning contraceptive knowledge, use, and availability provide the results for use by policymakers, service providers, and A.I.D. The surveys, which will be conducted as part of the Contraceptive Prevalence Studies project (9360624), will be designed to collect not only contraceptive data, but also data pertaining to pregnancies which are of high risk to mothers and infants. Information may also be collected on various other topics, including other reproductive variables, health, and nutrition.

Title: Fertility Impact Development
AID Project No: 9300068
Program Area: Program and Policy Coordination
FY Year Begin: 1978
FY Year End: 1995
Total Cost: 1546000 (US dollars)
Status: ACTIVE

Project to assist efforts of The Population Council (PC) to support policy-relevant research on the fertility impact of development programs in Asia. The PC will: foster or support ongoing research by Asian scholars and collaborative U.S.-Asian research on the social, economic, and cultural determinants of fertility; conduct policy roundtables and technical workshops for Asian researchers and interested LDC policymakers on country-specific determinants of fertility and sector-specific factors influencing the demand for family planning services in Asia; undertake a publications program to disseminate information to Asian researchers and policymakers; and provide leadership and guidance to Asian program planners and policymakers, including USAID's.

Title: Population Policy Research
AID Project No: 9320643
Program Area: Population and Humanitarian Assistance
FY Year Begin: 1979
FY Year End: 1988
Total Cost: 12665000 (US dollars)
Status: ACTIVE

Project to conduct research on the determinants of changes in fertility in developing countries. The project consists of the following subprojects: (1) a state-of-the-art review of existing knowledge of fertility determinants (to be conducted by the U.S. National Academy of Sciences); (2) an awards program to support research in promising areas identified by NAS (to be implemented by the Population Council); and (3) research on specific policy issues at the country or regional level.

Title: Fertility Determinants Policy Studies (subproject of: Population Policy Research)

AID Project No:	932064302
Program Area:	Population and Humanitarian Assistance
FY Year Begin:	1979
FY Year End:	1988
Total Cost:	12665000
Status:	<u>ACTIVE</u>

Subproject to establish a program to assist scholars and research organizations in conducting research on the determinants of fertility in LDC's. The subproject will be implemented through a grant to the Population Council (PC). Under its International Awards of Population Research program, PC will award a total of 15-20 contracts to finance research proposals submitted by LDC or developed-country research organizations working individually or together. Proposals may focus on sociological, economic, psychological, anthropological or other social science perspectives on fertility behavior; cultural factors influencing fertility; the proximate determinations of fertility, such as contraception and age of marriage; factors associated with high or increased fertility; and interrelationships among fertility determinants, other population parameters, and economic development. Contractors will be urged to pay particular attention to data analysis and to the use of existing data in designing research proposals. Prime consideration will be given to research that applies innovative methods to advance the understanding of fertility behavior and that show promise of applicability for improving population policy. Contracts will stipulate that one or more reports detailing adequately documented research findings are to be produced. These findings will be disseminated to governments, scholars, and policy planners through publications, seminars, and briefings. Contracts will be awarded on an open competition basis. A small number of closed-competition pilot study awards may also be made. PC will undertake a strong advertising effort on behalf of the program and will establish both a Program Committee to guide and implement the program and a Peer Review Committee to assess the scientific merit of proposals and to make selections among proposals of merit. PC will, as needed, provide recommendations on forms of information dissemination and assistance in project implementation.
< Problem > Within an overall 2% annual increase, fertility in LDC's varies widely, ranging from significant decreases to near stability. The causes of this fluctuation are unknown. The National Academy of Sciences has made a first step in overcoming this knowledge gap by identifying areas where the fertility data base can be increased. Still lacking is a mechanism for collecting the data and

APPENDIX B
POPULATION POLICY PROJECTS DATABASE

developing analytical methods for interpreting it for use in designing policies aimed at reducing fertility in LDC's.
< Strategy > Three-year project consists of a grant to the Population Council to establish a program to finance research proposals submitted by LDC and developed country research organizations on the determinants of fertility in LDC's.
< Goal > Design of population policies for LDC's improved. (I)
<Purpose > Understanding of the causes of fertility behavior in LDC's increased (I).

< Outputs > 1. Fifteen to twenty research proposals from LDC and developed-country research organizations funded. 2. A small number of research pilot projects undertaken. 3. Research findings disseminated to population planners, government officials, and scholars.

Title: Program for Voluntary Sterilization
AID Project No: 9320968
Program Area: Population and Humanitarian Assistance
FY Year Begin: 1972
FY Year End: 1990
Total Cost: 145331000 (US dollars)
Status: ACTIVE

Project to assist the Association for Voluntary Sterilization (AVS) to increase the number of LDC's in which high quality voluntary sterilization (VS) services are institutionalized and accessible to the poor majority. The project will be implemented by AVS through its International Project (IPAVS) and the World Federation of Health Agencies for the Advancement of Voluntary Surgical Contraception (WFHA-AVSC). AVS, as primarily a funding agency, will subgrant funds to public and private institutions through IPAVS to support VS service delivery and through WFHA-AVSC to foster changes in national VS policies and to improve VS guidelines. Facilities for outpatient surgical contraception (laparoscopy, culdoscopy, and minilaparotomy) will increase from 153 locations in 32 countries to 365 locations in 58 countries; the number of training facilities will grow from 81 in 21 countries to 193 in 39 countries; and the number of trainees will increase from 360 medical and 156 paraprofessional personnel to 867 and 617 personnel, respectively. Equipped clinical space devoted to VS will grow from 11 locations in 9 countries to 25 locations in 15 countries; the number of repair and maintenance centers for endoscopic equipment will increase from 10 to 23. WFHA-AVSC will increase the number of national and regional leadership groups from 32 and three to 42 and four, respectively. Also, a total of 16 professional publications - guidelines, standards, study reports, conference monographs, and promotional materials - will be produced. It is expected that one international and 17 national or regional VS conferences will be held and that VS subjects will be included in 14 other international meetings. In addition, WFHA-AVSC will develop guidelines and standards on services, regulations, education, and organizational development; will provide technical leadership and assistance to government and other VS programs; will disseminate technical and scientific information on service delivery systems; and will develop a consortium through collaborative relationships with related international agencies.

< Problem > Currently, there are numerous institutions and individuals in LDC's which have the potential to promote and/or conduct large-scale voluntary sterilization programs. In most cases, however, these institutions and individuals lack the funding, adequate staff, and expertise in both modern sterilization techniques and techniques for promoting sterilization to be able to implement viable and expanding programs and gain governmental and other donor support for these efforts.

< Strategy > Four-year project consists of a grant providing operating expenses to develop an institution's capability for conducting a worldwide voluntary sterilization program. Recipient institution provides overall project administration, operational staff, and complementary funding for expenses.

< Goal > Improved maternal and child health and decreased fertility in LDCs.

< Purpose > To increase the number of LDCs in which voluntary sterilization is acceptable to the majority of the population. !OUTPUTS 1. Service facilities in operation. 2. Training facilities in operation. 3. Persons trained: a. medical; b. paraprofessional. 4. Dedicated clinical space equipped. 5. Repair and maintenance (RAM) centers functioning. 6. National/ regional leadership groups functioning. 7. Professional publications produced: a. guidelines, standards, policies; b. study reports; c. conference monographs; d. promotional

< Outputs > 1. Service facilities in operation. 2. Training facilities in operation. 3. Persons trained: a. medical; b. paraprofessional. 4. Dedicated clinical space equipped. 5. Repair and maintenance (RAM) centers functioning. 6. National/regional leadership groups functioning. 7. Professional publications produced: a. guidelines, standards, policies; b. study reports; c. conference monographs; d. promotional materials. 8. Conferences conducted: a. international; b. national, regional. 9. VS subjects included in international meeting programs. 10. Changes reported: a. National policy, laws, regulations, "climate"; b. Program improvements (e.g., standards, staff competence, administration).

< Inputs > 1. Subgrants: a. services, training, IEC; b. equipment, RAM centers; c. national leadership groups. 2. Conferences: a. international; b. other. 3. Printed materials - production, distribution. 4. Technical assistance to LDCs (consultants).

5. International leadership network development (select study groups, standing committees, international meetings). 6. Management: a. headquarters; b. regional offices.

Title: Programmatic Grant to Population Council
AID Project No: 9363005
Program Area: Development Support
FY Year Begin: 1978
FY Year End: 1990
Total Cost: 36587000 (US dollars)
Status: ACTIVE

Grant to Population Council (PC) to support family planning (FP) research and action programs. Activities will include: (1) institutional development projects at the Universities of Indonesia, Zaire, and Cape Coast; (2) PC publications and information services; (3) research on voluntary sterilization, contraceptive technology, and adolescent fertility; (4) implementation of national marketing research program on FP methods, knowledge, use, attitudes in Mexico plus assistance to government of Mexico in establishing a large-scale commercial distribution system; (5) TA and program support for rural community based distribution (CBD) program in Columbia and for governmental delivery system in Peru; (6) research on child spacing and FP methods in sub-Saharan Africa; (7) follow-up on training workshops begun in 1977 on population, demography, development in Near East Asia; (8) projects of the international committee on applied research in population (ICARP). ICARP will fund small applied research projects for FP administrators and conduct studies on the relation between population and development in selected aid projects in Africa and Latin America in order to establish minimal guidelines to attain low fertility rates and establish FP delivery systems. Amendment of 8/19/82 supports activities for the period 1983-87 in four areas (contraceptive development, policy studies, international programs, and communications) and funds a subproject to help the Government of Tunisia implement a national program to expand FP services, with emphasis on rural outreach (especially in 23 delegations in 9 governorates) at 35 peri-urban clinics. Key outputs include: (1) training rural outreach workers from the Ministries of Health and Social Affairs, rural animatrices (20), and male educators (40); (2) improving or, as needed, establishing, FP mobile units; (3) expanding information, education, and communication (IEC) activities by designing materials for the nonliterate and semiliterate, revising mass media programs, and strengthening person-to-person activities; (4) operational research aimed at improving Tunisia's information management and program monitoring system (to include results of the

World Fertility Survey and similar surveys); and (5) establishing a rural management system and coordination unit. Select Tunisian personnel will receive short--term training overseas. (PD-AAL-714) Amendment of 6/26/85 provides funding for increased contraceptive development research (e.g., research on NORPLANT subdermal implants, the levonorgestrel IUD, the gonadatropin-surge inhibiting factor, and the contraceptive vaginal ring). (PD-AAR-312)

< Problem > The Population Council, Inc. is a New York-based private organization which has pioneered in the field of population and family planning among ldcs. Activities of the council have been supported by aid since the inception of population programs within the agency. In order to meet new ldc population and family planning needs, expanded aid support is needed by the council in the areas of applied research, innovative service delivery systems and technical assistance to program administrators.

< Strategy > Three year programmatic grant to the Population Council, Inc., (PC), a New York-based private organization, will provide staff, technical assistance, equipment & supplies to further PC family planning (FP) activities among ldcs in areas of institutional development; discernment of LDC FP attitudes; dissemination of FP information; provision of technical assistance for projects aimed at delivery of FP services; basic & applied research; publication of research findings.

< Goal > Improvement of quality of life in families in less developed countries through reduction of fertility and child spacing by improving delivery of health/family planning services.

< Purpose > Improvement of family planning services of population council through applied research, innovative service delivery systems and technical assistance to program administrators.

< Outputs > Establish programs of family planning/population in universities; quality publications of family planning/population; voluntary sterilization services and training; rural community based distribution (C.B.D.) project expansion; delivery system for family planning services in peru; marketing research for commercial program in Mexico; selective investigation on improved service delivery in conjunction with program administrators; investigation and guidelines for development projects as indicated in Section 104 (D)

< Inputs > Staff; technical assistance; equipment and supplies.

Title: Population Policy Initiatives
AID Project No: 9363035
Program Area: Development Support
FY Year Begin: 1985
FY Year End: 1995
Total Cost: 29703000 (US dollars)
Status: ACTIVE

Project to help LDC policymakers develop population policies/programs consistent with their development goals. The project (no implementing agency is specified) will support new policy initiatives to promote market-based population policies by the private sector and to disseminate population research findings to LDC decisionmakers and will support and provide TA for applied research in the area of population policy. Under a first policy initiative, the project will encourage private health managers and public officials to incorporate family planning (FP) into private health care systems; analysis of the costs and returns on investments of adding FP to existing programs will be a major activity. Under a second policy initiative, the project will draw on the experience of the communications and marketing industries to develop new approaches to making population research findings available to LDC decisionmakers in a timely and useful manner. Applied research projects will be designed to increase the near-term usefulness of research to LDC policymakers, especially with respect to resource allocation. Under the final component, the project will provide short- and long-term TA, seminars, and observation tours to strengthen the policymaking capacity of public population agencies such as population commissions. For further details, see the abstracts of individual subprojects.

Title: Technical Information on Population for the Private Sector (TIPPS)
(subproject of: Population Policy Initiatives)
AID Project No: 936303501
Program Area: Development Support
FY Year Begin: 1985
FY Year End: 1995
Total Cost: 29703000
Status: ACTIVE

Subproject (SP) to help private businesses and health care systems incorporate family planning (FP) services into their health care programs. The chief audiences of this SP are business owners, private health system managers, and administrators, as well as private businesspersons who manufacture or distribute FP products. Activities consist of country assessments, seminars, workshops, business analyses, study tours, and management fellowships. A minimum of 20 business analyses examining the cost and health benefits of FP will be carried out in 10 LDC's. The SP will be implemented by John Short and Associates with help from University Research Corporation. (Abstract derived from 1987 User's Guide to A.I.D.'s Office of Population, PN-AAZ-840, p. 19).

Title: Innovative Materials for Population Action (IMPACT)   (subproject of: Population Policy Initiatives)
AID Project No: 936303502
Program Area: Development Support
FY Year Begin: 1985
FY Year End: 1995
Total Cost: 29703000
Status: ACTIVE

Subproject to improve the use of population information and research findings by policymakers in up to 7 LDC's and the donor community. Besides helping LDC institutions improve their use of research findings, the subproject will collaborate with other organizations in preparing special materials for conferences and seminars and will respond to ad hoc requests for materials on population and family planning. The Population Reference Bureau, Inc. and The Futures Group will be the implementing agencies.

Title: Expert Studies on Population Issues (subproject of: Population Policy Initiatives)

AID Project No:	936303503
Program Area:	Development Support
FY Year Begin:	1985
FY Year End:	1995
Total Cost:	129703000
Status:	ACTIVE

Subproject to support research by the National Academy of Sciences' Committee on Population on population issues of special interest to the international donor community. The Committee will conduct four main activities: (1) workshops for researchers and policymakers on up to five topics; (2) in-depth assessments of 3-4 major population issues; (3) 1-2 day meetings of experts addressing up to eight important policy questions; and (4) two large conferences for U.S. and foreign researchers, policymakers, development specialists, and population program managers to discuss the work of the Committee on Population. During 1987-88, the Committee will continue to assess the health consequences of contraceptive use and controlled fertility. A conference on the demographic and programmatic consequences of new contraceptive technology is also planned. (Abstract derived from 1987 User's Guide to A.I.D.'s Office of Population, PN-AAZ-840, p. 15).

Title: Options for Population Policy (OPTIONS) (subproject of: Population Policy Initiatives)

AID Project No:	936303504
Program Area:	Development Support
FY Year Begin:	1985
FY Year End:	1995
Total Cost:	29703000
Status:	ACTIVE

Subproject to help: (1) LDC governments develop national population policies; (2) public and private sector institutions formulate operational policies for achieving national policy objectives; and (3) institutions conduct policy analyses supporting the national and operational policies. Assistance will take place through policy analysis subprojects, staff training, observational travel, and the provision of long-term advisors. The Futures Group will be the implementing agency.

Title: Demographic Data Initiatives
AID Project No: 9363046
Program Area: Development Support
FY Year Begin: 1991
FY Year End: 1995
Total Cost: `   20262000 (US dollars)
Status: ACTIVE

Umbrella project to strengthen LDC awareness of, and ability to use, population and family planning (FP) information in relation to development planning. Elements from projects 9320502/ 0547/0658 and 9363000/3017/3027 will be integrated into two components: RAPID III; and census and data support. RAPID III will provide public and private LDC policy institutions with computer-based policy models for evaluating the development impacts of population issues. These will include: (1) RAPID models, which assess the effects of alternative population growth scenarios on health and development; (2) planning models, which evaluate the effect of such scenarios on sector development; and (3) financial/program planning models (a new emphasis), which include cost-benefit analysis and target-setting models for use in planning FP programs.

INDEX

A

B